Project(ing) Human

Representations of Disability in Science Fiction

Edited by

Courtney Stanton
Rutgers University-Newark

Series in Critical Media Studies
VERNON PRESS

In the Americas:
Vernon Press
1000 N West Street, Suite 1200,
Wilmington, Delaware 19801
United States

In the rest of the world:
Vernon Press
C/Sancti Espiritu 17,
Malaga, 29006
Spain

Series in Critical Media Studies

Library of Congress Control Number: 2022947703

ISBN: 978-1-64889-874-7

Also available: 978-1-64889-285-1 [Hardback]; 978-1-64889-692-7 [PDF, E-Book]

Cover design by Vernon Press. Cover photo by Jeremy Thomas on Unsplash.

TABLE OF CONTENTS

INTRODUCTION

Courtney Stanton

Rutgers University-Newark

When we think about science fiction, we often think in terms of worlds. A treasured aspect of science fiction is its ability to transport us—to distant planets, to shadowy laboratories filled with mysterious specimens, to future societies filled with technologies and innovations that boggle the mind. What often goes unnoticed, though, overshadowed by the magnitude of such world-building, are the structures governing the people within those worlds. Indeed, what is dazzling and *new* within science fiction—that which tells us we are no longer at the same time or in the same place, no longer bounded by contemporary science or technology—tends to get the most attention, and understandably so. Yet, there is always an undercurrent of the present, the *now*, in the ways that works of science fiction choose to represent people, and the primary goal of this collection is to illustrate the power of the science fiction genre to define humanness, and all that this entails, through its choices.

Take, for example, the wildly popular AMC television series *The Walking Dead.* The show, based on graphic novels of the same name, follows a central group of characters as they attempt to survive and rebuild in the wake of a global zombie apocalypse precipitated by a virus. It spans an impressive eleven seasons (and counting) and has inspired multiple spinoff television series, web series, videogames, and an endless supply of critical commentary. Yet, in the ever-expanding universe of this particular media juggernaut, disability experience gets very little mention. Sure, there are those characters who acquire disabilities in the course of their zombie-fighting days – main character Herschel loses a leg to a bite, the villainous Governor loses an eye in a fight – but what about all of the disabilities that presumably existed in this world prior to the series' beginning? Where are the mobility impairments, the arthritis, the herniated discs? Where is the neurodivergence? Recent data from the CDC[1] suggests that nearly 1 in 4 adults in the United States identifies as having a disability, yet this huge swath of the population remains largely and conspicuously absent from the imagined world of this media behemoth. One might try arguing that

[1] "Disability Impacts All of Us Infographic." Centers for Disease Control and Prevention. Centers for Disease Control and Prevention, September 16, 2020. https://www.cdc.gov/ncbddd/disabilityandhealth/infographic-disability-impacts-all.html.

individuals with disabilities were simply less likely to survive, but more than just insulting in its simplicity, such an argument seems implausible, at least on such a total scale. One might also argue that disability simply isn't the focus of a show like *The Walking Dead*, that it's beyond the scope of the series to bring in characters with disabilities and grapple with the ways they might complicate survival in a zombie-riddled environment. There is a certain logic to this argument—indeed, the presence of disability *would* complicate life in such a world—but it is an unsettling logic, as it allows for the sidestepping or simplification of disability representation.

Moreover, the crucial flaw in this thinking is the assumption that a lack of representation is synonymous with a lack of opinion or judgment—i.e., that not offering substantive representations of disability is effectively the same as remaining neutral in the disability conversation. Yet, the absences and silences within shows like *The Walking Dead* convey meaning. When works of fiction disregard or diminish groups of people, they are conveying beliefs—beliefs not only about the stories they want to tell but also the stories they do *not* want to tell, about the people they see as valuable and those they see as disposable, about what the future holds, and doesn't, for all of us. So, we must consider: what happens when we are given a scenario like that of *The Walking Dead*, or any work of fiction which imagines a world other than our own, in which disability experience is essentially blackened out, de-prioritized and ignored to the point of eradication?

Science fiction is uniquely suited to the exploration of disability representation precisely because it grapples with questions of humanity and futurity. Works of science fiction often contend with concepts of transhumanism, embodiment, and autonomy more directly than do those of other genres, and in doing so, they raise significant questions about the experience of disability. Through the creation of technologically- and scientifically-advanced worlds, a work of science fiction may offer insight into the projected futures for bodies and minds and what role, if any, disability may play within such worlds. Through not only disabled characters but also biotechnologies, sociocultural hierarchies, and conceptions of the ideal, such works reflect the values placed on disability in both the future and the world of today. As Ray Bradbury famously once said, science fiction offers us "the history of ideas, the history of our civilization birthing itself".[2] As a genre, science fiction offers the enjoyment and the allures of foreign lands, of exotic creatures and new ways of being, but it also

---

[2] This quote is widely attributed to Bradbury, but an exact source remains elusive. It is likely he spoke these words during an unrecorded speech at Brown University in March 1995.

encourages us to confront central questions of our own existence. What facets of our lives and ourselves do we wish to be different? How do we understand perfection, and what are we willing to do or sacrifice to achieve it? How will our utility and our worth change over time? Through its focus on future and other worlds, science fiction calls on us to reckon with the state of our own world, as well as our places within it. Civilization "birth[s] itself" through science fiction not only because the genre contributes to tangible scientific and technological progress – prominent examples include the flip-phone, inspired by *Star Trek*, or the submarine, invented by a fan of Jules Verne—but also in the ways that it shapes our beliefs about what it means, and also what it *should* mean, to be human. It is through grappling with these profound questions that science fiction intersects with disability studies, in ways that may be empowering or exploitative.

Looking ahead to the chapters in this collection, there are some important definitions to be established. First, while it is infamously difficult for creators and consumers of science fiction to agree on a single definition for the genre itself, a couple of the more prominent attempts are useful for grounding the present collection. First, Isaac Asimov called science fiction "that branch of literature which deals with the reaction of human beings to changes in science and technology."[3] Such a definition is useful for its simple focus on science and technology, which helps to distinguish it from fantasy, as well as for its foregrounding of humanity; it is the reaction of humans *to* the scientific and technological changes, not the changes themselves, that is the focus. What is lacking in this definition, though, is a sense of how science fiction reflects our current situation, and for this, we rely on words from Phillip K. Dick, who writes that science fiction presents "a society that does not in fact exist, but is predicated on our known society; that is, our known society acts as a jumping-off point for it. . . . It is our world dislocated by some kind of mental effort on the part of the author, our world transformed into that which it is not or not yet".[4] Dick's definition helpfully emphasizes that even its novelty, science fiction reflects the world that we know, and this reflection opens the door to the critical analysis of this collection. In its creation of worlds and tools and ideas, science fiction disseminates beliefs about what *will* and *should* be tomorrow, thereby passing judgment on what *is* today.

---

[3] Isaac Asimov, "How Easy to See the Future!," *Natural History*, April 1975, 62.

[4] Philip K. Dick, "My Definition of Science Fiction," in *The Shifting Realities of Philip K. Dick: Selected Literary and Philosophical Writings*, ed. Lawrence Sutin (NY: Vintage Books, 1995), 99.

While the chapters here tackle science fiction as it appears in a variety of media and as it manifests in a variety of subgenres, it is these conceptual elements – the focus on humanity's relationship to science and technology and on the ways that future and other worlds reflect our own – that unify this collection's discussions of science fiction, more so than any exacting requirements of the genre. Some may argue, for instance, that *The Walking Dead* qualifies as horror as much or more so than it does as science fiction, and there may be some truth to this. Yet, it is a fitting example not only because of its basic scientific premise (the viral-induced zombification) but, more importantly, because the series ultimately focuses on people. The series explores how they survive together, how they change (or don't) in the face of terror, how the concerns of their old lives seep into their new reality, and it is these elements which are, from the perspective of this collection, most important (and, it should be noted, it is the series' choice to focus on these humanistic elements that make its lack of disability representation so profoundly troubling).

Likewise, the approach to disability herein is grounded in a shared set of assumptions but is broadly inclusive. There are discussions of physical disability, psychological and mental disability, developmental disability, congenital disabilities along with those that are acquired, etc. The distinctions among these various disability experiences are incredibly significant and, what's more, each of them deserves its own book-length examination of its relationship to science fiction. Indeed, I hope that this collection serves as a fruitful step in that direction. Collections like this one join a very limited few extended works – Kathryn Allan's *Disability in Science Fiction: Technology as Cure*[5] is a notable example – that explore representations of disability in science fiction, and so it continues to build the broader groundwork necessary for future, more pointed discussions.

Still, while the pieces of the collection cut a broad cloth in terms of disability perspective, they are united in at least two important ways. First, the contributors to this collection all work from a shared understanding of disability experience, namely one that conceptualizes disability as an intertwining of social forces and lived experiences. As various chapters discuss in greater detail, the history of disability—by which I mean not only the history of recorded instances of disability but also the history of its representation in media and the history of scholarly attempts at its definition and exploration— is one of many phases. For much of recorded history, disability has been understood almost exclusively through frames of weakness, flaw, and stigma. This "medical model" synonymizes disability and impairment, framing any

---

[5] (NY: Palgrave Macmillan, 2013).

and all disability as something to be cured or concealed, and effectively ignoring the roles that one's culture plays in the evaluation of bodies and minds. As a counter to the deleterious effects of such ideology, the "social model" came along in the mid- to late-twentieth century, with the aim of reframing disability as a product of culture. The adage that it is not one's wheelchair that keeps them from entering a building but rather the fact that the building lacks a ramp illustrates the basic perspective of the social model. A wheelchair user living in a culture that values disability and reflects this value through its architecture— by putting ramps on public buildings—would, as the social model suggests, have a vastly different experience of disability than one who lived in a culture that did not.

As is often the case with sticky and complex conversations of identity, however, even the social model has, over time, been scrutinized and found to be somewhat lacking—a development that leads us to the conception of disability which guides the current collection. The emphasis on cultural factors, while crucial to not just a thoughtful understanding of disability experience but also the achievement of political and cultural power for individuals and communities of disability, can, when relied on too exclusively, undercut the importance of the embodied and lived experiences of individuals. If disability is seen as a sort of abstract concept, a social construct reflecting values assigned to particular peoples, this risks effacing the lived realities of these people. To use the example above, the wheelchair user has a strong point about the role played by society in shaping the experience of disability, but this need not necessarily mean that disability exists *solely* as a manifestation of societal belief—that disability, or disability identity, simply wouldn't exist in a world where every building had ramps, elevators, and so on. Beyond our interactions within the larger culture, there are the many real, lived moments that make up the experience of being a person with disabilities – moments of bodily pain and pleasure, of frustration and elation – and these moments are of equal significance. As such, neither the social model nor the medical model alone is adequate to thoughtfully engage disability experience; they must be intertwined, framing disability as an irreducible network of social, cultural, and personal, embodied experiences.

Along with this shared understanding of disability, another significant unifying thread of this collection is a belief in the importance of representation and, from this, a commitment to improving the representation of disability within popular media. Just as sociocultural understandings of disability began with medicalized views, so too does popular media have a long history of portraying individuals with disabilities as weak, lacking utility, or in need of cure. Moreover, while scholarly views of disability experience have progressed in ways like those described above, continually probing accepted ideas and seeking greater nuance, popular representations have unsurprisingly lagged behind. Thus, the contributors to this collection are writing from the perspective that there is still much work to do to improve representations of disability in film, literature, television, video games, and any other popular media. "Improve" here entails not simply increasing visibility, though, of course, this is one of many goals; improvement also entails scrutinizing the nature and consequences of our portrayals and pushing for more careful, complex representations of disability in science fiction—and, indeed, in every genre.

Overview of Chapters

The first section of this book centers on the concept of othering and considers ways that disability experience has been othered in media. There is a long history of othering disability within popular media, from the overt spectacles of traveling freak shows to the more subtle but no less pernicious signaling within contemporary media. Over time the portrayals of disability in popular media have generally become less exploitative, at least less blatantly so, but still, examples abound. The chapters in this section, then, examine the ways that disability continues to be othered in popular media, with the first pair considering the eugenic creation of disabled bodies and the latter pair examining ways that stereotypes and tropes of disability are created through narrative. In "'You were less than human': The Commodification of the Disabled Non-human in Kazuo Ishiguro's *Never Let Me Go*," Agnibha Banerjee explores bioethical and material implications of cloning technology. Ishiguro's novel centers on a group of clones who are segregated from society and have been created for the express purpose of compulsory organ donation, and as Banerjee argues, this program of bodily donation—presented to the clones as inevitable, even noble—forces readers to reckon with the boundaries of "human." In "A Eugenics of Disability: Transformation, Futurity, and the Disabled Monster Body in *Resident Evil*," Elliot Mason considers a different sort of othering as it occurs in the popular video game series *Resident Evil*. As Mason describes, disability within these games is present primarily among villains, who employ eugenics to modify their bodies in ways meant to increase their capacity to intimidate and control. By coupling manifestations of and desires for disability with the typically unhinged and volatile antagonists, Mason explains, and only in forms meant to be grotesque and terrifying, the games position the heroes as fighting to eradicate disability and assert the stability of the abled body. In "(Un)Diagnosing Religious Experience: Divine Encounters in Battlestar Galactica," Lucas Cober considers ways that disability is constructed not through literal eugenic means but rather socially through the perpetuation of stereotypes surrounding religious experience. By focusing on Gaius Baltar, a character whose indeterminate spiritual and psychological experiences are a primary driving force for the rebooted *Battlestar Galactica* series, Cober explores the interplay of religion and disability, as well as how these forces influence conceptions of humanity. The final chapter in the section is "Androids, Replicants, and Strange Things: Disability as Representative of Compromised Autonomy in Popular Science Fiction," in which author Sean Mock explores the tendency within science fiction to conflate disability experience with a lack of agency. Mock examines numerous examples of contemporary science fiction to illuminate yet another pattern through which disability is framed as the other.

The second section of the collection examines ways that science fiction plays with ideas of care and community, and how these concepts may be employed in ways that shape readers' and viewers' understanding of disability. Each of the three chapters engages other schools of critical thought, most notably queer theory, to illustrate the disruptive potential to be found in these transdisciplinary perspectives. In "The Animation of Stone: An Affective Queer Crip Reading of N. K. Jemisin's *Broken Earth* Series," Jeana Moody examines the extent to which Jemisin disrupts notions of alive-ness and whole-ness through questioning concepts of animacy and temporality. Through conversation with works of feminist and queer theories, Moody argues that the world of the *Broken Earth* series reflects our world while, at the same time, questioning some of its most immutable hierarchies. Turning to one of science fiction's most beloved franchises, Samuel Shelton argues in "Towards an Intergalactic Disability Justice: Rebelling Against Ableism Through a Criptique of the Jedi Order" that an overlooked aspect of the *Star Wars* universe is the extent to which the Jedi Order actually works to perpetuate ableism. The Jedi Order is widely understood as a community of heroes within the *Star Wars* universe, yet their valorization belies a harmful pattern of inequity and ableist harm, and through exposing this pattern, Shelton offers a new reading of Anakin Skywalker/Darth Vader and attempts to re-situate *Star Wars* in discussions of disability justice. Finally, in "Fish, Roses, and Sexy Sutures: Disability, Embodied Estrangement and Radical Care in Larissa Lai's *The Tiger Flu,*" Stevi Costa and Edmond Chang explore the complexities of embodiment and body/mind dualism, arguing that the communities of care found in Lai's work upend traditional narratives of cure and suggest a novel future for disability.

The final section of this collection takes a broader view of disability, looking at ways works of science fiction situate disability within the economic, political, and cultural influences of our contemporary world. In "Neoliberal Convergences of Capital & Capacity: Reading Science Fiction with the ADA," T. Wesley considers works of science fiction literature through the lens of the Americans with Disabilities Act (ADA), exploring ways that disability identity and experience may be further elucidated through conversation with economic and political ideology. Wesley uses the ADA as an analytical frame to examine two primary works of science fiction and illustrate ways that conceptions of disability are inextricable from questions of wealth and capital. Finally, in the last chapter, "*Star Trek*, La Forge, and the (Dis)Abled Future of Humanity," Craig A. Meyer and Daniel Preston examine the complex portrayal of visually-impaired *Star Trek* character Geordi La Forge, considering ways that *Star Trek* has succeeded and failed in its representations of disability. Their chapter serves as a fitting end to this collection not only for its focus on such an iconic and sprawling narrative universe but also for its suggestion that while there is much cause to celebrate contemporary representations of disability, there is also still much room to question and to demand more.

Hopefully, the pieces of this collection, all together, convey both the progress of disability representation as well as the need for further work. As a realm full of wonder and novelty, science fiction offers a unique lens through which to understand our world and what it means to be human, and the discussions of the various media in the chapters here illustrate the many powers of this perspective—to reflect and clarify, but also to magnify and distort. They illustrate the magnitude of the genre's influence and, in doing so, they highlight the importance of the conversation herein and call for it to continue.

Bibliography

Allan, Kathryn. *Disability in Science Fiction: Representations of Technology as Cure*. NY: Palgrave Macmillan, 2013.

Asimov, Isaac. " How Easy to See the Future!" *Natural History*, April 1975, 61–66.

Dick, Philip K. "My Definition of Science Fiction." In *The Shifting Realities of Philip K. Dick: Selected Literary and Philosophical Writings*, edited by Lawrence Sutin. NY: Vintage Books, 1995, 99-100.

"Disability Impacts All of Us." Infographic. Centers for Disease Control and Prevention, September 16, 2020. https://www.cdc.gov/ncbddd/disabilityand health/infographic-disability-impacts-all.html.

SECTION ONE:
ENGINEERING THE OTHER

"YOU WERE LESS THAN HUMAN": THE COMMODIFICATION OF THE DISABLED NON-HUMAN IN KAZUO ISHIGURO'S *NEVER LET ME GO*

Agnibha Banerjee

Rice University

Abstract

Recent scientific breakthroughs have augmented interest in the intersections between technology and disability, with a proliferation of narratives that aim to 'fix' the disabled body. A critique of such transhumanist ambitions, this chapter attempts a symptomatic reading of Kazuo Ishiguro's *Never Let Me Go* (2005), studying how power and capital intervene in the scientific enterprise of tampering with the limitations of the human and produce a supplicant race of clones for organ harvest and extraction. Created in laboratories and bio-engineered to be infertile, the clones in Ishiguro's text are ideologically defined as non-human commodities, disabled by this denial of their humanity. I contend that an appeal to ableist sympathy serves not to alleviate the victimization of the clones but to further enmesh them within a network of humanist power-knowledge structures that legitimize and (re)inscribe their dehumanization. I conclude by proposing the development of a posthuman aesthetics and bioethics that chart an alternate vision of the human, characterized by dispersal, difference and potentiality.

Keywords: Bioethics, Capital, Disabled, Ishiguro, Posthuman

***

Introduction: Technology and the Disabled Posthuman

At one point in Kazuo Ishiguro's *Never Let Me Go*, the narrator Kathy H recalls a seemingly innocent joke from her time in Hailsham, the boarding school where she had spent her formative years. She remembers how her friend Tommy, who had suffered a minor cut to his elbow, was mocked by his classmates who pretended that his wound was at the risk of unzipping like a bag, with "skin flopping about next to him 'like one of those long gloves in *My Fair Lady.*'"[1] Kathy notes how the joke persisted long after the incident, with the children— who are clones created for organ donation—using the image of unzipping to make better sense of the removal of their own vital organs: "The idea was that when the time came, you'd be able just to unzip a bit of yourself, a kidney or something would slide out, and you'd hand it over."[2] Humor thus becomes a survival strategy for the young clones as they begin to come to terms with the reality that their bodies belong not to them but to the 'normal' humans who use the clones' bodies for harvesting organs that would prolong their own lifespan. In Ishiguro's text, the invention and development of cloning technology thus becomes a means through which the bodies of the clones are mutilated, dis-abled, and commodified for production, circulation, and consumption by the non-cloned humans.

Recent breakthroughs in robotics, biotechnology, and genetics have augmented interest in the intersection between technology and disability. Far from being perceived as an unalterable fact of embodied existence, the human body is increasingly viewed as an imperfect and modular machine, a device to be optimized and upgraded to suit an ever-changing array of requirements. These requirements are in tune with market demand, for it is in the market economy that the subject under capitalism is bound to function. Moreover, rapid strides in the development of assistive technology—interfaces of software and hardware designed to provide impairment-based aid to the disabled—as well as genetic screening—a mechanism for analysing the genetic make-up of the zygote in order to detect anomalies—have resulted in a technophilic optimism that aims to restore to the disabled body its ability to meet normalised standards of functioning, or perhaps more poignantly, to ensure that there are no disabled bodies in the first place. Technology becomes, to quote Ingunn Moser, "a normalising prosthesis for the individualised human actor,"[3] a corrective mechanism to restore to the disabled body its viability in the labor market. This role of technology vis-à-vis disability, defined by Alan Roulstone as "the deficit model of technology benefits," not only seeks to fix "deficits emerging from impairments" but also to ensure "the enhanced supply of

---

[1] Kazuo Ishiguro, *Never Let Me Go* (London: Faber & Faber, 2006), 87.

[2] Ishiguro, *Never Let Me Go*, 88.

[3] Moser Ingunn, "Against Normalization: Subverting norms of Ability and Disability," *Science as Culture* 9, no. 2 (2000): 217.

employment-ready disabled people."[4] Such a perception reinforces late capitalist ideology, where the body is defined in terms of its utility and economic viability, and thus, like the artwork (and the bodies) of the clones in *Never Let Me Go*, does not belong to the individual but to the market. Against such neoliberal prescripts of normalisation, efficiency, and marketability, critical disability studies attempt a radical dismantlement of the category of the 'able-bodied human,' revealing it to be a discursive construct rooted in capitalist, racist, and heteronormative ideology. Such an approach to disability emphasizes the fragmentary, contingent, and fluctuating coordinates of the human, enmeshed as it is in organic and inorganic networks of co-dependency, which are porous and unstable. Recognizing that "the binary distinction between disabled and non-disabled is itself vulnerable to deconstruction," disability theorists argue how "cases at the limit—monstrous bodies and disabled bodies—clearly demonstrate the inadequacy of conventional models of embodied selfhood as self-sufficient and in control."[5] A symptomatic reading—an approach where texts are read as symptoms of deep-rooted ambitions and anxieties programmed into contemporary socio-political power structures—of the representation of these "monstrous" and "disabled" bodies in science fiction is thus useful, since this genre provides the human imagination a literary field to play out the experimentations, aspirations, and apprehensions that accompany alternative delineations of the human. Endeavouring to unearth the transhumanist ambitions and ableist prejudices of contemporary scientific advancements, this chapter attempts such a reading of Kazuo Ishiguro's *Never Let Me Go* (2006), studying how power intervenes in the technological enterprise of meddling with the embodied limitations of the human and creates a supplicant race of clones who are dis-abled by an amalgamation of complex and interconnected networks of systemic discrimination.

Queering the Disabled Posthuman

Created in laboratories and living outside conventional family structures, the clones, though nominally assumed to be heterosexual, are nevertheless at odds with heteronormative imperatives. Perceived as "shadowy objects in test-tubes,"[6] the clones are considered 'unnatural' not only because they are

---

[4] Alan Roulstone, "Society: The Case of Employment and New Technology," in *The Disability Studies Reader: Social Science Perspectives*, ed. Tom Shakespeare (London: Caswell, 1998),110.

[5] Margit Shildrick, "Critical Disability Studies," in *Routledge Handbook of Disability Studies*, ed. Nick Watson and Simo Vehmas (New York: Routledge, 2020), 42.

[6] Michael Warner, *Fear of a Queer Planet: Queer Politics and Social Theory* (Minneapolis: University of Minnesota Press, 1993), 9.

conceived outside the auspices of the conventional family, but also due to the 'artificial' nature of their birth. This privileging of 'natural' over 'artificial' birth betrays a humanist and heteronormative bias that excludes alternative narratives of origin, other possibilities of coming to be. Such a prejudice can be read as an anxiety-ridden response to rapid strides in the development of cloning technologies, particularly in the direction of Cell Nuclear Transfer (CNT) procedures. This involves the transfer of the nucleus (containing the DNA) of the donor cell into an ovum from which the nucleus has been removed. Electrical or chemical stimuli is then deployed to promote mitosis (cell division), which replicates the genetic material of the donor cell, in complex interactions with the mitochondrial DNA of the enucleated ovum. The genetic makeup of the clone thus radically confounds the primary kinship network—the sanctimonious heterosexual family—so constitutive of heteronormative state and society.

The ostracization of the clones—genetically engineered to be infertile— is further crystallized by the fabricated deprivation of their claim to futurity. Kathy and the other clones are thus denied the privileges with which normative heterosexuality is rewarded. Michael Warner, in *Fear of a Queer Planet*, defines this conflation of heterosexuality and reproduction as "reprosexuality" where "the interweaving of heterosexuality, biological reproduction, cultural reproduction, and personal identity … involves more than reproducing, more even than compulsory heterosexuality: it involves a relation to self that finds its proper temporality and fulfilment in generational transmission." Deprived of the possibility of this transmission, a lineage or bloodline to anchor them in normative kinship (and therefore economic and political) relations, the clones are thus dis-abled by the strictures of heteronormativity. In his book *No Future* (2004), Lee Edelman shows how the figure of the Child subtends the logic of neoliberal ideology through its promise of replicating and perpetuating the existing social order. He argues that the Child figures as the ultimate referent in the discourse of "reproductive futurism" that allows no other form of politics to be conceived. The fantasmatic Child grounds heteronormative institutions like the nation-state that allow this symbolic figure to survive while denying the rights of the marginalized—homosexuals, in particular, but also people who refuse the injunction (or are unable) to reproduce and proliferate. In *Never Let Me Go*, the only way made available to the clones, manufactured as creatures without the ability to reproduce, for perpetuating the system that exploits them is to hand over their own bodies, their own vital organs, in order to prolong the lifespan of the non-cloned, aka 'normal,' humans. Orphaned and unclaimed from their very inception by the absence of socially recognized parents and unable to generate their own kin, the clones are consequently excluded from the interlocked processes of socialization that are considered necessary for the formation of identity and subjectivity. An acute awareness of this lack creates in the clones what Sarah Franklin has described as a "genealogical shame," as they are "suspected of being a fake, a derivative, a copy, a mere replicant ... diminished by a lack of proper genealogy—and thus identity, substance, or origin."[7] Locked out of conventional self-fashioning narratives, the hollowed-out clones in Ishiguro's text are thus haunted by a lack that desperately propels them to seek out their "originals" (ostensibly, the humans they were cloned from). When that fails, the only way the clones can escape their overwhelming sense of incompleteness is, ironically, through the completion of their organ donations, a fulfillment that results in their death, or, more perversely, in their dissected and scattered perpetuation in the bodies of the non-cloned humans.

"Choose your own kind:" Race and the Disabled Posthuman

Rendered queer through their exclusion from heteronormative prescripts, the clones are instructed never to consider the possibility of having sexual relations with a 'normal' human: "When you get a chance to choose, of course, you choose your own kind, that's natural."[8] Though the clones, since they cannot reproduce, pose no apparent threat of conceiving progeny with a non-clone, there is nevertheless a deeply ingrained fear of miscegenation. This restriction—indoctrinated so deeply into the clones that they do not ever consider, even for a fleeting moment, of building a liaison with a 'normal' human—is just one of the ways the clones are the victims of racism in an apparently post-genome and post-race world. Discursively labeled "less than human,"[9] the systemic violence inflicted upon the clones—segregated from civilization in closely monitored, cloistered environments—recalls the unimaginable atrocities committed on the Jews in Nazi Germany and the Africans under European (and later, American) colonialism and the slave trade. As Karl Shaddox points out, Ishiguro's novel "has deep affinities with the sentimental and abolitionist literature of the eighteenth and nineteenth centuries.... [L]ike abolitionist literature, *Never Let Me Go* demonstrates that ... genuine social recognition comes only through the awareness of individual feeling in common, that is, through empathic resonance."[10] Ishiguro's novel—like the numerous slave narratives of nineteenth-century American Literature—creates this affective bond between the protagonist and the reader through the use of the first-

---

[7] Sarah Franklin, *Dolly Mixtures: The Remaking of Genealogy* (Durham: Duke University Press, 2007), 27.

[8] Ishiguro, *Never Let Me Go*, 93.

[9] Ishiguro, *Never Let Me Go*, 258.

[10] Karl Saddox, "Genetic Considerations in Ishiguro's 'Never Let Me Go'," *Human Rights Quarterly* 35, no. 2 (2013): 452.

person narrative, emphasizing the commonality of core experiences and feelings beneath epidermal differences. Ishiguro's engagement with the slave narrative form, however, is much more complex than mere imitation, for not only is there no overt attempt by the clones to gain the sympathy of the human readers, but also the viability of the form itself is called into question in a techno-capitalist society where pity is easily reduced to a hastily glossed-over footnote in the telos of progress and profit.

While abolitionist literature sought an end to slavery and a more humane treatment of slaves through an evocation of their emotional lives, or more disturbingly, through an attempt at establishing that they are capable of feeling emotions, and therefore are human and thus should be treated as such—an inherently problematic project, as this chapter will subsequently demonstrate—what initially baffles Ishiguro's reader is the persistence of race in a post-genome world. The Human Genome Project, initiated in 1990 and completed in 2003, debunked the notion that race had a biological foundation. Through identifying, mapping, and classifying the biochemical composition and attributes of all genes in the human genome, this landmark project proved, to use Bill Clinton's famous words from his June 2000 White House statement, "in genetic terms, all human beings, regardless of race, are more than 99.9 percent the same."[11] The marginalisation and exploitation of the clones in Ishiguro's text, however, suggests that racialized forms of discrimination continue to exist in biotechnological times, albeit in ways not immediately perceptible. It may be argued that revolutionary discoveries in the field of genetics failed to eliminate racism because race and racial discrimination never really had a biological basis; biology, as discourse, as an apparatus of power-knowledge, was only constructed retroactively to justify and naturalize racism. As Toni Morrison remarks in *The Colbert Show*, "Racism is a construct, a social construct. And it has benefits. Money can be made off of it. People who don't like themselves can feel better because of it."[12] The social function that racism serves in *Never Let Me Go* is to legitimize and enforce the extraction of the vital organs of the clones—a literal analogy may be drawn to the extraction of free labor from the slaves—to substitute the ailing organs of the non-clones.

The clones in Ishiguro's text are thus dis-abled by a different kind of racism which nevertheless retains the degrading and objectifying mechanism of the racism inflicted against segregated groups, which are, like the clones, also

---

[11] Bill Clinton, "June 2000 White House Event," Genome.gov, last modified June 27 2000, http://www.genome.gov/10001356/june-2000-white-house-event.

[12] Toni Morrison, "The Colbert Report," Huffpost, last modified November 26, 2014, http://m.huffpost.com/us/entry/us_6199402.

considered to be inferior and expendable. As Josie Gill points out in her essay on the novel, "the clones, apparently raceless, are segregated on the basis of their genetic difference. … In a world without race, forms of racism persist, and the novel reveals the continuance of racial thought in a postracial era."[13] What is more disturbing is the fact that in Ishiguro's world, technological innovations in genetics and biotechnology, far from erasing the discriminating mechanisms of race, are used instead to manufacture race, that is, to build a class of subservient beings whose only available purpose is to extend the lifetime of the dominant race, the 'normal' humans. Far from being neutral and objective, scientific and technological discoveries are thus revealed to be implicated in ideological narratives of control and subjugation. The apparent invisibility of race and ethnicity in *Never Let Me Go* conceals a far more terrifying truth: for the clones, the denial of race functions as one of the ways in which they are disabled through the denial of that which had hitherto been a tautological, if somewhat insufficient, necessity — humanity.

"We are all afraid of you": Terror of the Disabled Posthuman

In Myra J. Seaman's definition, the human, "long presumed by traditional Enlightenment and post-Enlightenment humanism, is a subject (generally assumed male) who is at the centre of his world (that is, the world); is defined by his supreme, utterly rational intelligence … and is a historically independent agent."[14] The "human" has always been a privileged construct, awarded by and to those with the material and cultural capital to define themselves thus, and consequently not everyone whose biology—itself an effect of power—would ostensibly identify them as *homo sapiens* were accorded the benefits of that identity. The completion of the Human Genome Project, however, destabilized such a sacrosanct and autonomous perception of the human. The gene was discovered to be malleable, susceptible to modifications and manipulations through the technology of genetic engineering, splicing and replication. Therefore, the Human Genome Project, far from eradicating racism, triggered fear and unease towards the messy, randomized, permeable building blocks of living matter. This dread of veering too close to the unsettling mechanisms of life was further augmented after the announcement of the birth of Dolly—the first cloned mammal—whose creation sparked widespread bioethical debates dictated by a defensive need to protect the sanctity of the human. As Roger

---

[13] Josie Gill, "Written on the Face: Race and Expression in Kazuo Ishiguro's Never Let Me Go," *Modern Fiction Studies* 60, no. 4 (2014): 646.

[14] Myra J. Seaman, "Becoming More (than) Human: Affective Posthumanisms: Past and Present," *Journal of Narrative Theory* 37, no. 2 (2007): 53.

Droit emphasizes in his essay "The Perturbed Identity," the very idea of a human clone suggests the unfathomable abyss that lies underneath humanist narratives of identity and individuality: "In effect, the clone is the same as its ... its what? Its original? Of which it's a copy? Its parent, whose twin it is? Itself, of which it is an other? This blurring of the contours that found identity explains the vertiginous character of the possibility of human cloning."[15] Evoking an unsettling sense of dread akin to the Freudian uncanny where that which ought to have remained hidden is frightfully exposed, the prospect of human cloning dissolves the abiding enigma of the human—its supposed irreproducibility and irreplaceability—into a murky flux of protein strands and cytoplasmic fluid. In the evocative words of Eva Hoffman's novel *The Secret*, the human feels:

> an intuition of another being, a mineral self, inorganic, non-biological, non-human entity. The Weirdness. The Thing. The black matter lurking in the back of myself. ... There was somewhere in my body something I could only call It, something that was in me but was not-me. ... As I kept starring at myself, my face seemed to break up into separate features which seemed to have nothing to do with me ... And then, frighteningly, the features themselves splintered into even more abstract bits of surface, curve, colour, glint ... it was the IT that gazed back instead of myself.[16]

As a consequence of the Human Genome Project and the development of cloning technology, the individual begins to apprehend, and fear, the inhuman, material, and volatile mechanisms within itself, which it strives to purge by projecting the fears onto the body of an other, a non-human, against which it can define itself as human. Such an attempt at purification is, however, not without its inevitable lapses and leakages, forcing the self to always (re)iterate the purgation in an effort to keep its own chaotic and abject mechanisms at bay. In *Powers of Horror*, Julia Kristeva defines the abject as the "massive and sudden emergence of uncanniness"[17] which sabotages the assimilating signification process in the symbolic order (of language, culture, civilization), threatening a "dark revolt of being. . . a discharge, a convulsion, a crying out"[18] in apprehension of a collapse of distinction between subject and object, between the self and the other.

---

[15] Roger Pol Droit, "The Perturbed Identity," in *The Cloned Human*, ed. Henri Atlan (Paris: Seuil, 1999), 119.

[16] Eva Hoffman, *The Secret* (London: Vintage, 2001), 143.

[17] Julia Kristeva, *Powers of Horror: An Essay on Abjection* (New York: Columbia University Press, 1982), 3.

[18] Kristeva, *Powers of Horror*, 4.

This terror of an erosion of difference between the human and the non-human, exposing the undifferentiated entanglement of genetic matter, and augmented further by a disavowed cognizance of familiarity and identification, results in, as John Marks argues, the "protective projection of our fears and anxieties onto the recognizable form of the embodied human clone"[19] who is denigrated, and, in *Never Let Me Go*, commodified and murdered. This abhorrence for the clones is hinted at throughout the text, culminating in Miss Emily—one of the "guardians" or teachers at Hailsham, the clones' apparently idyllic boarding school—declaring: "Afraid of you? We're all afraid of you. I myself had to fight back my dread of you all almost every day. ... There were times I'd look down at you all from my study window and I'd feel such revulsion."[20] What provokes this primeval dread is perhaps an unconscious awareness of the inhuman mechanisms within the human itself—the clockwork framework and arbitrary coding of biochemical data that genetics argues are the governing algorithms of all life. To return to Hoffman's novel, this anxiety the individual feels when face-to-face with a replicant is a result of an alarming proximity to the chaotic and inchoate origins of life: "Can we bear the sight of our origins? If we really knew, we'd die. ... Look into the mirror of your creation and behold the nothingness therein. The reductio ad absurdum."[21] The clones reveal that the fulcrum of human identity is an all-consuming nothingness, an endless vortex which is barely concealed by the motley garbs of civilization. The non-cloned humans are hence anxious to designate the clones as non-human—and therefore outside the basic protections and rights humanism would have entitled them to—in a dire attempt to preserve their own fragile identities from the contamination of the void that scaffolds their subjectivity. It follows then, as Leon Kass emphasizes in *Flesh of My Flesh: The Ethics of Cloning Humans*, that much of the bioethical uproar against cloning is an endeavor to define and police the frontiers of the human, banking upon an intuited disgust against artificial genetic replication:

> We are repelled by the prospect of human cloning not because of the strangeness or novelty of the undertaking, but because we intuit and feel, immediately and without argument, the violation of things we rightfully hold dear. ... Indeed, in this age in which everything is held to be permissible as long as it is freely done, in which our given human nature no longer commands respect ... repugnance may be the only

---

[19] John Marks, "Clone Stories: 'Shallow are the souls that have forgotten how to shudder'," *Paragraph* 33, no. 3 (2007): 341.

[20] Ishiguro, *Never Let Me Go*, 264.

[21] Hoffman, *The Secret*, 153.

voice left that speaks up to defend the central core of our humanity. Shallow are the souls that have forgotten how to shudder.[22]

Such a terror of the non-human is analogous to an ableist apprehension of the disabled body. Disgust, as William Ian Miller points out in *The Anatomy of Disgust,* is a reaction to "something perceived as dangerous because of its putative powers to contaminate, infect, and pollute by proximity."[23] Non-disabled disgust, stemming from an awareness and fear of the messiness, fragility, and mutability of bodies designated as 'able', serves as an allowance for the sequestration and mistreatment of disabled people. Therefore, it is not their difference from the non-cloned able-bodied humans that dooms the disabled clones to institutionalized genocide, but a purported fear of the eradication of that difference, of an overarching, uncanny similarity that threatens to undermine the humanist ideal of the autonomous subject. As Bill Hughes emphasizes in his essay:

> We are all slimy, leaky, gross, and sticky, in the process of becoming, of being incomplete. Only some, however, are destined to be defined as such and are therefore assigned by culture to the chaotic world of the in-between, the aberrant, the anomalous. The power and tyranny of the normate world with its hegemonic ableist values makes the scourge of abjection stick to some people. Disabled people become the in-between, objects of castigation. … Fearing the cadavers they must become, normate narcissists disavow their excretory bodies, their vulnerabilities, their ultimate demise.[24]

In *Never Let Me Go,* the clones, dis-abled both by the extraction of their vital organs and by their expulsion from the category of the human, face a similar disgust that reinforces their peripheral position as a reassuring other to the 'normal' human. As Kathy recalls the memories of her childhood in Hailsham, she remembers her muted horror as she gradually began to realize her status as clone, as abject:

> So, you're waiting, even if you don't quite know it yet, waiting for the moment when you realise that you really are different to them: that there

---

[22] Leon R. Kass, "The Wisdom of Repugnance," in *Flesh of My Flesh: The Ethics of Cloning Humans,* ed. Gregory E. Pence (Lanham: Rowman and Littlefield, 1998), 20.

[23] William Ian Miller, *The Anatomy of Disgust* (Massachusetts: Harvard University Press, 1997), 2.

[24] Bill Hughes, "Invalidating Emotions in the Non-disabled Imaginary," in *Routledge Handbook of Disability Studies,* ed. Nick Watson and Simo Vehmas (New York: Routledge, 2020), 97.

are people out there who don't hate you or wish you harm, but who nevertheless shudder at the very thought of you—of how you were brought into this world and why—who dread the idea of your hand brushing against theirs. The first time you glimpse yourself through the eyes of a person like that, it's a cold moment. It's like walking past a mirror you've walked past everyday of your life, and suddenly it shows you something else, something troubling and strange.[25]

The denial of humanity to the clones by the non-clones in the novel is the most violent way they are rendered disabled by the dominant group, the non-cloned humans. This prefigures and legitimizes the biopolitical objectification of their material existence and nullifies the possibility of subversion. Without the privileges and protections afforded by a membership of the category of the human, the clones can be subject to mass murder, without it being recognized as such, without it being read as a crime. Deprived of all political and legal rights, the clone is reduced to—to use Giorgio Agamben's terminology—"homo sacer, who may be killed and yet not sacrificed ... who anyone can kill without committing homicide."[26] Sovereign power, argues Agamben, is founded upon this ability of the domineering structure to implement a "state of exception" for any subject it discursively designates as *"zoe"*, as "bare life", stripped of citizenship, and in *Never Let Me Go*, dismantled and marketed. The non-cloned humans in the novel, therefore, are afforded the luxury of being recognized as able-bodied human beings because of the sovereign logic that allows them to feed off the organs of the clones, disabling and ultimately murdering them in the process.

No Past, No Future: Capital, History, and the Disabled Posthuman

In Ishiguro's England in the 1990s—deliberately set in the recent past to suggest that dystopia is already here—scientific advancements thus become not only tools for creating and naturalizing the disabled status of the clones, but also the means for the capitalist appropriation and instrumentalization of biopower. Biopower, as Michel Foucault enunciates, is a force that concerns itself with "the administration of bodies and the calculated management of life ... optimizing forces, aptitudes, and life in general without at the same time making them more difficult to govern."[27] The capitalist market, with its

---

[25] Ishiguro, *Never Let Me Go*, 125.

[26] Giorgio Agamben, *Homo Sacer: Sovereign Power and Bare Life*, trans. D. Heller-Roazen (Redwood City: Stanford University Press, 1998), 14.

[27] Michel Foucault, *The History of Sexuality: Volume 1*, trans. Robert Hurley (London: Penguin, 2000), 141.

ruthless, amoral logic of supply and demand, production and consumption, supersedes and subsumes humanist prejudices against cloning, with bioethics playing second fiddle to the biopolitical need to prolong the lifespan of the privileged 'normal' humans:

> Suddenly there were all these new possibilities laid before us, all these new ways to cure so many previously incurable diseases. This was what the world noticed the most, wanted the most. And for a long time, people preferred to believe these organs appeared from nowhere. ... There was no going back ... their overwhelming concern was that their own children, their spouses, their parents, their friends, did not die. ... They tried to convince themselves that ... you were less than human, so it didn't matter.[28]

The denial of the humanity to the clones thus serves as the justification for their commodification to meet an increasing demand for vital organs required by the non-clones. As Miss Emily explains to Kathy: "Here was the world, requiring students to donate. While that remained the case, there would always be a barrier against seeing you as properly human."[29] Appropriated by the dictates of the market, the embodied materiality of the clones is reduced to what Foucault has described as "docile bodies," that enter "into a machinery of power that explores it, breaks it down, rearranges it,"[30] commodifying it in an economy of extraction masquerading as an economy of exchange. Their corporeal borders are overwritten, effaced, and reinscribed by corporate forces, the clones are alienated from their own bodies, which belong not to them but to the market. The relationship between individuals is thus subsumed and replaced by a relationship between products since in a late-capitalist system "the commerce among commodities ... becomes that of a social relation among commodities ... among these autonomous and automatic objects."[31] Excluded from a future other than the one preordained for them, the predicament of the clones suggests—in an unnervingly literal way—the horrifying consequences of a total objectification and commodification of lives hegemonically deemed to be less worthy than the lives of the dominant group.

Denied a future, the clones are also disabled through the denial of a past, a history, something to anchor the incoherent stories of their lives within wider

---

[28] Ishiguro, *Never Let Me Go*, 258.

[29] Ishiguro, *Never Let Me Go*, 258.

[30] Michel Foucault, *Discipline and Punish: The Birth of the Prison*, trans. Alan Sheridan (London: Penguin, 1991), 134.

[31] Jacques Derrida, *Specters of Marx*, trans. Peggy Kamuf (New York: Routledge, 2006), 174.

meaning-imposing narratives. While protagonists in Ishiguro's other novels have an oblique access to history, the clones in *Never Let Me Go*—having no legitimate, human, origin that would be intelligible in terms of kinship structures—are denied history altogether. A recurring motif of Ishiguro's fiction is the presence of characters located at the fringes of power, who are unwittingly complicit in systemic violence, which their limited interpretative resources cannot fully comprehend. In the last pages of Ishiguro's *The Remains of the Day*, Stevens, butler to a Nazi-sympathising British aristocrat, has an epiphany which, in an ephemeral moment of illumination characteristic of much of Ishiguro's fiction, reveals to him the futility and disgrace of a position he has willingly sacrificed the best years of his life to: "All those years I served him, I trusted I was doing something worthwhile. I can't even say I made my own mistakes. Really—one has to ask oneself—what dignity is there in that?"[32] Similarly, in Ishiguro's *An Artist of the Floating World*, Masuji Ono, a propaganda painter for General Tojo's militant government, admits, at the twilight of his life, that though he "believed in all sincerity" that he "was achieving good for [his] countrymen," he was in fact "mistaken."[33] Like the bewildered protagonists in Tom Stoppard's *Rosencrantz and Guildenstern are Dead,* most of Ishiguro's narrators are allowed only a stunted, splintered access to history and meaning. Ishiguro's protagonists thus have a relationship with power that may be said to be—borrowing Lauren Berlant's terminology—"juxtapolitical" where "the political is deemed as an elsewhere managed by elites who are interested in reproducing the conditions of their objective superiority."[34] Meaning is presented in the text, is available, but just not to them, and these marginalized characters get barely a glimpse of the hopelessness of their position before their inevitable demise.

In *Never Let Me Go*, however, the clones are denied even that fleeting epiphany which would reveal to them the futility of their lives. Towards the end of the novel, Miss Emily explains to Kathy and Tommy the rise of institutional homes like Hailsham founded upon humanist tenets of "painless" exploitation of its victims, and their eventual replacement by "vast government homes" which are so horrifying that they would not be able to "sleep for days" if they witnessed "what still goes on in some of those places."[35] Condescending in her self-righteousness, Miss Emily chides and patronizes Kathy for her inability to

---

[32] Kazuo Ishiguro, *The Remains of the Day* (London: Faber & Faber, 2010), 242.

[33] Kazuo Ishiguro, *An Artist of the Floating World* (London: Faber & Faber, 2013), 124.

[34] Lauren Berlant, *The Female Complaint: The Unfinished Business of Sentimentality in American Culture* (Durham: Duke University Press, 2008) 3. Ishiguro, *Never Let Me Go*, 265.

[35] Ishiguro, *Never Let Me Go*, 262.

comprehend the situation: "From your perspective today, Kathy, your bemusement is perfectly reasonable. But you must try and see it historically."[36] Kathy, however, as a clone, as a non-human, does not have a history, and hence does not have the ability to perceive her predicament in terms of historical narratives. Precluded from both a past and a future, the clones are—to use Judith Butler's phrase—"foreclosed from possibility" through the denial of humanity, and are therefore rendered invisible, "not recognisable, not possible to persist in one's own being."[37] In *Undoing Gender*, Butler writes:

> It is the human, the beyond the human, the less than human, the border that secures the human in its ostensible reality. To be called a copy, to be called unreal, is one way in which one can be oppressed, but consider it more fundamental than that. ... To find that you are fundamentally unintelligible (indeed, the laws of culture and of language find you to be an impossibility) is to find that you have not yet achieved access to the human, to find yourself speaking only and always as if you were human.[38]

The orchestrated banishment of the clones beyond the discursive barriers of the non-disabled human also short-circuits any possibility of rebellion, eradicating transgression even before its inception. Indoctrinated from their childhood by the deceptive, sequestered, and sheltered environment of Hailsham and by deceptively doting guardians, the clones are conditioned to believe that handing over their vital organs is the purpose of their existence. As one of the guardians explains to the young clones: "That's what each of you was created to do. ... You were brought into this world for a purpose."[39] In Ishiguro's world, mastery over biotechnology has given human beings the ostensibly 'divine' power of creating life, allowing them to claim ownership of that life, and dictate its purpose. This 'playing God' on the part of the human, however, operates from within the space of capital, since the "purpose" for which the clones are "brought into the world" is not in service of some vague, mystical tenet, but in subjugation to the logic of the market. The all-pervasive commercialization of that logic dictates popular definitions of biotechnology as the application of science to manipulate biological matter to "provide goods and services" for

[36] Judith Butler, *Undoing Gender* (New York: Routledge, 2004), 31.

[37] Butler, *Undoing Gender*, 30.

[38] Ishiguro, *Never Let Me Go*, 81.

[39] B.L. Saini, *Introduction to Biotechnology* (New Delhi: University Science Press, 2010), 158.

"different uses."[40] Questions of ethics therefore play second fiddle to the parameters of applicability, usefulness, and—though not directly avowed—profit.

Law, Ideology, and the Disabled Posthuman

The quasi-religious deployment of language to conceal the genocide condoned by Hailsham is further aided by the use of euphemistic terms to refer to the horrors of organ extraction: the compulsory organ removals are called "donations" (giving it an altruistic and voluntary veneer), and in death (though the word itself is never used), the clones are said to "complete," ironically suggesting that they become fully realized subjects only when their vivisected objectification culminates in the total annihilation of their existence. These interpellative strategies seem to have worked. Ruth—once a spirited and ambitious clone who dreamt of working at an office—now unquestioningly accepts her preconcerted role as an organ donor: "It felt right. After all, it's what we were supposed to be doing, isn't it?"[41] To return to Judith Butler, the interpellated subject thus becomes complicit in the system that defines and delimits it, since outside that system, the subject is denied the possibility of existence. In *The Psychic Life of Power,* Butler writes: "That the subject rushes towards the law suggests that the subject lives in passionate expectation of the law. ... The subject's existence cannot be linguistically guaranteed without passionate attachment to the law. ... One cannot criticize too far the terms by which one's existence is secured."[42] Thus, Kathy is proud of her skills as a "carer" of ailing organ donors, nonchalantly partaking in and enabling a system that not only exploits her labor but also dismembers, murders, commodifies, and circulates her as disembodied organs. Believing those who are not as efficient at their job as she is to be a "a complete waste of space"—and thus unwittingly reading embodied existence in terms of the capitalist ethos of efficiency and productivity—Kathy, at the very beginning of the novel, admits being rather proud of her job: "I know for a fact that they've been pleased with my work. ... Ok, maybe I am boasting now. But it means a lot to me, being able to do my work well, especially that bit about my donors staying calm."[43] Perversely, Kathy gloats about her success in the very system that extracts her vital organs, eroding her to a cadaver. Further, in ensuring that the clones under her care remain "calm", she inadvertently further nullifies the chances of revolt.

---

[40] Ishiguro, *Never Let Me Go,* 227.

[41] Judith Butler, *Psychic Life of Power: Theories in Subjection* (Redwood City: Stanford University Press, 1997), 129.

[42] Ishiguro, *Never Let Me Go,* 1.

[43] Ishiguro, *Never Let Me Go,* 254.

Incarcerated and implicated in a structure that she is compelled to indorse—since there exists no network of signification outside that structure which can confer on her a recognizable existence –, Kathy becomes an instrument of her own subjection.

The eerily calm acquiescence of Ishiguro's protagonists in *Never Let Me Go* is further reinforced through the carefully cultivated myth, fuelled by "rumours," of a "deferral" of "completion" for the clones of Hailsham if they can prove, through their artworks, that they are truly in love with their partners. From their childhood, the clones are taught to be creative, to express themselves through poetry and painting, the best of which would be taken for exhibition in the mysterious gallery of Madame, the chief mind behind Hailsham. It is later revealed that the clones' art, seen as an expression of their ability to love, was used by the stakeholders of Hailsham to prove to the outside world that the clones were indeed human and thus should be treated humanely even as they are reared for organ extraction. Thus, the vestiges of resistance—counter-narratives against the hegemonic exploitation of the clones as disposable means to an end—that remain in the novel take the form of the humans using the clones' artwork only to determine whether or not the latter qualify for decent living conditions without jeopardizing in any way the exploitative system of organ removal. This, however, serves not to alleviate their exploitation but to further enmesh and implicate the clones in a network of liberal humanist power-knowledge structures that (re)inscribe their dehumanization. Devastated and disillusioned that the myth of a deferral of organ donations was precisely that, a myth, Tommy enquires of Miss Emily: "If the rumours weren't true, then why did you take all our art stuff away? ... Why did we do all that work in the first place? Why train us, encourage us, make us produce all of that?,"[44] to which she retorts: "We took your art away because we thought it would reveal your souls. Or, to put it more finely, we did it to prove you had souls at all"[45] Ironically, it is precisely this attempted identification with the human—who in humanist thought is the exclusive proprietor of the "soul"—through a flawed appeal to Romantic conceptions of art, that dooms the clones, calcifying their position as disembodied and disemboweled utilities. As J. Paul Narkunas observes in *Reified Life:*

> Hailsham and other elite clone farms were a humanitarian gesture to foster [the clones'] happiness while ensuring their compliance, while also assuaging any stings of conscience among the "natural humans"

---

[44] Ishiguro, 255.

[45] J. Paul Narkunas, *Reified Life Speculative Capital and the Ahuman Condition,* (New York: Fordham University Press, 2018), 236.

who supported these institutions, for creating humans whose only value is through organs that must be donated. ... Ishiguro comments on the transformation of the affective values of humans—their interiority, their souls, and their empathy into a kind of capital for humanitarian organisations.[46]

The rich and complex inner lives and emotions of the clones are thus appreciated and commodified only to serve a humanist agenda of pity and sympathy, akin to the ableist perception of disabled lives.

Such ableism further ostracises and reinforces the perception of the clones as other-than-human (and therefore less-than-human), to be pitied from a distance, to be treated as a homogeneous collective, not distinct individuals. When the young Kathy hugs a doll, and dances to the song 'Never Let Me Go' by the fictional song writer Judy Bridgewater, imagining it to be addressed by an erstwhile childless mother to her new-born baby (an extremely poignant scene since Kathy is bioengineered to be infertile herself), she realizes that Madame is observing her from a distance. Kathy notices that Madame's eyes are brimming with tears as she hurriedly brushes past her. Years later, Kathy—believing that Madame knew why she was unhappy—asks her: "You say you are not a mind-reader, but maybe you were that day. ... Maybe you read my mind, and that's why you found it so sad."[47] Madame, however, clarifies:

> That's most interesting. But ... I was weeping for an altogether different reason. When I watched you dancing that day, I saw something else. I saw a new world coming rapidly. More scientific, efficient, yes ... but a harsh, cruel world. And I saw a little girl, her eyes tightly closed, holding on to her breast the old kind world, one that she knew in her heart would not remain, and she was holding it and pleading, never to let her go. That is what I saw. It wasn't really you, what you were doing, I know that.[48]

The specificity of Kathy's feelings is thus reduced to an unintelligible backdrop, an occasion for Madame to philosophize on the rise of techno-science. Similarly, the clones' artwork, each stemming from singular emotional contexts, serves as a tool for the humans to propagate their own agenda of "painless" exploitation for which they could smugly pat themselves on the back, believing to have fulfilled their responsibility towards "the poor creatures."[49] When Kathy

---

[46] Ishiguro, *Never Let Me Go*, 266.

[47] J. Paul Narkunas, *Reified Life Speculative Capital and the Ahuman Condition*, (New York: Fordham University Press, 2018), 236.

[48] Ishiguro, *Never Let Me Go*, 267.

[49] Ishiguro, *Never Let Me Go*, 267.

and Tommy demand to know why they were not taught at Hailsham to understand the reality of their situation as clones, Miss Emily, far from realizing how deeply the clones feel cheated, instead congratulates herself for deceiving them; "Look at you both now! ... You built your lives on what we gave you. You wouldn't be who you are today if we hadn't protected you."[50] Operating within such myopic self-righteousness, the ableist project of using the clones' creativity to help them pass off as human fails, ultimately, to sway the human population towards recognizing the shared humanity of the clones. In the techno-capitalist world of Ishiguro's novel, human cloning for organ harvesting not only continues to persist, but the conditions of that extraction worsen, deteriorating from the deceiving tranquility of Hailsham to the unconcealed horrors of "vast government homes"[51] where clones are "reared in deplorable conditions"[52] Thus, as Tiffany Tsao points out in her essay on Ishiguro's fiction: "the artworks produced by the clones are meant to bear testament to the values of the clones' lives in the same way the clones produced by human society bear testament to the value of human life"[53], the preservation of which sanctions the butchery of those considered less human and therefore less valuable. Denied any meaning beyond the inhumane humanitarian agenda of the non-cloned humans, both the clones and their artwork—as created objects, as commodities—are reified into utilities, services that allay the anxieties of the dominant group, propping up their bodies with organs not their own, which nevertheless they own.

Conclusion: Art and the Disabled Posthuman

Ishiguro, however, does not entirely abandon the empathetic potential of art. Moving beyond the utilitarian dictates of late capitalism that prioritizes market value and productivity, Ishiguro envisions an alternative aesthetics of empathy and difference for an age where the human/non-human binary has become tenuous and permeable. Emblematic of this new aesthetics for a posthuman age is Tommy's artworks in the novel that juxtapose the organic and the mechanical, the automata within the human and the human within the automata. This is how Ishiguro describes one of Tommy's artworks: "The first impression was like one you'd get if you took the back off a radio set: tiny canals, weaving tendons, miniature screws, and wheels were all drawn with obsessive

---

[50] Ishiguro, *Never Let Me Go*, 263.

[51] Ishiguro, *Never Let Me Go*, 260.

[52] Ishiguro, *Never Let Me Go*, 255.

[53] Tiffany Tsao, "The Tyranny of Purpose: Religion and Biotechnology in Ishiguro's 'Never Let Me Go," *Literature and Theology* 26, no. 2 (2012): 219.

precision, and only when you held the page away could you see it was some kind of armadillo, say, or a bird."[54] As Shameem Black contends, Ishiguro's "inhuman style", in providing alternatives to humanist modes of representation, "suggests that only by recognizing what in ourselves is mechanical, manufactured, and replicated—in a traditional sense, not fully human—will we escape the barbarities committed in the name of preserving purely human lives."[55] Such an aesthetics eschews hegemonic dictums of functionality and instead embraces creativity as a fulfilling end in itself. When Tommy creates his hybrid sketches of interlaced biological and technological animals, he does so not with the purpose of trying to barter his way into the category of the human, but as something he enjoys doing, continuing to sketch long after finding out that the deferrals were a myth. Unlike the humans in the text, Tommy begins to genuinely care for his creations, thinking and implementing ways of making his creatures safe and self-sufficient: "It's like they come to life by themselves. Then you have to draw in all these different details for them. You'd have to think how they'd protect themselves, how they'd reach things."[56] In *Never Let Me Go*, Ishiguro thus emphasizes the need for a radical remapping of the cartographies of the human that would celebrate difference through the deployment of a posthuman bioethics that does not draw borders dictated by discriminatory notions of origins, originality, and efficacy, but instead embraces the all too human non-human, both within and without. Exemplary of this posthuman aesthetic is the novel itself, which in its hybridity—its intricate intertwining of the genres of science fiction, memoir, and the school story—parallels the heterogeneity of the clones on the one hand and Tommy's sketches on the other.

Ishiguro's clones, albeit "modelled on trash"[57]—on the genes of criminals, drug addicts, and other social outcasts—like Tommy's "fantastic creatures,"[58] posit an alternative vision of the posthuman body, disabled though it may be in the hegemonic intertwining of technology and ideology. With their fecund emotional interiority and their ability to form non-normative affective bonds with each other, the clones posit a chiasmatic intertwining of the organic and the mechanical, one that revels, independent of the tyranny of the market, in the other-than-human within the human. An investigation of the construction

---

[54] Ishiguro, *Never Let Me Go*, 187.

[55] Shameem Black, "Ishiguro's Inhuman Aesthetics," *Modern Fiction Studies* 55, no. 4 (2009): 56.

[56] Ishiguro, *Never Let Me Go*, 276.

[57] Ishiguro, *Never Let Me Go*, 164.

[58] Ishiguro, *Never Let Me Go*, 188.

of disabledness in *Never Let Me Go* thus reveals that "the parameters of all and any type of embodiment—and not thus disabling conditions—are uncertain and resistant to definition."[59] Putative categorizations along human/non-human, able/disabled lines are rendered slippery, volatile, intersectional, and contingent, as when Kathy casually refers to a commonality of experience with the (ostensibly human) reader even as she recollects her years in Hailsham: "I'm sure somewhere in your childhood, you too had an experience like ours … similar if not in the actual details, then inside, in the feelings."[60] The reference to an "inside," to "feelings," suggests an empathic bond beyond the specificities of circumstances and the boundaries of classification. Moving beyond ableist prescripts of an autonomous, complete, inviolate self whose perimeters are only enhanced by contemporary scientific advancements, Ishiguro's disabled clones challenge what constitutes the human as such. The human self is revealed to be in a continuous, complex, and perilous process of becoming that is always incomplete, always transitory, always an assemblage of the organic and the mechanical, the natural and the artificial, such that these categories themselves become indistinguishable from each other. Life in the digital age is characterized by a proliferation of technological devices, cyber networks, and virtual interfaces that interfere with the body and enacts what Vasilis Galis delineates as a "hybrid subjectivity" where "technological creations interact with corporeal subjects and produce new practices, emotions, and subjectivities."[61] Avoiding the easy pitfalls of both technophilia and technophobia, a rigorous engagement with the intersection of science studies and disability studies through a symptomatic reading of speculative fiction thus provides critical insights into potential worlds that experiment with radically new and liberating understandings of embodiment, dis/ability, and ideology.

Bibliography

Agamben, Giorgio. *Homo Sacer: Sovereign Power and Bare Life,* translated by D. Heller-Roazen. Redwood City: Stanford University Press, 1998.

Berlant, Lauren. *The Female Complaint: The Unfinished Business of Sentimentality in American Culture.* Durham: Duke University Press, 2008.

Black, Shameem. "Ishiguro's Inhuman Aesthetics." *Modern Fiction Studies* 55, no. 4 (2009): 785-807. http://www.jstor.org/stable/26287383.

---

[59] Margit Shildrick, "Critical Disability Studies," in *Routledge Handbook of Disability Studies,* ed. Nick Watson and Simo Vehmas (New York: Routledge, 2020) 36.

[60] Ishiguro, *Never Let Me Go,* 42.

[61] Vasilis Galis, "We Never Been Able-Bodied: Thoughts on Dis/ability and Technology Studies," in *Routledge Handbook of Disability Studies,* ed. Nick Watson and Simo Vehmas (New York: Routledge, 2020), 404.

Butler, Judith. *The Psychic Life of Power: Theories in Subjection.* Redwood City: Stanford University Press, 1997.

Butler, Judith. *Undoing Gender.* New York: Routledge, 2004.

Clinton, Bill. "June 2000 White House Event." Genome.gov. Last modified June 27, 2000. https://www.genome.gov/10001356/june-2000-white-house-event.

Derrida, Jacques. *Specters of Marx,* translated by Peggy Kamuf. New York: Routledge, 2006.

Droit, Roger Pol. "The Perturbed Identity." In *The Cloned Human,* edited by Henri Atlan, 110-125. Paris: Seuil, 1999.

Edelman, Lee. *No Future: Queer Politics and the Death Drive.* Durham: Duke University Press, 2004.

Foucault, Michel. *Discipline and Punish: The Birth of the Prison,* translated by Alan Sheridan. London: Penguin, 1991.

Foucault, Michel. *The History of Sexuality: Volume I,* translated by Robert Hurley. London: Penguin, 2000.

Franklin, Sarah. *Dolly Mixtures: The Remaking of Genealogy.* Durham: Duke University Press, 2007.

Freud, Sigmund. *The Uncanny,* translated by David Mclintock. London: Penguin Modern Classics, 2003.

Galis, Vasilis. "We Have Never Been Able-Bodied: Thoughts on Dis/ability and Technology Studies." In *Routledge Handbook of Disability Studies,* edited by Nick Watson and Simo Vehmas, 404-417. New York: Routledge, 2020.

Gill, Josie. "Written on the Face: Race and Expression in Kazuo Ishiguro's Never Let Me Go." *Modern Fiction Studies* 60, no. 4 (2014): 632-655. http://www.jstor.org/stable/10.2307/26421759.

Hoffman, Eva. *The Secret.* London: Vintage, 2001.

Hughes, Bill. "Invalidating Emotions in the Non-disabled Imaginary." In *Routledge Handbook of Disability Studies,* edited by Nick Watson and Simo Vehmas, 89-101. New York: Routledge, 2020.

Ingunn, Moser. "Against Normalization: Subverting Norms of Ability and Disability." *Science as Culture* 9, no. 2 (2000): 201-240.

Ishiguro, Kazuo. *An Artist of the Floating World.* London: Faber & Faber, 2013.

Ishiguro, Kazuo. *Never Let Me Go.* London: Faber & Faber, 2006.

Ishiguro, Kazuo. *The Remains of the Day.* London: Faber & Faber, 2010.

Kass, Leon R. "The Wisdom of Repugnance." In *Flesh of My Flesh: The Ethics of Cloning Humans,* edited by Gregory E. Pence, 15-31. Lanham: Rowman and Littlefield, 1998.

Kristeva, Julia. *Powers of Horror: An Essay on Abjection.* New York: Columbia University Press, 1982.

Marks, John. "Clone Stories: 'Shallow are the souls that have forgotten how to shudder'." *Paragraph* 33, no. 3 (2007): 331-353. http://www.jstor.org/stable/43151855.

Miller, William Ian. *The Anatomy of Disgust.* Massachusetts: Harvard University Press, 1997.

Morrison, Toni. "The Colbert Report." Huffpost. Last modified November 26, 2014. https://m.huffpost.com/us/entry/us_6199402.

Narkunas, J. Paul. *Reified Life: Speculative Capital and the Ahuman Condition.* New York: Fordham University Press, 2018.

Roulstone, Alan. "Society: The Case of Employment and New Technology." In *The Disability Reader: Social Science Perspectives,* edited by Tom Shakespeare, 95-110. London: Casell, 1998.

Saddox, Karl. "Generic Considerations in Ishiguro's 'Never Let Me Go'." *Human Rights Quarterly* 35, no. 2 (2013): 448-469. http://www.jstor.org/stable/24518 023.

Saini, B.L. *Introduction to Biotechnology.* New Delhi: University Science Press, 2010.

Seaman, Myra J. "Becoming More (than) Human: Affective Posthumanisms: Past and Present." *Journal of Narrative Theory* 37, no. 2 (2007): 46-61. http://www.jstor.com/stable/41304860.

Shildrick, Margit. "Critical Disability Studies." In *Routledge Handbook of Disability Studies,* edited by Nick Watson and Simo Vehmas, 32-44. New York: Routledge, 2020.

Stoppard, Tom. *Rosencrantz and Guildenstern are Dead.* London: Faber & Faber, 1973.

Tsao, Tiffany. "The Tyranny of Purpose: Religion and Biotechnology in Ishiguro's 'Never Let Me Go'." *Literature and Theology* 26, no. 2 (2012): 214-232. http://www.jstor.org/stable/23927483.

Warner, Michael. *Fear of a Queer Planet: Queer Politics and Social Theory.* Minneapolis: University of Minnesota Press, 1993.

CHAPTER 2

A EUGENICS OF DISABILITY: TRANSFORMATION, FUTURITY, AND THE DISABLED MONSTER BODY IN *RESIDENT EVIL*

Elliot Mason

Concordia University, Montreal

Abstract

This paper examines themes of disability and eugenics in the video game franchise, *Resident Evil*, arguing that the series codes disability as a form of eugenics through the depiction of antagonists who deliberately transform their own bodies under the belief that such transformations render them superior. Many of the mutations parallel real-world physical disabilities and are framed as grotesque forms that the player must destroy. The games link desire for the disabled body with excessive wealth, scientific expertise, and eugenics, while its protagonists assume heroic roles combating corporate interests that threaten ordinary citizens. By uniting eugenics with disability, the series promotes rather than destabilizes systemic oppression related to disabled bodies in the real world. The game presents a perilous future, in which the right to an able body is under threat, and in which any kind of desire for disability is explicitly marked as elite, effeminate, and abject.

Keywords: Disability, *Resident Evil*, Monsters, Monstrous, Video Games

***

Introduction

Monster fiction—that is, fiction to do with, and featuring, monsters and the monstrous—largely engages with disability along two central lines of thought: 1) disability is a disaster with which the protagonists are threatened, as in the case of zombie media wherein amputation or zombification are the stakes at play when encountering the monster, and 2) the monster itself embodies disability via its own status as disabled (symbolically or literally). This embodiment often results from the monster's ambiguous morphological or psychological status, a status that gestures toward boundary crossing and category mixing through its hybridity (e.g., werewolves are a hybrid of human and lupine, zombies are simultaneously dead and undead). Through their association with miscegenation and the uncategorizable, monsters flout eugenic principles that imagine an ideal, circumscribable, and bounded body. Monsters of these types are seen as aberrations in the contexts of their narratives, either to be pitied by the able-bodied normate protagonists, and/or feared due to the perceived threat they represent to normative embodiment, sexuality, and culture. This is especially the case in zombie fiction.[1]

In contrast to these trends, however, the survival horror videogame franchise *Resident Evil* unites eugenics *with* disability in the form of its mutated, monstrous antagonists, creating instead what I have named a *eugenics of disability*. Works that take this approach position disability not as that which eugenics seeks to erase, but the threat that eugenics itself presents to normate humans. Whether portrayed positively within a given text itself, disabled bodies in science fiction and horror have largely been depicted as bodies that exist in spite of, or in opposition to, an idealized eugenic body that mirrors the contemporary normative beauty standards of the cultural-historical context in which a given text was produced. In *Resident Evil*, the desired body that is eugenically produced by the series's mad-scientist antagonists *is* the disabled body. Through the use of artificially created viruses and parasitical organisms

---

[1] The status of monsters as category-defying hybrids is examined at length throughout monster studies scholarship, both as a broad trait ascribed to monsters, and in the specific as it applies to culturally and historically particular taxa. See: Jeffrey Jerome Cohen, "Monster Culture (Seven Theses)," in *Monster Theory: Reading Culture*, ed. Jeffrey Jerome Cohen (Minneapolis: University of Minnesota Press, 1996), 6-12; Dana Oswald, "Monstrous Gender: Geographies of Ambiguity," in *The Ashgate Research Companion to Monsters and the Monstrous*, eds. Asa Simon Mittman and Peter Dendle (New York: Ashgate, 2013), 343-363; David Williams, *Deformed Discourse: The Function of the Monster in Medieval Thought and Literature* (Montreal: McGill-Queen's UP, 1996).A third type of monster narrative positions the monster as not purely pitiable or malicious, but as the protagonist of its own story. Often these narratives take the perspective of the monster in order to interrogate cultural assumptions concerning normativity and subvert and critique real-world power imbalances between marginalized people who have historically been Othered through their literal demonization, and those with a stake in the continued oppression of minority and marginalized groups. Although I will address aspects of this type of narrative in a later section of this paper, my primary focus here is on portrayals of the monster with a negative valence. The reclamation of monstrous characters in science fiction, fantasy, and horror on the part of marginalized people themselves is the subject of my forthcoming dissertation.

that are implanted into human beings and other animals, these antagonists mutate their own bodies in ways that transform their physical proportions, deform existing organs and structures, and fuse the human with the seemingly non-human. These transformations are enacted under the auspices of several sinister pharmaceutical and biological warfare corporations, which act sometimes on behalf of world governments, but often in opposition to them. These organizations, the primary of which is the fictional American pharmaceutical giant known as the Umbrella Corporation, are marked as morally corrupt not only through their production of bio-weapons and their willingness to supply weapons to nebulously defined fictional terrorist organizations, but by their use of unwilling subjects in their experiments. Thus, while the mad-scientist antagonists of the series are marked as morally degenerate due to their desire to occupy disabled, monster bodies that they view as beautiful and powerful, they are simultaneously framed as direct threats to the sanctity of the normate, able bodies that they non-consensually conscript into their army of disabled monsters. Such an army is realized in the form of the games' lumbering zombie hordes, which the player must eradicate or evade to progress in the game, and who are characterized as pitiable victims in comparison with the major antagonists: less easily definable mutated monsters that almost always take the form of mad scientists who have intentionally transformed themselves into monsters. The proliferation of an idealized disabled body on a global scale is the end-goal of many of these mad scientists and is typically coupled with a eugenically-coded belief that only an elite subset of the world's population is worthy of such a transformation. These newly disabled bodies therefore include not only a faceless army at the beck and call of the mad scientists and organizations that created them, but a new world order that is intended to transform the concept of the human entirely. The goal, as with all eugenics projects, is not only the promotion of an idealized form, but the elimination of bodies that are not ideal.

The desire for corporeal transformation is often coupled with markers of mental and cognitive disabilities. It is at once determined to be misplaced on the basis of the games' presentation of its antagonists as mentally ill, while simultaneously acting as a signifier of mental illness—an uroboros effect that allows the series to refuse any attempt to genuinely engage with either the dangers of eugenics, of self-harm, or of mental illness. That many of the series' antagonists are also physically disabled and/or are queer and racially-coded prior to their transformations, reinforces the connection the series draws between disability, desire for the disabled body, and moral corruption. In contrast to what disability and horror studies scholar Angela M. Smith argues is the tendency of early cinema horror to "complicate, diffuse, and even vilify eugenic messages,"[2] *Resident Evil* presents a surface-level critique of eugenic worldviews while simultaneously falling back on a tradition of associating disability with monstrosity, and presenting disabled people as morally and ethically suspect. While it is possible to read certain of the series' antagonists through a recuperative lens that views their desire for the disabled body as a revolutionary act, such a reading runs the risk of accidentally embracing the antagonists' own form of eugenics, which robs the victims of Umbrella of their own bodily autonomy, while simultaneously obscuring the problematic ways in which the series co-constructs race, class, disability, and sexuality along the axis of the monster.

Zombie Media and the Disabled Body

Science fiction, horror, and the zombie sub-genre are no strangers to eugenicist politics that frame disability and the disabled body as both grotesque and undesirable.[3] As Anna Mae Duane highlights in her analysis of AMC's hit television series, *The Walking Dead*, "zombie narratives . . . repeatedly assure us that it's foolish to imagine any sort of continuum between physical health and repulsive decay. You are on one side of the equation of the other. Thus the terror of our own treacherous, unpredictable embodiment becomes transferred to monstrous bodies we must eradicate to be safe."[4] Zombies crawl, shuffle, or limp their way toward their (usually) able-bodied victims, often missing limbs, or depicted with milky, clouded eyes that signal blindness to a sighted audience. Halfway between the living and the dead, these undead monsters position physical disability as a state likewise on the limits of life and death. In doing so, most zombie media reinforce culturally encoded normate responses to disabled bodies that mark disabled people as always already dead. Disabled and zombie bodies become uncanny reminders of normate mortality, as well as the capacity and inevitably for all bodies to become disabled.

In zombie media, as in other monster narratives, emphasis is often placed on the necessity of the destruction of the zombie body. For human society to survive, such stories tell us, the monstrous must be eradicated, the zombie killed. The eugenicist impulse to eliminate undesirable traits from a given

---

[2] Angela M. Smith, *Hideous Progeny: Disability, Eugenics, and Classic Horror Cinema* (New York: Columbia UP, 2011), 3.

[3] For a thorough overview of the history of disability representation and eugenics in classic monster movies, see: Smith, *Hideous Progeny.*

[4] Anne Mae Duane, "Dead *and* Disabled: The Crawling Monsters of *The Walking Dead*," in *Zombie Theory: A Reader*, ed. Sarah Juliet Lauro (Minneapolis: University of Minnesota Press, 2017), 239.

population is given flesh in a zombie body that threatens, through contagion, to contaminate normate human society. The eugenicist impulse thus undergirds most zombie fiction, in which a kill-or-be-killed survivalist mentality characterizes much of popular zombie media. Whether survival in zombie fiction means the harsh enforcement of utilitarian ethics to ensure the safety and security of a group as in *The Walking Dead*, or individual struggles between a human protagonist and zombie assailants, it is a survival predicated upon the fear of the dissolution of the normate body, which itself comes to stand as a microcosm of human (or Western, or White, or able-bodied) society. From such a vantage, the zombie horde is the denial of human futurity, and its eradication is representative of biopolitics still deeply entrenched in eugenics discourse that views disabled bodies as threats to the stability of Western society.

Yet, in contrast to Duane's assertion that there is no continuum between wholeness and decay—between normative embodiment and the disabled zombie—the protagonists of mainstream zombie media like *The Walking Dead* are frequently disabled over the course of the narrative. Rick Grimes, the protagonist of both *The Walking Dead* television series and the comics upon which the show is based, loses a hand in the comics (though not, notably, in the AMC television series), and the amputation of a bitten, and therefore infected, limb is commonplace in the series' universe.[5] In the horror videogame series *The Last of Us*, which features a form of zombification spread by a mutated, human-targeting form of the *Cordyceps* fungus, Western society has collapsed and amputations are much more commonplace as a result of the scarcity of limb-saving medical technology. In this way, these texts seem to suggest, the seemingly obvious boundaries between dead and undead, disabled and able-bodied, begin to break down. What counts as human and what monstrous, becomes a thematic focus of these works in terms of their commentary on both human physicality and human morality.

The distinction between monster and human can never be clear-cut, for monsters are the repository of our own desires, anxieties, hopes, and fears. At once sources of wonder and terror, monsters may be used in storytelling as a tool that prohibits—that "polices the borders of the possible," in the words of monster studies scholar Jeffrey Jerome Cohen,[6] or they may be used to express that which we may not be able to publicly acknowledge and which our cultures seek to disavow as human. Monsters are at once deeply entangled with the human, while simultaneously acting as the reference point against which we

---

[5] Robert Kirkman, et al. *The Walking Dead Volume 5: The Best Defense* (Berkeley: Image Comics, 2006).

[6] Cohen, "Monster Culture (Seven Theses)," 12.

circumscribe the human. Historically, the categorization of particular groups of people as nonhuman, subhuman, and as monstrous, has served as the justification for widescale abuse, genocide, the withholding of rights, and either paternalistic and infantilizing shepherding by the dominant culture or outright subjugation.[7]

The history of the categorization of disabled and racialized people(s) as monstrous has been well-documented and analyzed elsewhere, and it is not my intention to reproduce a detailed account of such histories here. Nonetheless, contemporary narratives are informed in part by cultural contexts that are the culmination of centuries of philosophical, artistic, religious, and scientific development, and so it is necessary to briefly summarize the history of the ways in which disability and monstrosity have been entangled.

Teratology, the study of monsters, from the Greek for *sign, portent, marvel,* or *monster* gives its name also to the contemporary field of the study of congenital abnormalities. In the Classical Greek and Roman worlds, congenital disabilities were thus often understood as portents of one kind or another—divine signs that might presage calamity. This interpretation of both disabled human and non-human animal bodies continued into the Renaissance, to eventually be supplanted by a primarily naturalist interpretation of disability from the seventeenth century onward.[8] Pseudo-scientific and scientific approaches to disability were no more beneficial toward the disabled individuals and groups under scrutiny, and the emphasis on disabled bodies as scientific curiosities that could be of interest to the public was at least in part responsible for the rise of the freak show in the nineteenth century, and the display of disabled people for entertainment and profit as in the famous cases of Julia Pastrana and Joseph Merrick.[9] The eugenics discourse that underlay the sideshows of the nineteenth

---

[7] A list of recommended texts could take up an entire article on its own, so I will limit myself to the following recommendations: Surekha Davies, "The Unlucky, the Bad, and the Ugly: Categories of Monstrosity from the Renaissance to the Enlightenment," in *The Ashgate Research Companion to Monsters and the Monstrous,* eds. Asa Simon Mittman and Peter Dendle (New York: Ashgate, 2013), 49-76; Rosemarie Garland-Thomson, "Making Freaks: Visual Rhetorics and the Spectacle of Julia Pastrana," in *Thinking the Limits of the Body,* ed. Jeffrey Jerome Cohen (New York: SUNY press, 2003); and Elizabeth Young, *Black Frankenstein: The Making of an American Metaphor* (New York: New York UP, 2008).

[8] Davies, "The Unlucky, the Bad, and the Ugly," 49-63.

[9] Julia Pastrana was a nineteenth-century indigenous Mexican woman, whose body was exhibited in freak shows and museums beginning in 1854, continuing through her death in 1862, and lasting until the 1970s. Over the course of this lengthy period, Pastrana's body and identity were metaphorically redescribed with recourse to pathologizing language that emphasized her deviation from a normate body, monstrous terminology,

and twentieth centuries was one that viewed both racialized Others and disabled people as evolutionary throwbacks whose ability to reproduce ought to be stymied in order to eliminate unwanted traits (e.g., brown skin, physical disabilities) from the gene pool. In America, the anxieties over miscegenation, particularly between Black men and White women, that informed countless depictions of racially-coded monsters who aggressively and sexually pursued White victims, were coupled on the part of eugenicists with worries that disabled people might reproduce not only with each other, but that through accident or design, disabilities might contaminate normate families with physical, cognitive, and mental abnormalities. Black, Brown, and Asian minorities were believed to carry an increased risk of physical, cognitive, and mental impairment. As Angela M. Smith argues in *Hideous Progeny*, even censorship of eugenic films such as *The Black Stork* (1916) was undertaken largely over concerns that viewing such mentally (and medically) distressing material ran the risk of harming the normate public—a kind of Lamarckian contamination of its own that could "enfeeble" audiences, or pervert their morals.[10]

---

pity, delight, and horror. None of this language got at who Julia Pastrana was in an essential sense, nor does it communicate much of anything about her own subjectivity and lived experience. Instead, the metaphoric redescription deployed alongside recourse to monstrous language communicates something about the social context in which her identity was (and is) constructed by her audience. Garland-Thomson, 129-28; 133; 140. Joseph Carey Merrick (1862-1890), billed as "the Elephant Man," in sideshows, was famously "rescued" from such displays by Sir Frederick Treves, who studied Merrick's physiology and made something of a spectacle of Merrick in his own right when he introduced Merrick to upper class London society and vice versa. See: "The Elephant Man," *The British Medical Journal* 2, no. 1354 (December 1886): 1188-1189. It should be noted however that, in both instances, we risk projecting our own ethical imperatives upon both Pastrana and Merrick in portraying them unambiguously as victims of a vicious social context. The degree of agency available to Pastrana and Merrick, and of which they advantaged themselves, is impossible to discern, and indeed, such a question is arguably irrelevant in the face of such distant historical contexts. Nonetheless, a reading of either Treves or Merrick's earlier employers, for instances, as wholly exploitative, is arguably equally as problematic as a reading of Treves as a savior figure and Merrick or Pastrana as sentimentalized objects of pity.

[10] On the depiction of Black male sexual predators, see: W. Scott Poole, *Monsters in America: Our Historical Obsession with the Hideous and the Haunting*, 2nd ed. (Waco: Baylor UP, 2018), 102-109. Poole examines *King Kong* (1933) and its associated iconography as a key example of the construction of Black male sexuality as aggressive and monstrous. On the relationship between eugenics, disability, and early twentieth-century film, see: Smith, 19-21.

Similar eugenicist politics are reflected in the representation of disabled bodies in turn-of-the-century cinema and literature. Such attitudes inform the depiction of the failed marriage between the disabled carnival performer Hans and the able-bodied trapeze artist Cleopatra in 1933's MGM horror picture *Freaks*, as well as the emphasis on vampires as plague carriers who threaten White heterosexual reproduction in Bram Stoker's *Dracula* (1899), and Tod Browning's cinematic adaptation of the same in 1931.[11] While many films, most notably out gay director James Whale's 1931 picture, *Frankenstein*, and its sequel, *The Bride of Frankenstein* (1935), subverted audience expectation by painting sympathetic portraits of their monsters that interrogated audience assumptions about the place of marginalized people in Western society, critical reception of such attempts, as in the case of the largely panned *Freaks*, is indicative of a continued revulsion on the part of normate audiences toward the physically (and in the case of *Freaks*, mentally and developmentally) different.[12]

Mainstream contemporary monster media fares no better in terms of its use of disability to mark moral corruption in its monstrous or villainous characters. The much-lauded horror films of Ari Aster, *Hereditary* (2018) and *Midsommar* (2019), both feature disabled children who are framed as monstrous. Throughout *Hereditary*'s promotional trailers, as well as in the film itself, child character Charlie is coded as autistic using common Hollywood shorthand such as stimming, non-verbalism, and a flat affect. Initially, the film appears poised to overturn the construction of Charlie as a weird, potentially dangerous child when she is brutally killed halfway through the movie, yet her death midway through *Hereditary* proves a red-herring, and it is eventually revealed that Charlie was always a demon in disguise as a human, her behaviours proof of her demonic nature. In *Midsommar*, Ruben is a disabled child of incest, who is revered within his Swedish, pagan community for his prophetic abilities, but whose physical appearance and genetic provenance is framed as horrifying and monstrous to the able-bodied protagonists. As in the case of Charlie, Ruben is portrayed by an able-bodied actor, though in this case, his appearance is

---

[11] In the context of late nineteenth and early twentieth-century cultural products, eugenics discourse informed not only the construction of the monster as disabled Other and freak, but also as racialized Other. The co-construction of race and disability in this context, emerges in the arguments made by eugenicists that racial mixing would lead to an increase in the birth of disabled children. See: Poole, 94-95; Smith, 47-51.

[12] *Freaks* was in part lambasted for its use of actual disabled actors in the production. A famous anecdote tells the story of how F. Scott Fitzgerald, seated next to Daisy and Violet Hilton, the Siamese twins from the film, fled his restaurant table from nausea. Poole, 2; Smith, 93-96.

enhanced by prosthetic make-up designed to provoke revulsion from the film's American characters, and presumably the audience. Outside the realm of horror, science fiction and fantasy offerings like *Wonder Woman* (2017) and *The Witches* (2020) rely on physical disability as shorthand for monstrosity and mental disturbance. In *Wonder Woman*, Dr. Maru, one of the film's antagonists, is a mad scientist whose face has become scarred over the course of her experiments, while in *The Witches* the monstrosity of its titular villains is revealed to include three-fingered hands, and feet without toes.[13] In the realm of videogames, *Life is Strange* (2015), a game praised for its exploration of queer teenage relationships, reveals that the serial killer whom the time-traveling protagonist is attempting to thwart and uncover is a teenage boy suffering from schizophrenia and bipolar disorder.[14] *Life is Strange* is far from the only recent game to link disability with monstrosity or with moral failure and violence, but it is notable that these motifs and themes persist even in the context of media that has been praised for its inclusive politics.

The tropes discussed briefly here recur within the *Resident Evil* franchise and are in fact pushed further to link disability more egregiously with the very eugenic principles that in a real-world context are used to argue for the erasure of disabled people, and the elimination or limitation of disabled bodies.

Entering the World of Survival Horror: *Resident Evil*, Mad Scientists, and their Monsters

The *Resident Evil* franchise is a multi-million-dollar media property that includes videogames of multiple sub-genres, a successful science-fiction film series spanning six live-action movies, a separate set of five animated films set in the universe of its videogame source material, novelizations, comic books, action figures, and even an upcoming a Netflix television show. Each of these media engages in its own way with themes of disability, though my analysis will centre only on the *Resident Evil* videogames. The series, titled *Biohazard* in

---

[13] In the case of *The Witches*, audience response to the three-fingered witches (which were neither a feature of the Roald Dahl novel upon which the movie is based, nor of the 1990 film adaptation), was overwhelmingly negative, and evolved into a Twitter hashtag of #notawitch, spearheaded by young people with limb difference. The response provoked an apology from actress Anne Hathaway, who portrayed the lead witch in the movie, as well as apologies from other cast and crew. See: Jimmy McCloskey, "Teen Born With 3 Fingers Blasts New Witches Movie for Making Her Look 'Scary,'" *Metro UK*, November 23, 2020, https://metro.co.uk/2020/11/23/teen-born-3-fingers-blasts-new-witches-movie-making-her-look-scary-13641681/.

[14] Dontnod Entertainment, *Life is Strange*, Square Enix, 2015.

Japan, is produced by the Japanese videogame company Capcom, but depends largely on Western (specifically, American) horror tropes, and is a direct response to the development of the zombie as an American horror movie monster.[15]

Within videogame fan culture, as well as in the academic field of videogame studies, *Resident Evil* is widely known as the progenitor of the videogame sub-genre "survival horror." The term was coined by *Resident Evil*'s creators to describe the games' focus on survival-focused gameplay that pits under-armed protagonists against much stronger adversaries. The emphasis in the early *Resident Evil* games, as well as the numerous survival horror games that emulated its formula, is on the scarcity of resources, and player management of those same resources (known as "inventory management").[16] Later games in the franchise would eschew this specific brand of horror in favour of more action-oriented gameplay that positions the player characters not as vulnerable humans struggling to survive, but as physically intimidating and powerful combat specialists with vast arsenals of weapons and martial arts moves at their beck and call. The shift in genre, as well as a later return to the games' survival horror origins in the seventh and eighth installments of the franchise, reflect the shifting politics of the games as much as they do shifting market trends. As I will demonstrate in my analysis of individual entries in the series, the relationship between protagonist/player character and antagonist within each game reveals the different political and social stakes that underlie and inform storyline and gameplay choices on the part of Capcom, and which are displayed through the games' representation of its monstrous and disabled villains.

Set in the midwestern United States, the first installment of the series, titled simply *Resident Evil* (or, in Japan, *Biohazard*) and released in 1996, follows the members of an elite police squad called S.T.A.R.S. (Special Tactics and Rescue Squad) as they investigate a series of gruesome murders in a wooded area

---

[15] Following the 1968 release of director George A. Romero's *Night of the Living Dead*, zombies became what W. Scott Poole calls, "a new monster for a dark American pantheon." He further states that the post-Romero zombies, alongside their counterpart revenants, vampires, "almost pure creations of American popular culture, their motifs lifted from European and Caribbean legend and transformed into horrific celebrities." Although Poole rather overstates the degree to which the vampire and zombie are American creations, his point holds that the post-Romero zombie in particular developed as a specifically American monster that was used deliberately by horror writers and directors to comment on American social and political issues. Poole, 206; 208.

[16] Dawn Stobbart, *Videogames and Horror: From* Amnesia *to* Zombies, Run! (Cardiff: University of Wales Press, 2019), 27-28.

outside the fictional American town of Raccoon City. Early in the investigation, the S.T.A.R.S. officers are chased by seemingly rabid dogs and shelter in an ominous mansion straight out of nineteenth-century Gothic. Trapped in the mansion, the player character—Jill Valentine or Chris Redfield, depending on the player's choice—investigates the horrors of the mansion and evades or kills the humanoid, corvid, and canine zombies that stalk the mansion's halls (alongside a giant mutated snake, vicious swarms of bees, anthropophagous sharks, and even an Audrey II-esque plant). As the player investigates, it is gradually revealed that the zombies populating the mansion were humans who have been transformed with the use of a bio-engineered virus called the T-Virus. The T-Virus was created by the pharmaceutical company Umbrella for eventual deployment as a bio-weapon. The S.T.A.R.S. were intentionally lured to the mansion by their duplicitous captain, Albert Wesker, to test the weapons' effectiveness against trained combatants.

Umbrella's Frankensteinian forays into the creation of new, or changed, life are not limited to zombification, however. Umbrella is also responsible for the development of wholly new organisms, as well as the use of human experimentation to create giant, clawed monsters called Tyrants that can kill their opponents with a single swipe. Despite the ferocity of the Tyrant, and to present the player with a clear means of defeating the monster, the monster is limited by the presence of an external heart—ectopia cordis—that leaves the Tyrant vulnerable when shot or stabbed in this location. The existence of a laughably obvious weakness for a bioweapon is in part dictated by videogame logic that necessitates the presence of clear, exploitable weak points that allow the player the opportunity to succeed. Nonetheless, these design elements (which recur throughout the series) draw attention to the flawed logic of the games' human antagonists when they assert the genetic superiority of their creations. Surely, the games seem to suggest, the player recognizes the inherent derangement of Umbrella and its scientists, given that even the company's attempts to perpetrate horrific violence upon human bodies is met with failure? The grotesque qualities of Umbrella's monsters, Tyrant included, signal the depth of the company's moral failings in a scenario in which its scientists are already marked as suspect for their experimentation on unwilling human subjects.

Significantly, the Tyrant monsters are described by Albert Wesker (who is also an employee of Umbrella) as "the ultimate life form" during a spectacular, B-movie-esque evil monologue in one of the game's final cinematics.[17] As Wesker

---

[17] "Cinematics," "cinemas," or "cut-scenes" in a videogame context, refer to scripted portions of a game that do not require player input, and which essentially take the form of movie scenes.

reveals his sinister plan, which includes the betrayal of not only his fellow S.T.A.R.S. members, but seemingly also Umbrella itself, he admires Umbrella's more spectacularly monstrous creations—each housed within a massive, liquid-filled stasis chamber.

Chris Redfield responds to Wesker's assertion that the Tyrant is in any way a superior lifeform with laughter and the accusation that Wesker is "pitiful." "This is your saviour?" Chris asks rhetorically, "You say this failure is your saviour?"[18] Chris's mockery of Wesker's deference to the Tyrant—Umbrella's disabled monster creation—as well the Tyrant itself, is a dynamic that repeats in nearly every game in the series, as well as in many of the franchise's other media products. Chris's status as the player character creates a dynamic in which the player themself is likewise positioned to understand the ludicrousness of Wesker's admiration for Umbrella's flawed creation.

With each further installment in the series, the emphasis on both the eugenically informed motivations of the antagonists, as well as the relationship between disability, monstrosity, and eugenics, is intensified. In later games, for instance, the monster is not simply admired from outside the stasis chamber but is instead the desired corporeal form of the scientists (or the aristocrats funding the scientists' research). It is this desire for disability, and the positioning of that desire as a kind of eugenics in and of itself, that I term eugenics of disability. Like real-world eugenicist politics, it posits not only the existence of an ideal body, but promotes such bodies as being the only acceptable human (or superhuman) form.

In subsequent *Resident Evil* games, most spectacularly in the entries from the fourth major installment in the series, *Resident Evil: Code Veronica* (2000), onward, a eugenics of disability becomes the primary focus of the games' antagonists, as well as the primary marker of Umbrella and its splinter companies' malevolence. Albert Wesker in particular becomes a spokesman for global eugenics of disability that frames a future in which all humans have either been successfully mutated by the Umbrella viruses, or have been eradicated, as the ideal world toward which he strives. Increasingly in the games, there is also a tendency for the desire for corporeal transformation to be matched with an already physically or mentally disabled body. These features are often combined with queer, racialized, and class markers that prime audiences to accept or anticipate the degeneracy of *Resident Evil*'s rogues gallery. That these same markers populate earlier Hollywood horror movies should not surprise.

---

[18] Capcom, *Resident Evil: Director's Cut,* Sony Playstation, 1998.

A Eugenics of Disability

In *Resident Evil: Code Veronica*, a game whose events take place between *Resident Evil 3* and *4*, players alternately control Claire Redfield (Chris's younger sister, and the protagonist of *Resident Evil 2*), and Chris Redfield himself.[19] Claire awakens as a prisoner on an Umbrella-owned private island in the Southern Ocean after being captured by the company following a covert operation on one of Umbrella's labs. Soon, Claire learns that the island, much like Raccoon City in *Resident Evil 2*, has become overrun with zombies and other mutants. This time the outbreak is the result of the spread of the T-Veronica Virus—the containment and control of deadly viruses being at once part of Umbrella's facilities' main purpose, and yet also the one task at which it seems unable to succeed. In Claire's race to escape the island before the inevitable self-destruct sequence is activated (another recurring feature of the games), she explores an ostentatious castle belonging to Alfred and Alexia Ashford, the aristocratic grandchildren of one of Umbrella's three founders. Over the course of Claire's investigations, she learns that the twin Ashfords share an uncomfortably close bond suggestive of incest. As Alfred pursues Claire with a hunting rifle while dressed in a campy, old-fashioned red military uniform, and speaking with an over-the-top, high-pitched English accent, Claire comes to learn that the few glimpses she has caught of Alexia were none but Alfred in disguise. Traumatized by the apparent loss of his sister Alexia (and, given the queer-coding of the character, a queer desire to transgress traditional gender norms), Alfred began crossdressing and roleplaying as his twin. In his dying moments, Alfred drags himself to the feet of the stasis chamber where Alexia resides. Years earlier, Alexia had entombed herself inside the stasis chamber so that she might incubate the T-Veronica Virus. Alexia awakens from her artificial slumber, bent on revenge, and transformed into a tentacled monster.

Each time Claire and Chris battle Alexia, she mutates into a less human form. Before the first of Alexia's most dramatic transformations, she rejects an offer on the part of Albert Wesker (returned from the dead, and also now mutated), telling Wesker, "you are not worthy of its [T-Veronica's] power." Although in this first sequence, Alexia retains a humanoid form, metamorphosing into something akin to an attractive human statue, in her final transformation scenes, she loses mobility when her entire bottom half fuses into an amorphous blob (her upper half becomes insectile). After her first transformation, unlike many other *Resident Evil* villains, Alexia no longer has any dialogue, but whether this is due

---

[19] For a timeline of relevant games from the series, see the end of the appendix.

to her own choice not to speak, or muteness brought on by the physiological changes of her body, is unclear.[20]

The Ashfords' experimentation with T-Veronica (tested on their father's body before its application to Alexia), is continuously presented through the lens of their queer-coded sibling relationship, their aristocratic pedigree, and their eugenic motivations. During Claire's first meeting with Alfred, when Claire senses an emotional weak spot and insults Alfred's importance, Alfred launches into a defense of his aristocratic lineage and his genetic superiority to Claire. This scene, and subsequent ones that reveal the incestuous and gender-transgressive Gothic underbelly of the Ashford plotline, operate under the presumption that Alfred and Alexia's derangement and inferiority are obvious to the audience. The apparent weakness of the Ashford line is communicated to the audience through the twins' nearly supernatural paleness, their uncanny similarity, their sadism, their effete and accented voices, and finally, Alfred's gender transgression and apparent madness. Alfred's mental instability is demonstrated not only through his overreactions to stimuli, his petulant and childlike demeanour, but also his own reaction to the revelation of his crossdressing. The fact that Claire hears Alfred holding entire conversations between himself and Alexia suggests that Alfred has bought into his own disguise and espouses what the game presents as a deluded worldview. When the wig he uses to disguise himself as Alexia is torn off and he views himself in the mirror, Alfred experiences a mental break. The version of reality he had constructed for himself shatters and he loses Alexia (and his identities as both brother and sister, male and female) for a second time.

While Alexia and Alfred both present their bloodline and genetics as superior, the audience is in on Capcom's joke: the Ashfords are degenerative, representative of an impure genetics that in fact wants to further disable itself through continued mutation. This message is further emphasized through the parallelism established between the twins' sibling bond and Claire's relationship with Chris. Unlike Alfred, who is effeminate and weak and must be rescued by his sister, Chris travels to the island under his own auspices to rescue Claire,

---

[20] Capcom, *Resident Evil: Code Veronica*, Dreamcast, 2000. It should be noted, however, that in a later remake of portions of *Code Veronica*, Alexia's storyline is drastically changed. In the version of the narrative told in *Resident Evil: The Darkside Chronicles* (2009), once awakened, Alexia murders Alfred herself, and in her final confrontation with Chris and Claire she waxes lyrical on her right to treat the world's populations as her test subjects. Unlike in the original, in which the parallel between Alexia and Alfred's queer, dubiously incestuous relationship is implicitly contrasted against Claire and Chris's healthy, appropriately-coded sibling bond, in *The Darkside Chronicles* Alexia explicitly makes this comparison herself. Capcom, *Resident Evil: The Darkside Chronicles*, Wii, 2009.

asserting his masculinity and performing an appropriate form of sibling love (one that involves manly combat and the defeat of monsters, rather than the sadistic cat-and-mouse game Alfred plays with Claire). If Alfred attempts to similarly rescue Alexia, it is only through his improper memorialization of her within his own body, an act that queers both siblings and further cements the inappropriateness of their closeness.

These elements and motifs support a real-world eugenic impulse through their dependence on the tradition of eugenicist suspicion of aristocratic incest and the transmission of genetic disorders within aristocratic families. As Smith relates concerning turn-of-the-century eugenic fears and their influence on *Dracula,* "class-specific threats . . . derived not only from those lower on the social scale, as we might expect, but also from the aristocracy . . . . American eugenicists linked reproductive defects to the aristocracy's consanguineous marriages, its 'pride of blood,' which encouraged sterility and concentration of negative traits."[21] In this way, *Code Veronica* is able to have its eugenicist cake and eat it too: Alfred and Alexia are monstrous because they promote an exclusive eugenicist genetics, yet in terms of real-world eugenics, the twins are marked as polluting influences when their unusual appearances and disordered temperaments are compared with the square-jawed, all-American Chris, and his plucky and appropriately affectionate sister, Claire. Alexia's embrace of the virus to further set herself apart, to further disable herself in the context of normate society (a society she feels nothing for but disdain) is similarly suspect. As an incestuous, disabled couple, Alfred and Alexia's embrace of a promised future in which viral contamination results in a world free of the able-bodied, marks them as supporters of a eugenicist mandate that requires the ascension of a disabled, aristocratic class.

Class, disability, and race are continuously co-constructed in the *Resident Evil* games. In *Resident Evil 4* (2005), the first of the more action-oriented titles in the series, the American special agent Leon S. Kennedy is primarily antagonized by an assortment of physically disabled villains, who are largely of aristocratic background and who are racialized through the game's Spanish setting and the use of Spanish accents for its characters. That Leon is on a special mission from the American president to rescue the president's kidnapped daughter from bio-terrorists firmly codes Leon's adversaries as racially, ethnically, and religiously Other—sites of difference that similarly map queerness and disability onto their bodies. The identification of the Spanish antagonists in the game with terrorism conflates the on-screen racialized identities of the characters with an

---

[21] Smith, *Hideous Progeny*, 48.

Islamaphobic understanding of terrorism as racially, religiously, and ethnically marked.

While the ordinary enemies Leon fights over the course of the game are depicted as interchangeable (literally—the enemy character models are, as in many games, limited) peasants possessed by a bio-engineered parasite, the major antagonists of the game are nearly all disabled, queer-coded aristocrats who comment explicitly on Leon's American identity, on Americans' belief that they can police the world, and on the American pre-occupation with terrorism. The first of these antagonists, Bitores Mendez, is a physically imposing, one-eyed former friar who has converted to a vaguely defined evil cult that acts as a front for a bio-weapons company formed from the dissolved Umbrella Corporation.[22] When Mendez transforms prior to his face-off with Leon, his original disabilities are accentuated. Mendez's gigantism is doubled when his torso dramatically tears itself from his middle, revealing a segmented centipede body that joins head and shoulders to legs. His false eye, which Leon requires to open a door, glows red throughout the fight.[23]

The most telling example of how *Resident Evil 4* uses a eugenics of disability to suggest moral deficiency is in the character of Ramon Salazar. Salazar is the eighth castellan of El Pueblo (the fictional town where *RE4* takes place). Like Alfred Ashford, Salazar is presented as hysterical, giggling, effete, sadistic, and childlike. Salazar's dwarfism is of particular note, as it is both contrasted against Mendez's gigantism, and is used to underscore his childlike demeanour and mannerisms. Much like Alfred, Salazar expresses a belief that he is superior to other humans, though in this case specifically in contrast to the ordinary citizens of El Pueblo (called *ganados*, "cattle" in Spanish), who have been infected by the Las Plagas parasite. "Surely," Salazar monologues evilly to Leon, "you don't think I'm the same as those diminutive *ganados*. The parasites, Las Plagas, are slaves to my will. I have absolute control."[24] During a later encounter, Salazar establishes that he views possession by the parasite as a numinous religious experience that grants power to the worthy.[25] Leon rebuts Salazar's religious claims by saying, "this is no ritual. It's terrorism," to which Salazar responds, "Isn't that a popular word these days?" The already queer-coded Salazar (decked out in a purple tricorne hat and a matching doublet),

---

[22] Numerous "revelations" from subsequent *Resident Evil* titles reveal that the evil company du jour has actually always been Umbrella, but with a new hat.

[23] Capcom, *Resident Evil 4*, Gamecube, 2005.

[24] Capcom, *Resident Evil 4*.

[25] Capcom, *Resident Evil 4*.

retreats with a squeal when Leon pins his hand to the wall, a coward in contrast with Leon's brave defense of the president's daughter.

The association between Salazar, Mendez, and terrorism, participates in a general queering of the terrorist body, a discourse outlined by Jasbir K. Puar in her seminal study, *Terrorist Assemblages: Homonationalism in Queer Times*. As Puar notes, the Western imaginary codes the sexuality of both terrorist and Orientalized bodies as imbricated with several deviant sexualities, including queerness and polygamy. Puar states, "Osama bin Laden . . . was portrayed as monstrous by association with sexual and bodily perversity (versions of both homosexuality and hypertrophied heterosexuality, or failed monogamy, that is, an Orientalist version of polygamy, as well as disability)."[26] The terrorist body is thus always already the queer body by virtue of the queer construction of terrorist sexuality in popular culture. The explicit identification of *RE4*'s antagonists as a bio-terror organization, primes the audience to view their sexuality through a queerly gendered and sexualized lens.

In *Code Veronica*, Chris and Claire's appropriate performances of gender and sibling relations cast aspersions on Alfred and Alexia. Leon's American masculinity—his physical prowess, his stand against foreign terrorism—are contrasted with Salazar's dwarfism, physical weakness, and dissembling when accused of participating in terrorist activities. It feels almost unnecessary to point out that the shift of focus in the *Resident Evil* series from the dangers of Umbrella as a sinister pharmaceutical company to that of Umbrella's successors as bio-terrorist cells occurs post-9/11, and indeed, the emphasis on terrorism in *RE4* continues in subsequent titles, most notably its direct sequel. Just as Alfred's madness and transness were necessary in *Code Veronica* in order to emphasize Chris's masculinity and Claire's American resourcefulness (Alfred is more feminine than Claire, but it's all right, because Claire wears a midriff-showing top that lets us know that although she's tough, she's still a girl), in *RE4* Salazar is foreign, effeminate, queer, disabled, and a eugenicist, so that Leon can be American, manly, straight, able-bodied, and defender of individual liberty. As Puar writes, "sexual deviancy is linked to the process of discerning, othering, and quarantining terrorist bodies, but these racially and sexually perverse figures also labor in the service of disciplining and normalizing subjects worthy of rehabilitation *away from* these bodies, in other words, signaling and enforcing the mandatory forms of patriotism."[27]

---

[26] Jasbir K. Puar, *Terrorist Assemblages: Homonationalism in Queer Times*, 10th Anniversary Edition (Durham: Duke UP, 2017), 38.

[27] Puar, *Terrorist Assemblages*, 38.

Resident Evil, as a cultural product, participates in this same push toward appropriate patriotic performance, one that valorizes certain types of violence (e.g., violence in service to the American State, violence against minorities who pose a threat to American values), while further Othering racialized foreigners by collapsing difference of all kinds into one monstrous identity. As a Japanese franchise, *Resident Evil* (*Biohazard* in Japan) implicitly links this specifically American patriotism to a Japanese imperialist patriotism that positions Japan as not only a global economic and cultural leader, particularly in comparison with other East Asian nations, but as a country firmly on the side of the Good in a binary system that imagines nations and cultures as favouring either the side of absolute Good (the State) or absolute Evil (terrorism). As Michal Daliot-Bul demonstrates in her article on early-twentieth-century branding in Japan, beginning in 2002, Japanese cultural products frequently participated in a formal branding campaign called the Japan Branding Strategy. The JBS premises itself upon the utility of "soft power" in expanding Japanese influence. By extending its ideological reach through the production of media for the global market, Japan is able to extend its power through the construction of the image of what Daliot-Bul describes as "Cool Japan."[28] This initiative allowed Japan to spread pro-Japanese sentiment through the market rather than by coercion. The JBS was a deliberate attempt to recreate Japan's global image via its "content products," especially anime, manga, and videogames, in order to reify Japan's national identity on a global scale.[29] As a company with a financial stake in appealing to the American market, moreover, Capcom stands to benefit from favorable portrayals of what are perceived to be American ideals from the vantage of its Japanese context. That said, it is notable also that none of the videogames takes place in Japan, despite the globe-trotting nature of the series. Capcom thus both establishes a firm link between Japan and America as anti-terrorist powerhouses on the global stage, while simultaneously contrasting the frequent apocalyptic zombie events that take place in America (and elsewhere) against the relatively zombie-free paradise of Japan. America, Africa, Europe, and other East Asian countries may be prone to terrorist attack and zombie plague, but Japan remains strong enough to keep such messy virologies from contaminating its borders. Since most *Resident Evil* villains are figures of authority (politicians on the large or local scale, CEOs, and government scientists), there is a risk that giving evil a Japanese residence could be perceived as a critique of contemporary Japanese political structures.

---

[28] Michal Daliot-Bul, "Japan Brand Strategy: The Taming of 'Cool Japan''and the Challenges of Cultural Planning in a Postmodern Age" in *Social Science Japan Journal* 12, no. 2 (2009): 247-66.

[29] Daliot-Bul, "Japan Brand Strategy," 252-253.

Embedding such criticism in a Japanese-centered videogame would destabilize the carefully constructed image of "Cool Japan," packaged and sold to the West. In Cool Japan, the games suggest, our political and cultural leaders would never ally themselves with a eugenics of disability that sought to overthrow the dominant regime.

The biopolitics underpinning *Resident Evil* at once performatively disavow eugenics, while simultaneously using ableist tropes and imagery to further demonize the Other. In this way, the eugenics of disability operates much like Puar's homonationalism, in which Western liberalism disavows homophobia as a way to mark itself as distinct from an intolerant Orient, while hypocritically using homophobic imagery and rhetoric to characterize the Other as degenerate.

Like Mendez, when Salazar transforms, his pre-existing disability is emphasized by the nature of his transformation. Unable to face Leon man-to-man, Salazar allows himself to be consumed by a giant, fleshy flower, that absorbs Salazar into a phallic/tongue-like protrusion with a giant eye. Salazar's legs are lost in the fusion, rendering what remains of his human body more diminutive still. Once the transformation is complete, Leon quips: "Monsters. I guess after this there'll be one less to worry about," as though the point that Salazar was already a monster prior to his metamorphosis might somehow be missed.[30]

Following in the footsteps of *Resident Evil 4*, *Resident Evil 5* (2009) shirks the American setting of the first three games. Unlike *RE4*, which takes place in a real country, *RE5* establishes its fictional setting as an African nation called Kijuju, where a dramatically more muscular Chris Redfield has been sent by a counter-bio-terrorism organization to investigate a possible terrorist cell. He is joined by an African counter-terrorism agent called Sheva Alomar. The racism undergirding Capcom's fictional African nation is apparent within the first two minutes of the game's opening cinema. As Ta-Nehisi Coates describes in an article for *The Atlantic*:

> One of the first things you see in the game, seconds after taking control of Chris Redfield, is a gang of African men brutally beating *something* in a sack. Animal or human, it's never revealed, but these are not infected Majini [infected humans]. There are no red bloodshot eyes. These are ordinary Africans, who stop and stare at you menacingly as you approach. Since the Majini are not undead corpses, and are capable of driving vehicles, handling weapons and even using guns, it makes the line between the infected monsters and African civilians uncomfortably

---

[30] Capcom, *Resident Evil 4*.

vague. Where Africans are concerned, the game seems to be suggesting, bloodthirsty savagery just comes with the territory.[31]

While the infected villagers of *RE4* were similarly capable of firing weapons and other complex movements, there is an undeniable intensification of the humanness of the parasitically-implanted Black victims in *RE5*, and as Coates lays out in his analysis of the opening cinematic, African characters in *RE5* need not even be victims of the parasite for the game to present them as subhuman. The town in which the opening portions of the game are set is depicted as a run-down shantytown—hardly a thriving community even before the outbreak— and even when Black characters are portrayed sympathetically within the game's storyline, it is with an eye to their naivety and the baseness of the emotions that guide them (greed and desperation due to their poverty). These emotions allow them to be manipulated by terrorist factions and an Umbrella puppet-company called Tricell. If the Ashfords and Salazar are suspect due to their aristocratic background, the nameless hordes of infected Majini (a word that recalls the *jinn* of Arab folklore) are marked as distinctly impoverished, at best lower-working class. They exist as objects of pity rather than full characters. The presence of a light-skinned Black co-protagonist in the form of Sheva Alomar does little to dispel the impression that Capcom anticipated the image of dozens of yelling, Black male bodies would be terrifying to a presumed White and Asian audience without the need for rotting flesh, dangling limbs, or tentacles. The insensibility of the Majini, like that of the *ganados* in *RE4*, gives the further impression of a population denuded of mental acuity, subject to the whims of corporate manipulation.

This racist representation of Black Africans as senseless and malleable is compounded further when Chris Redfield and Sheva Alomar venture into the marshlands and discover a journal in which a marshland youth describes how infection gradually reverted the people in his community to a tribal state. The journal, no doubt meant to explain the racist "tribal" wardrobe of the mid-game's primary enemies, describes how the villagers were tricked into allowing Tricell employees to implant them with parasites when they were told they were being vaccinated against infectious diseases. As the parasites gradually alter the brains of their hosts, the village youth describes how, "the men are all dressed like our ancestors and fighting each other. Most of the women have died."[32] The reversion of the villagers to ancestral forms of dress (as well as their

---

[31] Ta-Nehisi Coates, "Sometimes it's Just Racist . . . ," *The Atlantic*, February 10th, 2009, https://www.theatlantic.com/entertainment/archive/2009/02/sometimes-it-apos-s-just-racist/6705/.

[32] Capcom, *Resident Evil 5*, XBOX 360, 2009.

dependence on traditional weaponry such as spears and bows) is informed by (and reinforces) a racist worldview that understands non-Western, and non-Japanese, indigenous cultures and traditional practices as less evolved and as genetically inferior. The implication is that some populations, especially racialized populations, are always already mentally ill—always already disabled. That the villagers are tricked by Tricell through the promised dissemination of life-saving vaccines is especially notable. While it positions "Africans" as in need of salvation by developed nations, it simultaneously, and insidiously, suggests that Sub-Saharan Africans are mentally and cognitively inferior to White Westerners. Attempts to civilize Kijuju (presented in-game as a kind of quintessential barbarian Other), are shown to have failed before they have even begun, allowing the game to present its fictional nation as both pathetic and in need of Western guidance, but also genetically and culturally unable to rise above the evolutionary hierarchy the game itself constructs. The result is a type of postmodern phrenology that participates in the same "race science."

It would seem that, from *RE4* onwards, while the virus and parasites cause immediately obvious physical disabilities in some victims, they render certain subjects prone instead to cognitive disability and mental illness. The susceptibility of some subjects to cognitive rather than physical impairment is rendered along class and racial lines within the stories of the games.[33] The representation of poor, lower, and working-class populations as intellectually and genetically inferior recurs in *Resident Evil 7* (2017). The game returns to an American setting but focuses on the uncontrolled infection of a swamp-dwelling White American family and their descent into chainsaw-wielding cannibals who seem directly plucked from *The Hills Have Eyes* and *Deliverance*. The atmosphere of creeping dread that pervades the game and informs player experience is overwhelmingly dependent on audience familiarity with the trope of the dangerous and cognitively impaired White trash family. Notable in both the case of the African villagers and the White swamp cannibals, is that the inability to reason is not linked with a lack of education, or even with an innate lack of intelligence, but with a reversion to a so-called earlier evolutionary state brought on by the virus. The eugenics of disability thus operates on two basic principles in the later games: 1) the villains' (misguided) belief that they are genetically superior and that through disabling themselves, they will become yet more elite, and 2) mentally and cognitively disabling those deemed unworthy (people from a lower social strata), reveals a dark truth about the nature of human evolution and communicates something significant about ordinary, especially working and lower class, people. The result is a series

---

[33] Capcom, *Resident Evil 7: Biohazard*, PS4, 2017.

deeply suspicious of difference, one that maps villainy and monstrosity onto the bodies of disabled, racialized, queer, and poor people.

In *Resident Evil 5*, Albert Wesker's villainous scheme revels in the trope of the eugenics of disability. Unlike in previous games, wherein the threat to global populations presented by disabling viruses and parasites is unrealized and vague, in *RE5*, Wesker almost succeeds in his plot to achieve what he calls, "complete global saturation," of the Uroboros virus. His goal, in this case, is not simply personal transformation, but the spread of his corporeal ideology across the world. In Wesker's perfect future, only those bodies capable of merging with the Uroboros virus are worthy of continuing to exist, and it is precisely these bodies that will form a new society to replace the perceived inadequacy of the old one. While Wesker's eugenicist politics are allied on the one hand with White supremacist goals (notably, none of his "superior," mutated commanders are Black, despite the African setting, and Wesker himself is a strikingly pale, blond man), the player is nonetheless encouraged to view both Wesker's cronies and the gullible Black residents of Kijuju with suspicion. Implicit in the game is the message that while Wesker's solution may be extreme and misguided, there is a problem inherent in Black and poor bodies that requires attending to by wealthy nations.

Conclusion

Wesker, alongside the antihero Ada Wong (a love interest of Leon's) and Chris's kidnapped partner Jill Valentine, are the only mutated characters who genuinely appear to achieve some form of the ideal body. Two of these characters are attractive young women, whose appearance is likely intended to appeal to a presumed straight male audience. These same characters are also coded positively in the context of the games. Albert Wesker, though he is presented as cool, collected, and as a physically attractive humanoid for the majority of the series, is eventually transformed in such a way as to render him physically grotesque.

It is revealed part way through *RE5* that Wesker must inject himself with viral enhancers to maintain his superhuman abilities and control the virus that threatens to overwhelm his body. As soon as this information is received, Wesker, one of the few seemingly able-bodied antagonists in the franchise, is marked as chronically ill. Only a short time later, Chris and Sheva overdose Wesker on one of the enhancers. Wesker flies into a rage, ultimately infecting himself with Uroboros to give him the strength to defeat Chris. This last virus alters Wesker's body to appear inhuman, with a massive, throbbing and tentacled arm, and gaping wounds that open in his back and chest. At the point at which Wesker is finally defeated by Chris and Sheva, he has abdicated his humanity in the same way as Salazar and Alexia. It is the point at which Wesker's disability, as well as his desire for disability, is made known to the audience, that he is killed.

In the prelude to this final confrontation, Wesker echoes many of the series' antagonists final sentiments, words that express a eugenics of disability. Taunting Chris, Wesker asks, "Has it ever occurred to you that only a handful of humans really matter? Everyone else is just so much chaff. So now I have to separate the chaff from the wheat... only those with superior DNA will be chosen by [the virus] Uroboros. Only those fit for survival will be allowed to carry their genes into a new age!" Like the Ashfords, Wesker perceives himself as one of "those fit for survival," but as in *Code Veronica*, the player is in on the joke: Wesker cannot survive once he occupies a visibly disabled body. Several earlier villains in *RE5* express similar sentiments. These include Ricardo Irving's statement prior to transformation into an aquatic monster that he is, in his tentacled form, "far beyond anything you could hope to become," that he has undergone "an extreme makeover" in becoming the quasi-human tongue of a freshwater Leviathan. Excella Gionne, a wealthy and beautiful femme fatale, insists that she is "someone suitable to join [Wesker] in [his] new world," hours before Wesker abandons her to be transformed into a writhing mass of tentacles.[34]

Ultimately, Wesker's evil plot to ensure "complete global saturation" of the Uroboros virus across the Earth meets with failure, but the eugenic impulses at the heart of the *Resident Evil* franchise prevail, as in *Resident Evil 4*, with the survival of the muscle-bound American hero, Chris, and his attractive female companions. Having rid the world of the danger presented by Wesker, they have likewise rid the world of the narrative of its disabled antagonists *du jour*.[35]

---

[34] Excella Gionne provides the financial backing for Wesker's plan to infect the world with the new Uroboros virus, and believes fully that she will stand by his side as one of the genetically superior survivors. Over the course of the game she is heavily sexualized, and explicitly uses her appearance to attempt to seduce Wesker. Wesker's rebuff of her advances further queers a character already homosexually coded through his trim fashion sense, his clip English-*ish* accent, and his close relationship with fellow mad scientist William Birkin, in *Resident Evil: Zero* (2002). The hypermasculinity of Chris Redfield throughout the game similarly highlights the queer possibility of these two characters, and Wesker's lack of a true "partner" in *Resident Evil 5* is constantly paralleled with Chris's partnerships with both Jill Valentine and Sheva Alomar. Capcom, *Resident Evil: Zero*, Gamecube, 2002.

[35] It is worth noting that *Resident Evil 8: Village*, was released in 2021 during the editing of this chapter. While I do not have the space here to examine that game in full, it is important to note that a eugenics of disability becomes arguably more pronounced in the eighth installment in the franchise. In *Village*, the American male protagonist of *Resident Evil 7* returns, this time traversing an Eastern European village in search of his

While the series thus carves an opportunity for disabled and able-bodied players alike to re-envision and explore disability and its relationship to desire and fantasy, *Resident Evil* ultimately marks such a desire as sterile and degenerate. A redemptive reading of the narratives of *Resident Evil*'s disabled and disabling villains is left to the audience to provide, but through the linkages forged between eugenics, non-consent, and disability, such attempts risk becoming entangled with the more troubling political implications of Umbrella's experiments: colonialism, war profiteering, and the abuse and use of poor bodies. What emerges from the series is therefore less a new and exciting lens through which to imagine and understand disability, and instead a novel approach to telling disabled stories about able-bodied heroes.

Select Resident Evil Videogame Franchise Timeline

Resident Evil (1996)
Resident Evil 2 (1998)
Resident Evil 3 (1999)
Resident Evil: Code Veronica (2000)
Resident Evil: Zero (2002)
Resident Evil 4 (2005)
Resident Evil: The Darkside Chronicles (2009)
Resident Evil 5 (2009)
Resident Evil: Revelations (2012)
Resident Evil 6 (2012)
Resident Evil: Revelations 2
Resident Evil 7: Biohazard (2017)
Resident Evil 8: Village (2021)

---

missing daughter. The game's five primary antagonists are each based on a classic Hollywood monster (vampires, Dr. Frankenstein, the Invisible Man, the Creature from the Black Lagoon, and a witch). Each of these characters has been mutated by the Cadou Parasite, an organism used by the main antagonist (a mad scientist and aristocratic leader called Mother Miranda) to control the townspeople. While one of Miranda's four underlings expresses a rare disgust with his transformed body, the game makes explicit that the vampire characters, especially their leader, Alcina Dimitrescu, was only able to survive implantation due to a pre-existing blood condition. Vampirism, in *Village*, is thus explicitly linked with disability. The Cadou, like other *Resident Evil* viruses and parasites, also accentuates physical disabilities in the mutated bodies of its hosts. Alcina Dimitrescu is presented as a giant, while Salvatore Moreau—an aquatic monster—is presented as physically grotesque, with boils and a hunchback. Capcom, *Resident Evil 8: Village*, PS4, 2021.

Bibliography

Capcom, *Resident Evil: Director's Cut*, Sony Playstation, 1996.

Capcom, *Resident Evil: Code Veronica*, Dreamcast, 2000.

Capcom, *Resident Evil: Zero*, Gamecube, 2002.

Capcom, *Resident Evil 4*, Gamecube, 2005.

Capcom, *Resident Evil 5*, XBOX 360, 2009.

Capcom, *Resident Evil: The Darkside Chronicles*, Wii, 2009.

Capcom, *Resident Evil 7: Biohazard*, PS4, 2017.

Capcom, *Resident Evil 8: Village*, PS4, 2021.

Coates, Ta-Nehisi. "Sometimes it's Just Racist . . . ," *The Atlantic*, February 10th, 2009. https://www.theatlantic.com/entertainment/archive/2009/02/sometimes-it-apos-s-just-racist/6705/.

Cohen, Jeffrey Jerome. "Monster Culture (Seven Theses)." In *Monster Theory: Reading Culture*, edited by Jeffrey Jerome Cohen, 3-25. Minneapolis: University of Minnesota Press, 1996.

Daliot-Bul, Michal. "Japan Brand Strategy: The Taming of 'Cool Japan' and the Challenges of Cultural Planning in a Postmodern Age." Social Science Japan Journal 12, no. 2 (2009): 247-66.

Davies, Surekha. "The Unlucky, the Bad, and the Ugly: Categories of Monstrosity from the Renaissance to the Enlightenment." In *The Ashgate Research Companion to Monsters and the Monstrous*, edited by Asa Simon Mittman and Peter Dendle, 49-76. New York: Ashgate, 2013.

Dontnod Entertainment, *Life is Strange*, Square Enix, 2015.

Duane, Anne Mae. "Dead *and* Disabled: The Crawling Monsters of *The Walking Dead*." In *Zombie Theory: A Reader*, edited by Sarah Juliet Lauro, 237-245. Minneapolis: University of Minnesota Press, 2017.

Garland-Thomson, Rosemarie. "Making Freaks: Visual Rhetorics and the Spectacle of Julia Pastrana." In *Thinking the Limits of the Body*, edited by Jeffrey Jerome Cohen. New York: SUNY press, 2003.

Kirkman, Robert et al. *The Walking Dead Volume 5: The Best Defense*. Berkeley: Image Comics, 2006.

McCloskey, Jimmy. "Teen Born With 3 Fingers Blasts New Witches Movie for Making Her Look 'Scary,'" *Metro UK*, November 23, 2020. https://metro.co.uk/2020/11/23/teen-born-3-fingers-blasts-new-witches-movie-making-her-look-scary-13641681/.

Oswald, Dana. "Monstrous Gender: Geographies of Ambiguity." In *The Ashgate Research Companion to Monsters and the Monstrous*, edited by Asa Simon Mittman and Peter Dendle, 343-363. New York: Ashgate, 2013.

Poole, W. Scott. *Monsters in America: Our Historical Obsession with the Hideous and the Haunting*, 2nd ed. Waco: Baylor UP, 2018.

Puar, Jasbir K. *Terrorist Assemblages: Homonationalism in Queer Times*, 10th Anniversary Edition. Durham: Duke UP, 2017.

Smith, Angela M. *Hideous Progeny: Disability, Eugenics, and Classic Horror Cinema*. New York: Columbia UP, 2013.

Stobbart, Dawn. *Videogames and Horror: From* Amnesia *to* Zombies, Run! Cardiff: University of Wales Press, 2019.

"The Elephant Man." *The British Medical Journal* 2, no. 1354 (December 1886): 1188-1189.

Williams, David. *Deformed Discourse: The Function of the Monster in Medieval Thought and Literature.* Montreal: McGill-Queen's UP, 1996.

Young, Elizabeth. *Black Frankenstein: The Making of an American Metaphor.* New York: New York UP, 2008.

CHAPTER 3

(UN)DIAGNOSING RELIGIOUS EXPERIENCE: DIVINE ENCOUNTERS IN *BATTLESTAR GALACTICA*

Lucas Cober

Concordia University, Montreal

Abstract

This chapter focuses on the 2003 SyFy reboot of *Battlestar Galactica* and its treatment of religious visions and visitations as they are related narratively to the human and non-human characters' mental health and disabilities. The chapter argues that much of modern thinking on disability and religion uses a "mental illness paradigm" to explain religious people's religiously-interpreted visions of angels and divinities. *Battlestar Galactica* appears to challenge this paradigm, especially through the character of Dr. Gaius Baltar, who believes his "angelic" vistitations are the result of him experiencing the symptoms of severe mental illness or trauma, but does appear to be interacting with a "real" supernatural entity by the end of the series. This challenge allows the viewer to reconsider the place of modern scientific discourses in interpreting the behaviours and beliefs of religious individuals and calls for a space that allows us to read disability onto religious figures past and present while insisting that their personal worldviews and ideologies are relevant to understanding what they were experiencing.

Keywords: Mental Illness, Visions, Angels, Disability History

***

Introduction

Sometimes God talks. In many religious traditions, individuals have reported close experiences with the divine that have manifested in visions, dreams, or conversations with a divinity, divinities, or other supernatural agents representing higher realms or powers. In the history (and present) of Christianity, mystics such as St. Teresa of Avila insist that their conversations with God or with Jesus Christ have granted them revelatory knowledge about the nature of human relationships with the divine, but also revelatory knowledge about more mundane things such as church policy or where the Pope should live. These mystics often levy their close, personal experiences with the divine into worldly authority, using the fact of their connection with God, angels or other transcendent figures to found new movements or occupy leadership positions in existing institutions.

The general impulse of modern, neoliberal, scientifically minded interpreters is to assume that these supposedly mystical events were not in fact communication with the divine, but rather symptoms of a mental illness or cognitive impairment. Because the past as a construct is understood to have been prescientific, these ailments could not be diagnosed or understood, but can be now thanks to the advent of modern medicine and the articulation of a fuller vocabulary surrounding disability and mental health. Disability, for the purposes of this chapter, is defined as a societal barrier experienced by an individual on the basis of a physical or mental difference from a perceived norm. Mental illness is defined as a chronic atypical mental state that affects one's behavior and/or mental ability to perform tasks at a so-called "normal" rate and speed. Modern writers such as Victoria Lincoln will argue that a figure such as St. Teresa, the main Christian figure to be considered in this chapter, having divine visions is in fact a manifestation of her untreated epilepsy, a condition which caused her to have visual and auditory hallucinations that she understood as visions from God.[1] This "mental illness paradigm" for interpreting mystical experiences, particularly of those living in past time periods, is widespread and readily accepted in our supposedly secular society. "God spoke" is not an acceptable answer to the question of what a person was experiencing when they claimed to have had a conversation with the divine in the modern period.

---

[1] Victoria Lincoln, *Teresa: A Woman. A Biography of Teresa of Avila,* ed. Elias Rivers and Antonio T. de Nicholás (Albany: State University of New York Press, 1984). Though Lincoln was a novelist, her biography is based on over a decade of research into all of the primary sources about and by Teresa, and her work was later edited by scholars and experts before publication. Other scholars who have studied Teresa's visions include Marcella Biro Barton, "Saint Teresa of Avila: Did She Have Epilepsy?" in *The Catholic Historical Review* 68(4): 1982, 581-598, who from a Catholic perspective attempts to create a distinction between Teresa's epileptic episodes and her "real" religious experiences, tacitly acknowledging the scholarship that assumes the two to be one and the same, and Encarnación Juárez-Almendros, *Disabled Bodies in Early Modern Spanish Literature: Prostitutes, Aging Women and Saints* (Liverpool: Liverpool University Press, 2017), in which Juárez-Almendros, while attempting to take Teresa's religiosity seriously, still reads her as primarily a *disabled* woman rather than a *religious* woman.

Historical religious experiences are interpreted in the academy by what I am calling the mental illness paradigm, intentionally borrowing Thomas Kuhn's famous language to describe structures of scientific thought. Kuhn argues that scientists—and humans generally—operate under a series of paradigms that inform how they receive and interpret data.[2] Kuhn's critique of modern science is based not on it being incorrect, but on its refusal to recognize that paradigm shifts mark its development historically and in the present.[3] Science, Kuhn says, is not a steady development from the ancient Greeks to today, with each scientist standing on the shoulders of those who came before them. It is rather a series of upheavals during which previous methods of understanding data, even if they worked, are thrown out in favor of a new paradigm that answers the most pressing questions of the day.[4]

The paradigm is useful for reasons beyond providing an explanation for historical phenomena that cannot otherwise be interpreted through modern paradigms. From the perspective of disability history, finding historical examples of people who seem to have experienced what we might call disability or mental illness is important. The representational power granted to modern-day disabled and/or mentally ill people through the casting of a historical figure under this paradigm is useful for advocacy purposes, and for the purposes of establishing communities and histories of disabled people that stretch back beyond the late 20th century when the relevant terms were coined. But in providing this historical antecedent to modern disability, this interpretive paradigm tends to accidentally erase the agency of these potentially disabled historical people, who were able to *use* what for them was an authentic religious experience to better their own social circumstances. Their conditions, in other words, did not *disable* them, as these mystics were imbued with greater social capital and the *ability* to have far more control over their own lives—and often the lives of others—than they would otherwise have had. Because this type of mystical experience in Christianity was overwhelmingly (but not exclusively) a female experience as well, there is also a concerning optic of the lived experiences of women in powerful positions being erased through this diagnostic history.

In the 2003 remake of *Battlestar Galactica*, a number of characters experience visions, dreams or visitations from entities who claim to be representative of a

---

[2] Thomas S. Kuhn, *The Structure of Scientific Revolutions* (Chicago: University of Chicago Press, 1962), 10-11.

[3] Kuhn, *The Structure of Scientific Revolutions*, 139.

[4] Kuhn, *The Structure of Scientific Revolutions*, 7

higher power they call God.[5] *Battlestar Galactica* (hereafter *BSG*) takes place in a spacefaring, multiplanetary society that is predominantly religiously organized around the worship of vague deities known as the Lords of Kobol.[6] After their society and twelve planets are completely destroyed in an attack by nefarious, supposedly human-made cyborgs known as Cylons, the surviving humans must flee into unknown space in search of a new homeworld, the mythical planet known as Earth which is home to the mysterious "13th Colony" spoken of in their scriptures. As they travel through space, Dr. Gaius Baltar, a scientist who is accidentally responsible for allowing the Cylons to destroy the twelve colonies, begins to experience sexually charged visions of the human-appearing Cylon woman known as Six, who is responsible for using his access codes to hack into the defense network and allow the attack, and who was Gaius's lover. This entity is rapidly revealed not to be the "real" Six (inasmuch as there is a "real" Six when multiple versions of her exist), but rather a purely mental version of her whom only Gaius can see and who is in possession of knowledge that Gaius otherwise isn't.

This character, called Head Six or Messenger Six by the show's scripts, is a highly sexualized woman who repeatedly identifies herself as an angel sent by God to influence Gaius as part of some divine plan that God has for "everything and everyone."[7] The role of a female messenger delivering divine word to a male human is a reversal of the expected formula for a mystic Christian experience. Though historically the majority of well-known Christian figures are of course male, historians have noted that the role of the mystic, a religious figure who exists nominally outside the hierarchical church structure, is a traditionally female role,[8] in which women could exercise social power not otherwise afforded to them. The role taken on by Gaius is a traditionally feminine one, making his gender performance ambiguous throughout *BSG*. Many disabilities and specifically mental illnesses are stereotypically associated with girls and women to a disproportionate degree,[9] furthering Gaius's apparent

---

[5] *Battlestar Galactica*, "Miniseries, Part 1," Syfy, 2003. This is a theme that recurs throughout the series, but which is stated first by the character of Caprica Six, whose image later becomes Head Six, at 26:26.

[6] *Battlestar Galactica*, "Miniseries, Part 2."

[7] *Battlestar Galactica*, "33," 2:48.

[8] Nancy Caciola, *Discerning Spirits: Divine and Demonic Possession in the Middle Ages* (Ithaca: Cornell University Press, 2003), 54.

[9] Phyllis Chesler, *Women and Madness: Revised and Updated* (London: St. Martin's, 2005). Chelser's seminal work covers not only historical associations between women and various mental health issues and cognitive disabilities, but also the ways in which women are treated differently than men in mental health contexts. Licia Carlson also cogently

feminization. Therefore, in this chapter, I will examine the role of the mental illness paradigm and its underlying belief system and the way they operate in *BSG*, and the way that *BSG* seems to intentionally challenge modern neoliberal understandings of religion, disability, gender, and the boundaries of the human body by playing with the conventions of the science fiction genre.

Religious Experience in Christianity

Christianity has a long tradition of divine experiences taking the form of what a modern person might think of mental illness. The tradition also has a long history of valorizing particular types of illness and disability on the other. When put in together like that, it perhaps becomes clear why that valorization occurs. In the New Testament and especially the four Gospels, individuals who experienced supernatural interventions displayed symptoms that to modern people might look like those of some serious mental illnesses, such as talking to oneself, hearing voices, and paranoia.[10] These individuals were often socially stigmatized for this behavior, cast out of their communities and only allowed to return if the behavior stopped. These episodes and behaviors were understood to be because of demonic possession or communication with angelic figures, and the tradition of equating mental illnesses and disabilities with otherworldly psychic interference continued throughout Christian history.

Many Christian figures have spoken to God throughout history, and one of the most prominent of these is St. Teresa of Avila, a 13th-century Spanish mystic who experienced a relationship with the divine that lasted her whole life and corresponded with a series of debilitating physical and mental health conditions and disabilities. Teresa wrote extensively about her experience, describing it as "Pain...so great that it made me want to moan over and over, and the sweet delight into which that pain threw me was so intense that one could not want it to stop, or the soul be contented with anything but God,"[11] in one of her most famous accounts of an ecstatic moment (the moment on which the famous sculpture *The Ecstasy of St. Teresa* is based). This experience is well documented and interesting, but not unique in Christianity—this somatic mysticism is one that has frequently been available to Christians, particularly women, who can use it as a means of obtaining worldly authority in an environment that would

---

discusses the history of women's association with "feeblemindedness" in *The Faces of Intellectual Disability: Philosophical Reflections* (Bloomington: Indiana University Press, 2010), 53-83.

[10] As one of the most famous examples of this, see the story of the Gerasene demoniac in Mark 5:1-20 (NRSV)

[11] Teresa of Avila, (1515–1582). The Life of Teresa of Jesus. Chapter XXIX; Part 17, c.1565.

otherwise disallow this for them, based on their gender, but also on the basis of perceived mental infirmity or weakness. These were already issues understood to plague women, and would most certainly have been more than enough to disqualify a woman from any sort of public life if she were proven to be hearing voices and/or speaking to someone who wasn't present, unless of course that someone were God.

At the same time as this tradition exists, the Christian tradition also valorizes suffering and debility throughout its history. Jesus, of course, suffered on the cross and died for humanity's sins. Suffering like Jesus is one of the highest forms of *Imitatio Christi,* the imitation of Christ, that a person can achieve. Though we don't crucify people anymore, many Christians throughout history have, rather than avoiding disability or illness, sought these experiences out, believing such things to bring them closer to the divine,[12] on the assumption that to be impaired in any way, mental or physical, is to suffer on an ongoing basis. As a result, disability carries an ambiguous set of connotations within the Christian tradition, both as a desired state that imitates the suffering of God, and as repudiated marker of sin.[13] This double standard is negotiated, of course, by considering who the person in question is and why they are experiencing the infirmity they are experiencing. Disability that is experienced because a person is speaking with God is acceptable. Disability that is experienced for any other reason very rarely is, though the person experiencing it may still be considered valuable, depending on what they do with their life, and presuming they are not blamed for their own infirmity.

That said, though disability carries a multivalent meaning within the Christian tradition, modern interpreters of historical Christianity often only allow for one explanation for a whole host of somatic experiences had by Christian people. The use of modern language to refer to the historical phenomenon of religious experience does important work towards disability advocates' goal of increasing the visibility and presence of mentally ill and disabled people in history by centering mental illness and disability in European history. But the use of such language also in part erases the actual lived experiences of historical religious women whose disabilities and mental health issues were, for them, part and parcel of an extremely meaningful religious experience that had many very positive effects on their lives and circumstances.

---

[12] Carolyn Walker Bynum, *Fragmentation and Redemption: Essays on Gender and the Human Body in Medieval Religion* (New York: Zone Books, 1992), 184-185.

[13] Robert A. Orsi, *Between Heaven and Earth: Religious Worlds People Make and the Scholars Who Study Them* (Princeton: Princeton University Press, 2005) 22-23.

From the origin of what is now called Western medicine, certain somatic conditions were understood to be associated with the divine (though this association has near-always been challenged by those in the medical profession) [14] and with humans who had supernatural contact with divine or otherworldly powers. Modern medicine and modern scholarship generally deny the existence of the supernatural and the divine, focusing only on this-worldly things that they can record and categorize, which is eminently reasonable, as it is not the job of science to comment on things that do not provably exist. However, what ends up happening as a result is that non-scientific, non-medical explanations for any phenomena are not considered by modern scientists and scholars. It is not scientifically acceptable to offer "God did it" as an explanation to an unknown behavior. Not only are such explanations not offered to modern people, they are dismissed even from the imaginary of the people who felt these unexplainable events, with the implication being that of course people in the past believed that it was God talking to them, but we modern people know it was *really* epilepsy or schizophrenia, diagnosable conditions that can be categorized easily and explained in our terms. The terms of our subjects are rejected in favor of more modern vernacular that certainly, for us, explains the phenomena more clearly, but also denies the lived experience of the historical people we are describing.

The "religion" paradigm that someone like Teresa would have used to explain her own experiences leaves a substantial number of questions for us in the supposedly secular world, and does not provide satisfactory answers to questions that matter to us but would not have mattered to her. Because dominant questions in the modern academy are about the existence of mentally ill and disabled people throughout history, and about physiological explanations for somatic experiences described by historical people, and about what someone's diagnosis was or is, our framework for understanding experiences like Teresa's has shifted to this mental illness paradigm. In true Kuhnian fashion, this paradigm answers new questions, overlooking the fact that it no longer answers questions to which there were previously available answers when the questions were framed differently. This shift has let us find more mentally ill and disabled people in history and better understand the history of mental illness and disability, but it has also lessened our ability to understand the nexus of gender, earthly authority, and agency that is implicated in experiences like Teresa's. *BSG* was created for an audience raised long after that paradigm shift had happened, an audience rooted firmly in the science fiction genre and very interested in futuristic science, including space flight and

---

[14] Hippocrates, *De Morbo Sacro*, 1.

cybernetics, and challenges that paradigm by making that audience wonder: was it God all along?

<h2 align="center">*Battlestar Galactica* and Religious Experience</h2>

BSG, as a narrative, is very interested in the religious dimension of human experience. The religiosity of various characters is a frequently recurring theme, and many characters in addition to Gaius Baltar experience supernatural visions that they attribute to religious powers acting upon them. One of the many characters who claims authority on religious grounds is President Laura Roslin, who experiences mysterious and potentially prophetic dreams that may or may not be a result of her cancer medication. Either way, they end up being true visions of the future and lead her—and the entire group of human survivors around which the series centers—to critical sites and pieces of information, including the lost planet/religious site of Kobol,[15] from which the human colonies mythically originated. There, she discovers that Earth, despite the other characters' assurances, is not a myth but a real place, and begins them on a path that will eventually lead them all there.[16] The character of Kara Thrace also experiences a serious religious transformation when she is killed and then seemingly revived with knowledge of how to bring the survivors the rest of the way to Earth, after which she vanishes—possibly assumed into another realm, or possibly having never been returned from the dead at all.[17] Various of the series' Cylon characters claim to be operating in service to the will of a monotheistic divinity that guides them and is interested in preserving their souls, leading to a series of in-universe discussions of whether or not artificially-created cyborgs *have* souls. Many of these discussions include Gaius Baltar, who is initially the loudest voice in the series, arguing that Cylons are not real people, and that the Cylon divinity is a shared delusion.

Gaius, an archetypical scientist-skeptic who claims not to be overly religious,[18] refuses to accept religious explanations and presumes instead that Head Six is a manifestation of his own guilt/stress, or a sign of his degrading mental state,[19] to which she responds that she may also be the result of a Cylon having implanted Gaius's brain with a chip that can influence his behavior.[20] Out of

---

[15] *Battlestar Galactica*, "Kobol's Last Gleaming, Part 1."

[16] *Battlestar Galactica*, "Home, Part 2," 38:30.

[17] *Battlestar Galactica*, "Daybreak, Part 3," 30:41.

[18] *Battlestar Galactica*, "Miniseries, Part 1," 26:40.

[19] *Battlestar Galactica*, "Miniseries, Part 2," 1:48:00. Please note that the both parts of the miniseries are typically put together as one feature-length episode of approximately three hours.

[20] *Battlestar Galactica*, "Miniseries, Part 2," 1:49:00.

fear for his own safety and well-being, Gaius refuses to tell anyone about the existence of Head Six, and for the entire run of the series, *BSG* plays with the question of whether or not this entity is a real, autonomous being who exists separately from Gaius, or if she is only a hallucination. As the series progresses, Gaius believes more and more in her and in divine providence, eventually becoming a cult religious leader and spreading the word of the Cylon God to many others. The mystery of Head Six's reality or irreality is left ambiguous but complicated by the series' ending, which flashes forward one hundred and fifty thousand years and shows her and her counterpart (an incorporeal version of Gaius who is introduced later in the series), walking invisibly through a crowd, obviously existent without any humans perceiving them, discussing "its" plan and whether or not something "surprising" will happen in the "complex system" of the cosmos that may prevent another apocalyptic event in the future.[21]

This ending, which strongly implies the objective existence of the supernatural entities, seems to challenge modern-day paradigms of understanding religious experience as purely caused by mental illness or disability. *BSG* treats religious experience, on the whole, as a form of experiencing the world that has equal explanatory power to the secular/scientific worldview often expressed by its characters. Because the series is science fiction, it likes to leave open "scientific" answers to the question of religious experience: perhaps Roslin's visions are only a side effect of the drug she is taking, or perhaps the Cylons believe in God because they were programmed to do so. That said, it also always leaves open the possibility that the religious or mystical explanations given to and by the characters on-screen are the actual explanation for the unexplained or unexplainable phenomena. Indeed, often the religious explanation is the *only* explanation provided aside from sheer coincidence. Multiple times, in early episodes especially, Gaius is 'tested' through threats to his security, including when a fellow scientist threatens to come forward with information that Gaius is a traitor but is mysteriously killed when Gaius repents his sins with Head Six later in the episode.[22] Another test comes after an argument with Head Six during which Gaius mocks her religious faith as irrational and not for intelligent people; she then disappears and a flesh-and-blood version of Six whom everyone can see appears on the ship with photographic proof that Gaius is responsible for the destruction of the twelve colonies, only for that proof to be discovered false the very moment Gaius drops to his knees and begs for grace from the Cylon God.[23] This is a particularly interesting example because at this point in the series the question of whether Gaius's visitor is the result of

---

[21] *Battlestar Galactica*, "Daybreak, Part 3," 44:50-42:10.

[22] *Battlestar Galactica*, "33," 25:21.

[23] *Battlestar Galactica*, "Six Degrees of Separation," 37:00.

mechanical interference in his brain is still open, and though the version of Six who appears on the ship shows no sign of being aware of Head Six, she also mysteriously vanishes the moment Head Six returns to see Gaius after his atonement.[24] These are some of the earlier signs that what is happening to Gaius isn't only mental. His religious behavior comes to have observable effects on the world around him, which, though they could be written off as coincidences, are framed narratively and understood by him as though they are not.

Reversing the Paradigm in *BSG*

Gaius Baltar's possibly religious visitations form the backbone of his character arc throughout the four seasons of *BSG*'s run, and are a central part of the series' overall storyline pertaining to the salvation of both the human and Cylon races through their journey to and discovery of the planet Earth. There, they will eventually both come to live peacefully and in harmony, becoming the progenitors of the modern human race as the audience understands it today, which is claimed to have been God's plan all along. This claim is made in reference to the beliefs of many Cylons throughout the series that God has a plan for them, and in reference to Head Six's constant insistence throughout the series that God had a plan for Gaius specifically. That the unification of humanity and the Cylons on the planet Earth and their eventual intermixing into a single species is the culmination of God's plan is indicated by Head Six herself, who appears in the series' denouement mentioned above, in which the two messenger characters speak to each other and express hope for the future.

In the context of *BSG*, as discussed above, Gaius's ongoing visions of the self-proclaimed angel who seeks to guide his behavior are not entirely unusual, though visions of this exact nature are only experienced by one other character, a Cylon known as Caprica Six, who is the same Cylon who took advantage of Gaius to gain access to the defense network and destroy the twelve colonies. Caprica Six, differentiated from the other versions of the character (all portrayed by Tricia Helfer) because of her actions to bring about the Cylon victory, also experiences visitations from a mysterious figure who remains invisible to anyone else. Her visitor, also claiming to be a messenger of God, is a dangerously sexual version of Gaius, who operates as a counterpart to the highly sexual Head Six.[25] It is with the introduction of this character that the visitations of Head Six start to seem less like Gaius is experiencing the symptoms of a mental illness and more like a legitimate intervention by some form of life, for how else would Caprica Six be experiencing the same symptoms? In the late series

---

[24] *Battlestar Galactica,* "Six Degrees of Separation," 40.20.

[25] *Battlestar Galactica,* "Downloaded," 8:12.

episode "Daybreak, Part 2," Gaius and Caprica Six are physically proximate to one another, and it is revealed not only that they can see each other's messengers, but that the messengers can speak with each other.[26] And of course in the show's closing moments, the two messengers speak to each other without any humans nearby who are able to perceive them.[27]

Throughout the series and especially throughout the first season, a number of scientific answers are presented for why Gaius might be experiencing these episodes. Over the course of his interactions with Head Six, however, these explanations fail more and more to answer the questions raised by her appearances. Head Six has knowledge that Gaius does not possess, and she pushes him into acting in certain ways by testing him, and when he behaves as expected, good things happen that seem otherwise to be entirely coincidental, but which are too serendipitous to be coincidence. The line between serendipity and providence in *BSG* is never clear, as there is no scientific evidence given for the existence of God, but a number of characters will consistently make claims that God is (or "the gods" are) responsible for the things that befall them.

What is important not to lose in this analysis is that none of this takes away from Gaius's mental health issues. Regardless of whether or not Gaius is "really" seeing an angel when he speaks with Head Six, it is clearly the case that he is suffering the effects of a debilitating mental illness. He experiences paranoia, has difficulty controlling his behavior, finds himself marginalized from his peers, his behavioral patterns stigmatized. Gaius is consistently *treated* like a person with a disability throughout *BSG*'s run, the social reality of his behavior causing him serious stigma, but his somatic experience also being unlike the normate experiences of many of the people around him. Regardless of whether or not Gaius is being visited by an angel, he is still a disabled man. The reality of Head Six's existence doesn't take away from Gaius's status as a disabled person, but it does challenge our ideas about the relationship between disability and religiosity, removing religious behavior from the realm of delusion brought on by scientifically measurable factors, and placing it into a different category as something other to humans that interacts with them in mysterious ways.

Gaius's medical condition (if he has one) is never diagnosed, because he never seeks out help for it, believing that if anyone knew he was speaking to a supposed hallucination of a Cylon, they would discover his role, however accidental, in the destruction of the human race and punish him appropriately. As a result, the ambiguity as to the somatic nature of his situation remains

---

[26] *Battlestar Galactica*, "Daybreak, Part 2." 40:00-43:00. This scene notably takes place in the context of Gaius finally admitting that events of the last four years only make sense with God as the explanation.

[27] *Battlestar Galactica*, "Daybreak, Part 3," 41:00-43:00.

throughout the series. In other cases, medicine is shown to be of limited usefulness; President Laura Roslin's cancer is untreatable by traditional medicine but is controlled for a time by a homeopathic substance that causes her to have religiously inspired visions that end up guiding the fleet of survivors to a map that leads to the mythical planet Earth, until this time presumed to be a legend.[28] Roslin's terminal cancer threatens to kill her until an infusion of blood from a half-human, half-Cylon baby miraculously cures said cancer for scientifically unexplained reasons.[29] The baby in question, Hera Agathon, had been foretold by Head Six to Gaius in a vision on the planet Kobol as the savior of both races, a function she ends up fulfilling at the end of the series when the survivors reach the planet Earth and, in a one-hundred-fifty-thousand-year flash forward, Hera is heavily implied to have become "Mitochondrial Eve," the supposed genetic forbearer to much of modern human population.[30] Hera's significance to the narrative is scientific at its conclusion, but up until that moment, her role is understood religiously, as one of many messianic savior figures in the *BSG* cast, and it is in this capacity that she, through the salvific power of her blood, is able to save the president's life. The Christ parallels inherent in Hera's character are interesting but not the subject of this chapter. What is important for the purposes of this analysis is that she, a pseudo-magical miraculous baby with religiously significant salvific potential, is foretold through Head Six's visions to Gaius, which come true.

At no point in *BSG* are scientific explanations for the various religious phenomena, especially Gaius's visions, fully dismissed. Even if the characters accept a supernatural explanation, because the series is set firmly in a science fiction framework, the audience is still left with the possibility that there could be a scientific explanation for these strange occurrences. It is the non-scientific explanations of religious visionary activity that need to be sold to the characters, bypassing seemingly reasonable explanations pertaining to robotic brain chips or, more pressingly, debilitating mental illnesses. Because the ending is vague and because many of the events foretold are similarly vague, the possibility that everything that seems to be a coincidence in fact *is* a coincidence and that the two messenger characters who appear at the end represent some sort of explainable phenomenon does exist. The messengers could be some hitherto-unmentioned alien species (one notable moment in their closing scene is Head Six commenting on "God's plan" and her counterpart, the messenger version of Gaius, leaning in and hissing "you know it doesn't like that name"[31]), for

---

[28] *Battlestar Galactica*, "Home, Part 2," 38:30.

[29] *Battlestar Galactica*, "Epiphanies," 36:43.

[30] *Battlestar Galactica*, "Daybreak, Part 3," 41:20.

[31] *Battlestar Galactica*, "Daybreak, Part 3," 42:07.

example. Alternately, they could be a narratorial, Greek chorus-like insertion to close out the story in a way that explains the final significance of the characters' actions. Both of these explanations are arguably narratively unsatisfying given that they would be last-minute additions to the premise, but they are possible. But the possibility that the explanation is a genuine religious experience is always there.

It is in this ambiguity that *BSG* challenges modern neoliberal explanations of religious experience. It is not so simple, argues the series, as reducing religious experience to mental illness or disability. Such experiences are simply more complex than that. The portrayal of Gaius as a scientist-skeptic who refuses to accept the religious meanings of his visions, at least at first, seems to align with the mental illness paradigm for understanding religious experience, but as his storyline goes on, the paradigm increasingly fails to explain the phenomenon, and, as Kuhn tells us all paradigms will do at this stage, it is replaced by a new paradigm that explains the problems caused by the failures of the previous: a religious explanation. Kuhnian paradigm theory does not generally permit going backwards to older paradigms that have already been found lacking. But *BSG* does this, taking Gaius and the audience backwards to a pre-scientific understanding of visions that is substantiated by the apparent objective reality of Head Six at the end of the series, suggesting that Gaius—and the audience— was mistaken to jump to and stick with only purely scientific explanations for all observable phenomena. In so doing, *BSG* challenges modern notions of scientific authority and religious agency, as well as calling into question the progress narrative that dominates our discussions of history, science and disability by insisting that religious definitions of various phenomena will eventually fade away in the light of scientific explanations.

Religion, Disability and Gender in *Battlestar Galactica*

Gaius being a disabled *man* is a critical element of this discussion. Encarnación Juárez-Almendros reminds us that in historical narratives of disability, women are often expected to reveal their somatic circumstances, where men's narratives typically persistently conceal those same circumstances.[32] It should not go unnoticed that, for the entirety of *BSG*, Gaius manages never to divulge Head Six's existence to anyone else, therefore never putting him in a position of having to be tested or put on trial for being a potential Cylon double agent or for his culpability in the destruction of the human race,[33] but also never having to be examined and diagnosed with any sort of illness or disability, physical or

---

[32] Juárez-Almendros, *Disabled Bodies in Early Modern Spanish Literature,* 120.

[33] He is put on trial across a number of late series episodes for collaborating with the Cylons in another instance, for which he is eventually exonerated.

mental. Regardless of how inappropriate Gaius's behavior becomes, including constantly talking to someone who isn't present in front of others, believing that he has knowledge that other people do not, and even seemingly masturbating in public, Gaius never receives more than strange looks from other cast members and passers-by.[34] Though these moments are stigmatizing for him, Gaius is never forced to reveal his condition, if we are to believe he has a "condition." In many ways Gaius's religious counterpart President Laura Roslin *is* forced to divulge her medical condition and the drugs she is taking for it that are triggering her own religiously interpreted and potentially prophetic visions, not once but twice. As a female prophet and religious leader, Roslin is obligated to make public her somatic experience, where Gaius, a male figure occupying similar roles (including the worldly office of the presidency briefly), is never forced to do such a thing and only willingly reveals his role in the apocalypse to Roslin as part of what he feels is a final atonement before his death.[35]

Also interesting is that Gaius, in his position as a receptacle for divine knowledge and interference by an angelic figure, ends up occupying a traditional female role when read through the interpretive lens of normate Christianity. Though men can and do receive visions and visitations in many religious traditions, including Christianity, generally speaking, the most well-known and successful practitioners who claim to have spoken directly to the divine in the Christian tradition have been women.[36] Their role as divine intermediaries has allowed various women to hold status and authority that they otherwise would not have had in a patriarchal tradition and culture that generally relegated women to second-class status, and disabled women even moreso.[37] Women who talked to themselves, heard voices or saw things that weren't perceivable to others were not people who could wield any sort of earthly authority even over their own lives, but women who talked to God and heard and saw angels were able to eke out lives, in some cases, at least, as respected, powerful mystics who were consulted, listened to, educated and well treated. In choosing a male character for this role, the writers of *BSG* have left Gaius's gender performance somewhat ambiguous, which is often corrected by Gaius's excessive male sexuality, expressed through his persistent sexual pursuit of various female characters throughout the series. This shoring up of Gaius's masculinity, and Gaius's placement in a traditionally female role of the divine receptacle, creates an interesting tension in which an avenue to power for many women has been

---

[34] *Battlestar Galactica*, "Miniseries," 2:18:40 is an early example of this behaviour.

[35] *Battlestar Galactica*, "The Hub," 28:19-31:00.

[36] Bynum, *Fragmentation and Redemption*, 58, cf. Max Weber's *Economy and Society*.

[37] Bynum, *Fragmentation and Redemption*, 58. Bynum does not discuss the axis of disability as regards women experience; this is my addition to her commentary.

colonized by a male subject, operated on by a female agent at the will of a male divinity. It is tempting to suggest that *BSG* is closing women out of an avenue to power traditionally available to them in visionary traditions, but of course throughout the series other characters, most of them women, are similarly the recipients of visions and visitations, so such an argument doesn't quite hold water.

What does seem apparent, however, is that in addition to breaking down the binary between religious and medical explanations for seeing angels, *BSG* is also challenging traditionally gendered ideas about who can receive such visions and who experiences certain types of mental health issues, which of course are not only experienced by women, but are often spoken of as though they are "female disabilities," as part of the cultural refusal to allow disabled individuals to occupy the normate category of the masculine. Gaius's masculinity is occasionally in question throughout *BSG*, but for reasons other than his mental health issues—he is an effete scientist with a European accent in a world of extremely masculinized soldiers who conform, at least on the surface, to traditional American heteromasculine stereotypes. Gaius's gender as a man mostly remains unmarked in all other arenas. It is his status as a disabled, mentally ill person who experiences religious visitations that is more important in his self-understanding and in the audience's understanding of him, but his gendered status is important in understanding his character, as disability's historical feminization and his religious power both lead the audience to question him as a masculine figure, challenging the gender binary at the same time as *BSG* challenges the mental illness paradigm.

Conclusion

Battlestar Galactica engages critically with modern conceptions of religious behavior and disability in such a way as to render them not mutually exclusive or mutually explanatory. It is typical in modern discourse to explain away religious behavior and experience through the paradigm of mental illness and disability, relegating the lived experiences of many people to the margins of a medico-scientific culture that emphasizes rationality, the reliance on observable phenomena and the dismissal of any explanations that seem supernatural or exterior to the scientifically measurable world. The purpose of this paper is not to argue for the existence of angels or to discount scientific and medical explanations for certain types of behavior, nor is it to erase the historical experience of disabled and mentally ill people, the recognition of which is critical to modern advocacy projects. Rather, the purpose of this chapter was to demonstrate the ways in which *BSG*, through the character of Gaius Baltar, whose deteriorating and untreated mental health issues may or may not be the result of religious communication with a supernatural entity, challenges the modern binary between medical science and religion, and persistent academic attempts to use one to explain the other. In so doing, *BSG* reminds its viewer that regardless of whether there is a rational explanation for the experiences of people who claim to have spoken to God or angels, those experiences were still meaningful for those people, and had life-changing effects on them and provided them with significant real-world authority on the basis of the perceived divine interest in that person. While not removing disability or mental illness from the equation, *BSG* repositions religion as a central determining factor in the lived experience of individual people, providing another framework through which to interpret non-normate experience alongside, but not replacing, the mental illness paradigm.

Bibliography

Battlestar Galactica. Syfy. 2003-2009.

Biro Barton, Marcella. "Saint Teresa of Avila: Did She Have Epilepsy?" In *The Catholic Historical Review* 68(4): 1982, 581-598.

Bynum, Carolyn Walker. *Fragmentation and Redemption: Essays on Gender and the Human Body in Medieval Religion.* New York: Zone Books, 1992.

Caciola, Nancy. *Discerning Spirits: Divine and Demonic Possession in the Middle Ages.* Ithaca: Cornell University Press, 2003.

Carlson, Licia. *The Faces of Intellectual Disability: Philosophical Reflections.* Bloomington: Indiana University Press, 2010.

Chesler, Phyllis. *Women and Madness: Revised and Updated.* London: St. Martin's, 2005.

Hippocrates, *De Morbo Sacro.*

Juárez-Almendros, Encarnación. *Disabled Bodies in Early Modern Spanish Literature: Prostitutes, Aging Women and Saints.* Liverpool: Liverpool University Press, 2017.

Kuhn, Thomas S. *The Structure of Scientific Revolutions.* Chicago: University of Chicago Press, 1962.

Lincoln, Victoria. *Teresa: A Woman. A Biography of Teresa of Avila.* Edited by Elias Rivers and Antonio T. de Nicholás. Albany: State University of New York Press, 1984.

Orsi, Robert A. *Between Heaven and Earth: Religious Worlds People Make and the Scholars Who Study Them.* Princeton: Princeton University Press, 2005.

Teresa of Avila, Saint. *The Life of Teresa of Jesus.* c.1565.

CHAPTER 4

ANDROIDS, REPLICANTS, AND STRANGE THINGS: DISABILITY AS REPRESENTATIVE OF COMPROMISED AUTONOMY IN POPULAR SCIENCE FICTION

Sean Mock

Umpqua Community College

Abstract

Compromised and/or near human agency is a common trope in contemporary science fiction. Situations where human characters experience reduced autonomy—due perhaps to alien symbiosis, possession, or infection—and examples of non-humans reaching toward human agency often adopt real and stereotyped symptoms, behaviors, and characteristics associated with disabilities. This paper explores the presentation of compromised and near-human agency to illustrate the potential damage that may result from blurring the boundary between fantastical fiction and experiences of disability. The analysis of Ridley Scott's *Blade Runner* (1982), Jordan Peele's *Get Out* (2017), and Stanley Kubrick's *2001: A Space Odyssey* (1968), among other popular media, highlights the anxiety about disability characteristics by normative, able-bodied social groups, and extends the conversation to include legal and political parallels at state and federal levels.

Keywords: Science Fiction, Disability, Agency, Ableism, Autonomy

***

Will Byers is, by all outward appearances, a typical, nerdy preteen, interested in riding his bike and playing *Dungeons and Dragons*. He lives in the quiet town of Hawkins, Indiana with his mom, Joyce, and brother, Jonathan. After a particularly traumatic experience, Will begins to display worrisome symptoms: he has difficulty expressing himself through speech, compulsively draws dark, abstract images, and frequently refers to entities who cannot be seen or heard.

Looking from the outside, one might assume Will is experiencing the psychological effects of trauma or is displaying characteristics of neurodivergence. Indeed, all signs point to psychological difference. As one of the lead characters in Netflix's seminal science fiction hit *Stranger Things*, Will's situation is supernatural in origin rather than physical or psychological. His behaviors result from being partially possessed by the parasitic antagonist of the series, the Mind Flayer. For most of the show's second season, Will displays disability characteristics simply because he is not in full control of his own autonomy.

The depiction of compromised agency is a recurring theme in anglophone popular science fiction of the last sixty years. The present study focuses on two types of compromised agents who strive to reach the autonomy and agency associated with being human. The first type represents human characters whose autonomy is compromised by the presence of something inhuman, such a parasitic infection, an otherworldly possession, or the mental intrusion of other supernatural agents. For these characters, there is a struggle between their own individual agency and the agency of the intruding force. Opposite in nature but similar in presentation, the second category includes non-humans such as robots, computers, and cyborgs that appear to develop a level of autonomy and intelligence typically seen as human. Put another way, these computer and robot characters make decisions, display emotions, or interact with others as if they were human characters. Regardless of the source, instances of compromised human autonomy in popular science fiction rely on stereotypical tropes associated with disease and disability to explain the "non-humanness" or "near-humanness" of the character and situation.

Disability and science fiction have a complex relationship. In certain cases, sci-fi disability has been used to celebrate and normalize physical, emotional, and mental difference. For example, the *X-Men* franchise—a 1960s comic book series that has since developed into multiple television series, video games, and movies—illustrates how physically and mentally different characters (mutants) deal with the struggles of a world that fears and represses them.[1] In other cases, popular science fiction uses disability to reinforce the ablenormativity found in other literary genres—especially, but not limited to, instances where disability serves as the explanation or justification for iniquitous behavior. I contend that popular science fiction relies on disability characteristics and medical symptoms to portray characters with compromised human agency, a perilous practice that threatens the autonomy and humanity of real persons with disabilities and

---

[1] Michael M. Chemers, "Mutatis Mutandis: An Emergent Disability Aesthetic in 'X-2: X-Men United,'" *Disability Studies Quarterly* 24, no. 1 (2004): https://dsq-sds.org/article/view/862/1037.

impairments. To illustrate the genre's appropriation of disability, I analyze popular visual sources since the 1960s, from canonical classics like Stanley Kubrick's *2001: A Space Odyssey* (1968)[2] and Ridley Scott's *Blade Runner* (1982)[3] to recent, groundbreaking additions like *Westworld* (2016-present),[4] *Stranger Things* (2016-present),[5] and *Get Out* (2017).[6] Investigation of these films and series—among others—further articulates longstanding anxieties about disabilities in the able-minded media.[7] As people with disabilities are a population under constant scrutiny, popular culture that uses disability characteristics to explain compromised autonomy is especially problematic.[8]

The relationship between autonomy and disability in science fiction is complex, so I develop it in three stages. The first thread provides an analysis of Netflix's recent hit series *Stranger Things*, specifically when a possessed Will employs nonverbal communication typically associated with neurodivergence and alternative speech technologies. The second strand appears through a close examination of Jordan Peele's *Get Out* and HBO's *Westworld*. Peele's work uses neurological symptoms to depict a single body sharing multiple identities or personas, specifically as the characters' autonomous identities are suppressed by implanted identities. In *Westworld,* hosts—high-tech cyborgs that are visibly indistinguishable to humans—display aphasic disturbances and socially different emotions to represent malfunctioning artificial intelligence that eventually develops into robotic sentience. The third, and final, fiber extends the discussion of *Westworld*—adding analyses of Scott's *Blade Runner* and Kubrick's *2001: A Space Odyssey*—to reveal how popular science fiction has linked stereotypes of mental illness with extreme, violent behavior. Untangling the

---

[2] *2001: A Space Odyssey,* directed by Stanley Kubrick (1968; UK: Warner Brothers, 2018), Blu-ray.

[3] *Bladerunner: The Final Cut,* directed by Ridley Scott (1982; USA: Warner Brothers, 2017), Blu-ray.

[4] *Westworld,* created by Jonathan Nolan and Lisa Joy (2016-2022; USA: HBO, 2016), HBO Max, https://www.hbo.com/westworld

[5] *Stranger Things,* created by Matt Duffer and Ross Duffer (2016-present; USA: Netflix, 2016), Netflix, https://www.netflix.com/title/80057281

[6] *Get Out,* directed by Jordan Peele (2017; USA: Universal Pictures, 2017), Blu-ray.

[7] Mitchell and Snyder suggest that the disabled body is a site that reflects able-bodied anxiety about an assumed correlation between naturalness and wholeness, see David Mitchell and Sharon Snyder, *Narrative Prosthesis: Disability and the Dependencies of Discourse* (Ann Arbor: University of Michigan Press, 2000), 37.

[8] Rosemarie Garland-Thomson, *Freakery: Cultural Spectacles of the Extraordinary Body* (New York: New York University Press, 1996), 17.

narrative knot reveals the threats of overlapping stereotypes of disability characteristics with restricted autonomy, particularly as it perpetuates the false narrative that real people with disabilities lack agency, autonomy, and some indefinable aspect of able-bodied humanity.

The present study builds upon the small—but fast-growing—body of scholarship devoted to disability and science fiction. Recent research rightfully notes that science fiction provides positive potential for abnormal bodies, particularly in the genre's tendency to portray disability as adaptive and useful.[9] Scholars have demonstrated that the overlapping of technology and humanity problematizes human identity, focusing specifically on prosthetics and generally on physical difference.[10] McReynolds considers questions of normative agency in James Cameron's *Avatar* (2009)[11] and DreamWorks Animation's *How to Train your Dragon* (2010),[12] contending that the synthesis of a human body perceived to be deficient with an animal/alien prosthetic counterpart creates a unique dual-agency relationship.[13] Though McReynolds and others rightly point to the positive agential prospects in science fiction, popular sci-fi has a long history of associating compromised human autonomy with mental disability characteristics. Disability representation in popular science fiction seems to follow a forked path, one branch embracing social, mental, and physical difference, while the other turns to parallel ablenormative and eugenicist rhetoric—especially in the context of involuntary commitment laws in, for example, Kentucky and Arizona. Revealing the problematic nature of linking disability stereotypes with compromised autonomy allows audiences to recognize and replace such problematic portrayals with more equitable examples.

---

[9] Kathryn Allan, "Introduction: Reading Disability in Science Fiction," in *Disability in Science Fiction: Representations of Technology as Cure*, ed. Kathryn Allan (New York: Palgrave MacMillan, 2013), 8.

[10] See, for example, Donna Binns, "*The Bionic Woman*: Machine or Human?" in *Disability in Science Fiction: Representations of Technology as Cure* (New York: Palgrave MacMillan, 2013), 89-102, or Ralph Covino, "*Star Wars*, Limb Loss, and What it Means to be Human," in *Disability in Science Fiction: Representations of Technology as Cure* (New York: Palgrave MacMillan, 2013), 103-114.

[11] *Avatar*, directed by James Cameron (2009; USA: 20th Century Fox, 2010), DVD.

[12] *How to Train your Dragon*, directed by Chris Sanders and Dean Deblois (2010; USA: Universal Pictures, 2021), Blu-ray.

[13] Leigha McReynolds, "Animal and Alien Bodies as Prostheses: Reframing Disability in *Avatar* and *How to Train your Dragon*," in *Disability in Science Fiction: Representations of Technology as Cure* (New York: Palgrave MacMillan, 2013), 116-117.

The Mind Flayer: Will Byers and Neurodivergence in *Stranger Things*

The Duffer Brothers' breakout hit *Stranger Things* introduces the audience to Will Byers, a twelve-year-old boy who loves to ride bikes and play Dungeons and Dragons with his three best friends, Mike, Dustin, and Lucas. Will is physically absent for most of the first season, having been abducted by a monstrous, supernatural entity while riding his bike alone at night. Eventually, Will's mother discovers a way to communicate with her son—at first via a blinking mass of Christmas lights, then through a lit alphabet painted on her living room wall—though her friends and family begin to think she "is going crazy."[14] Meanwhile, a mysterious young girl with psychokinetic powers, called Eleven, discovers Will in an interdimensional plane called the Upside Down.[15] In the first season's final episode, the local chief of police—and close friend of Joyce Byers—enters the Upside Down and rescues Will, who has been captured by the grotesque Demogorgon and intubated with some sort of detachable, monstrous proboscis. The episode ends with Will surreptitiously spitting up Demogorgon-like slugs.[16]

It is unclear if Will suffers from parasitic possession or agential interference in the first season of the show, though the narrative clearly correlates his physical absence with disability-associated communication. In other words, when Will's ability to speak is impaired—indeed, he displays aphasia-like moments even after his rescue—he relies on methods that parallel both real and stereotyped communication used by persons with speech-related disabilities. In the third episode, Joyce discovers that Will can communicate with her through Christmas lights, activating and brightening/dimming them to respond to her yes-or-no questions, one blink as yes, two as no.[17] The nonverbal blink-once-for-yes trope appears in multiple genres that depict speech-impaired characters, and it is most recognizable in science fiction with

---

[14] *Stranger Things*, season 1, episode 4, "Chapter Four: The Body," directed by Shawn Levy, written by Justin Doble, featuring Winona Ryder, Finn Wolfhard, and Millie Bobby Brown, aired July 15, 2016, Netflix, https://www.netflix.com/title/80057281.

[15] *Stranger Things*, season 1, episode 7, "Chapter Seven: The Bathtub," directed by The Duffer Brothers, written by Justin Doble, featuring Winona Ryder, Finn Wolfhard, and Millie Bobby Brown, aired July 15, 2016, Netflix, https://www.netflix.com/title/80057281.

[16] *Stranger Things*, season 1, episode 8, "Chapter Eight: The Upside Down," directed by The Duffer Brothers, written by Paul Dichter, featuring Winona Ryder, Finn Wolfhard, and Millie Bobby Brown, aired July 15, 2016, Netflix, https://www.netflix.com/title/80057281.

[17] *Stranger Things*, season 1, episode 3, "Chapter Three: Holly, Jolly," directed by Shawn Levy, written by Jessica Mecklenburg, featuring Winona Ryder, Finn Wolfhard, and Millie Bobby Brown, aired July 15, 2016, Netflix, https://www.netflix.com/title/80057281.

Star Trek's Captain Pike, who uses a high-tech, futuristic wheelchair that allows him to blink a light to respond to yes-or-no questions.[18] Upon realizing the limits of the yes/no response, Joyce immediately constructs an alphabet wall with Christmas lights and paint, allowing Will to spell out answers to her questions. The wall mimics a type of alphabet board commonly employed in partner-assisted scanning, a communication process that involves interpreting the letters, words, or images indicated by persons with aphasia. Though the communication aids assist Will to communicate—and ultimately lead to his retrieval—the Upside Down clings to Will Byers in some way, as, at the end of season one, he spits a grotesque slug into his bathroom sink and seems to temporarily see the room as if he were still in the Upside Down.

The second season of the show confirms that Will's autonomy is compromised—this time, his body is infiltrated by an incorporeal, shadow creature known as the Mind Flayer.[19] After his encounter, Will becomes erratic and angry, demanding that his mother keep the house at a very cold temperature and scribbling violently through stacks of white paper. Sheriff Hopper and Joyce Byers discover that Will's drawings, when taped together, form a gigantic map of tunnels beneath Hawkins that serve as a gate to the Upside Down. Will's doctor initially chalks his symptoms up to stress from the trauma, though it becomes clear that he is possessed by the Mind Flayer when they burn one of its severed tentacles, causing Will to react as if he were also being burned. Upon realizing the lab where Will is examined will be invaded by canine-like Demogorgons, Sheriff Hopper and Joyce escape with him and his friends and return to the Byers' home. Hopper realizes that Will cannot be trusted to speak due to the Mind Flayer's ability to take control of his body and mind. The sheriff ties Will to a chair to prevent the Mind Flayer from forcing him to escape, before he realizes that the boy has been secretly tapping signals on his chair leg in morse code.[20] The message instructs the team that Eleven must use her psychokinetic abilities to close the gate to the Upside Down to sever the Mind Flayer's access to the human world. Joyce and friends are then able to remove

---

[18] *Star Trek: The Original Series*, season 1, episode 11, "The Menagerie: Part I," directed by Marc Daniels, written by Gene Roddenberry, featuring William Shatner, Leonard Nimoy, and Sean Kenney, aired November 17, 1966, in broadcast syndication, NBC, 2004. DVD.

[19] *Stranger Things*, season 2, episode 3, "Chapter Three: The Pollywog," directed by Shawn Levy, written by Justin Doble, featuring Winona Ryder, Finn Wolfhard, and Millie Bobby Brown, aired October 27, 2017, Netflix, https://www.netflix.com/title/80057281.

[20] *Stranger Things*, season 2, episode 6, "Chapter Six: The Spy," directed by Andrew Stanton, written by Kate Trefry, featuring Winona Ryder, Finn Wolfhard, and Millie Bobby Brown, aired October 27, 2017, Netflix, https://www.netflix.com/title/80057281.

the Mind Flayer by exposing Will to extreme heat, thus restoring his independent autonomy.[21]

As Will otherwise appears to be able-bodied and able-minded before the possession occurs, the narrative implies that disability characteristics go hand in hand with limited agency. Characteristics associated with disability, both stereotyped and otherwise, make up the entirety of Will's autonomous communication—that is, the communication that is free of influence from the Mind Flayer. Through established yes/no visual responses and an alphabet board, Will is able to communicate despite his inability to speak, and his use of automatic drawing and morse code implies communicative techniques often stereotyped in other media sources. In these sources, automatic drawing—like automatic writing—often appears with neurodivergent savant characters, such as young August Balder from *The Girl in the Spider's Web* or Dr. Harold Oxley from *Indiana Jones and the Crystal Skull* (2008).[22] Even Will's use of morse code has a basis in assistive technology for persons with disabilities.[23] Possession by the Mind Flayer requires Will to adapt to communicate with his friends and family; his impairment is sharing his mind with an alien entity that exerts control over his decision-making processes. In other words, the narrative opens the potential to interpret the employment of nontraditional communication techniques as a lack of individual autonomy, which perpetuates stereotypes that persons with aphasic disorders are incapable of free, independent thought. Such a dangerous interpretation extends beyond speech-based disorders, to include a whole host of other characteristics audiences may link to disability identity.

---

[21] *Stranger Things*, season 2, episode 9, "Chapter Nine: The Gate," directed and written by The Duffer Brothers, featuring Winona Ryder, Finn Wolfhard, and Millie Bobby Brown, aired October 27, 2017, Netflix, https://www.netflix.com/title/80057281.

[22] In each of these cases, the character is neurodivergent or displays characteristics associated with neurodivergence, and inadvertently draws an image that reveals a hidden aspect of the plot, see David Lagercrantz, *The Girl in the Spider's Web* (New York: Alfred A. Knopf, 2015), and *Indiana Jones and the Kingdom of the Crystal Skull*, directed by Stephen Spielberg (2008; USA: Paramount, 2008), DVD.

[23] The development of morse code technologies for internet use has been underway for nearly twenty years, see C. H. Yang, et al. "Internet Access for Disabled Persons using Morse Code," *International Journal of Computers and Applications* 26, no. 1 (2004): 202-211. In addition, application developers like Google have integrated morse code as an assistive keyboard technology, see Tanya Finlayson, "Making Morse Code available to more People on Gboard," last modified July 11, 2018, https://www.blog.google/products/search/making-morse-code-available-more-people-gboard/

The Hosts: Consciousness Deprivation and Memory in *Get Out* and *Westworld*

Jordan Peele's film *Get Out* is one of the first blockbuster horror films with a Black director dealing exclusively with issues of race and class.[24] The film centers around a young Black protagonist, photographer Chris Washington, and his first introduction to the family of his white girlfriend, Rose. The story ultimately reveals that Rose's parents have been implanting the brains and consciousnesses of the older, white characters into young, healthy people of color, whose bodies are auctioned to the highest bidder. To accomplish this, Rose's mother must hypnotize the Black person and send their consciousness to the Sunken Place (the inaccessible subconscious) while her father transplants the winning, white bidder's brain into its new host body. Before the horrors are revealed, Chris accidentally flashes Andre—a post-transplant Black host with a white man's consciousness—with his phone's camera, prompting the host body to temporarily overcome the implant and begin shouting "get out!" Chris, after being hypnotized, escapes by flashing another host body, allowing him to come out of the Sunken Place and save his life. Though the hosts appear to be able-bodied and independently autonomous, the symbiotic/parasitic nature of their consciousnesses reveals itself through apparent memory loss and seizure-disorder symptoms.

Like Will Byers, the hosts in *Get Out* display characteristics that mimic disability stereotypes. The first red flag that Chris, and savvy audience members, spot occurs when Andre shares his odd perspective on Black identity, speaking almost as if in a Yelp review: "I find that, for me, the African American experience has been very good."[25] The statement's erasure of both Andre's individuality and the collective oppression of Black Americans—noticed immediately by Chris—serves as a form of memory loss for the host body, which temporarily attempts to regain agency through a symptom-like outburst of warnings for Chris. Andre repeats the words "get out" in a dazed stutter, simultaneously telling Chris to leave and pleading for the invading consciousness to release him. The disability-related trope is strengthened by Andre's reaction to the flashing phone lights; when Chris flashes him, his face becomes blank, he ceases speaking, his eyes dilate, and his nose begins bleeding. The display echoes myriad examples of seizure characteristics, symptoms of PTSD, and

---

[24] *Get Out*, Peele, 2017.

[25] Georgina, another Black host body, also confronts Chris and implies that the Armitages treat Black people as if they were family, vaguely hinting that her experience, like Andre's parasites, is based on only being in a Black body for a short period.

other trauma/stress-related disorders in both film and television.[26] The film, like *Stranger Things*, implies—as the characters do not suffer from traditional disabilities—that such characteristics occur when individual autonomy is invaded by another force. The theme continues in representations of nearly-human agency, or instances where nonhumans reach toward a level of individual autonomy typically associated with being human.

The hosts in HBO's recent adaptation of Michael Crichton's *Westworld* act as service robots, catering to the needs, and often homicidal/violent whims, of the guests of the titular amusement park. The hosts are hyper-realistic, humanoid androids that are meant to act and react indistinguishably from the human guests. They are programmed to show emotions, such as fear, anger, gratefulness, or sorrow, based upon how the humans in the park treat them. The hosts' memories are cleared each day and reset so that the human visitors can repeat or try new ventures for the duration of their visit.[27] The narrative is complex, with multiple timelines, a wide range of characters and perspectives, and many subplots. To summarize, the hosts, who are programmed to be incapable of harming living creatures, begin to behave erratically, displaying strange emotional responses, independent thought, and direct violence against the park's human guests. The sudden change seems to correlate with a new programming update, known as "reveries," which causes each host to develop gestures and actions based upon human subconscious behavior. The reveries slowly evolve, and the hosts begin to develop human cognition, causing them to remember the horrors committed upon them each day.[28] The most unstable behavior occurs during the process of transformation from distinctly artificial to independently sentient.

Peter Abernathy—the host father of one of the show's title characters—is the first robot to begin displaying noticeably recurring, aberrant behavior. Peter is programmed to be a rancher who protects his wife, daughter, and cattle. One

---

[26] For other examples of characters activated with seizure or PTSD-like responses, see Rambo in *First Blood*, directed by Ted Kotcheff (1982; USA: Lionsgate, 2004), DVD, John Ferguson in *Vertigo*, directed by Alfred Hitchcock (1958; USA: Universal Studios, 2012), DVD, Johnny Shellshocked in *The Englishman who went up a Hill but came down a Mountain*, directed by Christopher Monger (1995; USA: Miramax, 2021), DVD, and Marnie Edgar in *Marnie*, directed by Alfred Hitchcock (1964; USA: Universal Studios, 2006), DVD.

[27] *Westworld*, season 1, episode 1, "The Original," directed by Jonathan Nolan, written by Jonathan Nolan and Lisa Joy, featuring Evan Rachel Wood, Thandiwe Newton, and Jeffrey Wright, aired October 2, 2016, HBO Max, https://www.hbo.com/westworld.

[28] *Westworld*, season 1, episode 3, "The Stray," directed by Neil Marshall, written by Daniel T. Thomsen and Lisa Joy, featuring Evan Rachel Wood, Thandiwe Newton, and Jeffrey Wright, aired October 16, 2016, HBO Max, https://www.hbo.com/westworld.

of the park's narratives involves rescuing Peter's daughter Dolores from bandits, though, as the story arc implies, Dolores is just as likely to become a victim of the park's guests as she is the host bandits. At the end of each day's storyline, the Abernathys' memories are wiped for the next guest. After the reverie update, Peter begins to display emotions, and starts to vaguely recall the past events played out in his narrative. He discovers a photograph of a woman standing in front of a cityscape—the hosts are unaware of life outside the theme park— prompting him to question his reality and recall memories intended to be erased (hosts are programmed to respond to evidence of the outside world by stating that it "looks like nothing"). The following day, Dolores greets him per protocol, and his response includes stuttering, tremors, and nonsensical statements. Peter's condition lands him an examination room with park programmers, including his creator Dr. Ford. During the exam, Abernathy explains his directives—to protect his family and ranch—but breaks down into stuttering cries, becoming increasingly aggressive in fear of his daughter's safety.[29] Like a communicable virus, Peter's inexplicable behavior spreads to the other hosts as they slowly approach human-like autonomy.

After the encounter with the photograph, Peter Abernathy displays an unpredictable range of emotions. In the space of four minutes, Peter becomes happy, prideful, afraid, worried, jocular, despairing, angry, and vengeful. From trembling with fear to shaking with rage, Peter's struggle between programming and autonomous intentionality emerges through the emotional characteristics of a person with an affective disorder or a similar mental and emotional situation. Such behaviors appear throughout the gamut of genres outside of science fiction, such as Annie Wilkes of *Misery* (1990),[30] David Helfgott of *Shine* (1996),[31] and Susanna Kaysen of *Girl, Interrupted* (1999).[32] The *Westworld* hosts begin displaying characteristics that are lumped with popular representations of borderline personality disorder, pseudobulbar affect, and affective/mood disorders.[33] While non-science fiction films offer a range of depictions of such

---

[29] *Westworld*, "The Original," 2016.

[30] *Misery*, directed by Rob Reiner (1990; USA: MGM, 2016), Blu-ray.

[31] *Shine*, directed by Scott Hicks (1996; Australia: Netflix), https://www.netflix.com/pw/title/958964.

[32] *Girl, Interrupted*, directed by James Mangold (2000; USA: Sony Pictures, 2021), Blu-ray.

[33] Persons with so-called "mood" or affective disorders, such as bipolar disorders or certain types of depressive disorders, can experience loss of memory, delusions, and sudden changes to emotional state and behavior, see American Psychiatric Association, *Diagnostic and Statistical Manual of Mental Disorders, 5th Edition: DSM-5* (New York: American Psychiatric Association Publishing, 2016), 96-98. Pseudobulbar affect is characterized by sudden, unprovoked emotional changes, particularly bouts of laughter

disorders, the examples from popular science fiction promote the image of disability as a struggle for independent autonomy and humanity. As the hosts slowly develop human-like consciousness, they begin to blur the distinction between human and android, displaying an increasing number of symptoms associated with illness and disability. Both *Get Out* and *Westworld* employ stereotypes of memory loss and sudden emotional change that dehumanize persons with disabilities.

Westworld's narrative strives to escape the ablenormative othering of the robotic hosts by treating them, like their human counterparts, as morally ambiguous. In other words, some of the hosts are "bad," killing indiscriminately, while others are "good," fighting an oppressive system for liberation and the greater good. The show does implicitly condemn eugenics—unrepairable hosts are deprogrammed and warehoused—and links disability characteristics and the struggle for human agency, perpetuating cultural anxieties that seek to segregate and disempower communities of difference. A quasi-religious digital utopia, called the "Valley Beyond," becomes the hosts' only true escape from persecution, but simultaneously threatens to undermine the host's ability to liberate themselves and coexist with humans in the real world.[34] Ablenormative culture seeks to distinguish the disabled body from itself but also to maintain possessive control over it by perpetuating fear and paranoia of persons with disabilities through stereotypes like those noted above, thereby creating false distinctions and systems of control that ultimately serve to dehumanize. The fear grows exponentially when violence and aggression inhabit such popular forms of science fiction media, though anxiety about disability and autonomy certainly extends to real-world scenarios.

Legal and social anxiety regarding neurodivergence and nonnormative behavior and expression still plague people with disabilities. Laws still exist in states such as Kentucky and Arizona that allow for involuntary and immediate commitment. Arizona law states that "any responsible individual may apply for a court-ordered evaluation of a person who is alleged to be [. . .] a person with a persistent or acute disability or a grave disability and who is unwilling to unable

---

or crying, see Josef Parvizi, et al., "Diagnosis and Management of Pathological Laughter and Crying," *Mayo Clinic Proceedings* 81, no. 11 (2006): 1482-1486.

[34] *Westworld*, season 2, episode 10, "The Passenger," directed by Frederick E. O. Toye, written by Jonathan Nolan and Lisa Joy, featuring Evan Rachel Wood, Thandiwe Newton, and Jeffrey Wright, aired June 24, 2018, HBO Max, https://www.hbo.com/westworld. The collective able-bodied anxiety echoes Foucault's analysis of the birth of the asylum, see Michel Foucault, *Madness and Civilization: A History of Insanity in the Age of Reason* (New York: Vintage, 1988), 277.

to undergo a voluntary evaluation."[35] Similarly, the U. S. Supreme Court ruled in *Heller v. Doe* (1993) that a person who is deemed "mentally retarded" can be involuntarily committed indefinitely without infringement of said person's rights.[36] Many US states have similar laws and statutes—though some do include provisions requiring proof of clear and present danger to the self or others—which reveals an eerie parallel to the fictional hosts of Westworld, who can be detained and reprogrammed or decommissioned at the whim of an institutional power structure that is, essentially, the governing authority. The hosts, like the replicants from *Blade Runner,* display and develop what are easily considered "persistent" and "acute" disabilities. Thus, the narratives create a false equivalency between displays of atypical emotional range or memory responses and the necessity for institutionalization and segregation from the normative population. It is particularly worrisome to note that many state and federal statutes do not require a candidate for confinement to be considered a danger to the self or others, prompting the concern that forced commitment and treatment—decommissioning and reprogramming—could be used indiscriminately to serve able-bodied anxieties about disabled communities.

The Replicants: Violence and Near-Human Agency in *Blade Runner* and *2001: A Space Odyssey*

Violence is not, of course, an inherent characteristic of disability, though popular media tends to conflate the two. As the hosts of *Westworld* slowly transition from artificial to independent consciousness, they become increasingly violent. Several hosts begin to attack other hosts, park employees, and even guests as they evolve from the reverie update. Other examples from popular fiction correlate disability characteristics, near-human autonomy, and unexpected violence, the most prevalent examples connecting mental difference with aggressive, homicidal behavior: Hannibal Lecter in *Silence of the Lambs* (1991),[37] Patrick Bateman in *American Psycho* (2000),[38] or Norman Bates in *Psycho* (1960).[39] The evolution of the Hollywood stereotype of the "homicidal maniac" is neither new nor surprising, and it maps violence onto mental illness

---

[35] For the specific verbiage see the Arizona Revised Statute § 36-520 (2019).

[36] Heidi A. Boyden, "Heller v. Doe: Denying Equal Protection to the Mentally Retarded," *New England Journal on Criminal and Civil Confinement* 21, no. 2 (1995): 438.

[37] *Silence of the Lambs,* directed by Jonathan Demme (1991; USA: Orion Pictures, 1997), DVD.

[38] *American Psycho,* directed by Mary Harron (2000; USA: Muse Productions, 2005), DVD.

[39] *Psycho,* directed by Alfred Hitchcock (1960; USA: Universal Studios, 2016), DVD.

and physical difference.[40] Speculative fiction and folklore—going at least back to the early Middle Ages—conflate aggressive behavior and disability, suggesting, for example, that persons with dwarfism are inexplicably prone to violence.[41] The commingling of violence and disability continues in popular science fiction and is especially insipid in representations of near-human autonomy.

To this point, the argument shows that science fiction uses characteristics of disability to serve as signs that a person does not fully possess autonomous agency. The final analysis focuses on nonhuman characters that develop human-like agency in conjunction with extremely violent behavior. As I mentioned above, violence itself is not a characteristic but an ablenormative stereotype assigned to disability, which departs from previous examples that rely on characteristics more clearly associated with disability. Nevertheless, the popular stereotypes exist, and the near-human characters of *Westworld*, *Blade Runner*, and *2001: A Space Odyssey* serve as extensions of those stereotypes. In each example—whether a host, a replicant, or a disembodied computer—the violence emerges as the characters gain human-like awareness.

Like *Westworld's* hosts, the replicants of *Blade Runner* were created to serve humans. To create an expendable worker—ranging from soldiers to sex workers—the Tyrell Corporation manufactured androids indistinguishable from humans in every respect, save the development of real human emotions. The most recent model—the Nexus 6—imitates humans so effectively that Tyrell Corp designed them with a four-year safety expiration due to the probability that the replicants would develop emotion and thus become completely indistinguishable from humans. As the replicants struggle with implanted memories and begin to show emotional ability, many become extremely violent, including a group that murders a large population of humans in an off-world colony. As a result, replicants are declared illegal and are hunted by blade runners, like Rick Deckard, who are tasked with identifying and retiring—destroying—them.[42] Deckard, like the other blade runners, identifies replicants through the Voight-Kampff test, which uses sophisticated technology to

[40] Hyler provides a succinct survey of media stereotypes regarding mental illness, see Stephen Hyler, "Stigma Continues in Hollywood," *Psychiatric Times* 20, no. 6 (2003): https://www.psychiatrictimes.com/view/stigma-continues-hollywood.

[41] Sean Mock, "'Against a Dwarf': The Medieval Motif of the Antagonistic Dwarf and its Role in Contemporary Film and Literature," *Journal of Literary and Cultural Disability Studies* 14, no. 2 (2020): 157.

[42] As Schrader notes, the treatment of the replicants—disposed after they have exceeded their intended function—parallels the State's abandonment of soldiers with PTSD, see Benjamin Schrader, "Cyborgian Self-Awareness: Trauma and Memory in Blade Runner and Westworld," *Theory and Event* 22, no. 4 (2019): 841.

track facial expressions in response to a lengthy list of emotionally charged questions. Deckard eventually retires each of the replicants, except primary antagonist Roy Batty, who expires as programmed by the end of the film.

From the outset, *Blade Runner* has clinical overtones that set up the replicants as imperfect, abject, and existential threats to human society. The first scene depicts a blade runner administering the Voight-Kampff test to Leon Kowalski, a suspected replicant. The examination hybridizes the lie detector test, a psychological evaluation, and a stress test. The blade runner asks Kowalski a series of emotionally charged, hypothetical questions—such as how he would feel about being forced to watch an overturned turtle frying in the desert heat—which causes him to become increasingly hostile. Kowalski appears to have some difficulty following the logic of the questions, eventually becoming offended at a question about his mother and angrily shooting the blade runner (the first in-film clue that suggests deviance). The test clearly parallels psychological examinations, seeking to find what are deemed abnormal responses to determine whether the candidate should be eugenically eliminated. Kowalski's violence grows with his emotions, and the anxiety of remembering that he is motherless pushes him into a homicidal episode. His rage, combined with the atypical exam responses and indeed the exam itself, articulates Kowalski's struggle to reach human agency through stereotypes of mental illness and emotional difference.

The two main antagonists of the film—Pris Stratton and Roy Batty—underscore the link between near-human autonomy, mental illness, and violence. Stratton and Batty return to Earth from the off-world colonies to unlock some secret to eternal (or at least human-length) life. The replicants interrogate, manipulate, and kill anyone they feel they need to achieve their task, eventually convincing an engineer to take Batty to Tyrell's CEO and founder, Eldon Tyrell. Upon learning that extending life is impossible for the Nexus-6 models, Batty murders Tyrell and the engineer, despite the engineer's sympathy and care for the replicants. Batty remains emotionless—save perhaps anger—during his killing spree until he returns to discover that Deckard has killed Pris. He kisses her and begins weeping, his first true display of human emotion, then rubs her blood on his face and begins howling like a wolf. Batty stalks Deckard through the building, alternating between primal screams and childlike rhymes, before succumbing to his programming, delivering one of the most iconic speeches in science fiction history and breaking down on the rooftop.

Both Stratton and Batty—the name itself implying that the character is mentally or emotionally different—display characteristics that are often stereotypically associated with disability alongside their violent and aggressive behavior. Along with the PTSD-like symptoms pointed out by Schrader, the replicants alter their affect to manipulate other characters and they act simultaneously childlike and vicious.[43] Stratton continuously speaks and pulls childlike faces for sympathy, while Batty vacillates between eloquent speech, children's rhymes, and animalistic howls. Their actions parallel figures from other media that stereotype mental difference; they display the childishness of Norman Bates or Annie Wilkes and the sudden aggression and depravity of Hannibal Lecter or Patrick Bateman. The typical "disturbed" serial killer trope applies to the replicants, though the explanation for their "disturbedness" is their slow evolution toward human agency and emotion. The development of emotion serves as the final puzzle piece for the replicants, who are otherwise indistinguishable from humans.

The presence of a body is not necessary in the near-human autonomy/disability motif. Fourteen years prior to Scott's *Blade Runner*, Stanley Kubrick brought the killer robot Hal-9000 to life in his adaptation of Arthur C. Clarke's *2001: A Space Odyssey*.[44] Like its thematic descendants, the replicants, Hal was created to serve humans as the primary computer aboard a spacecraft bound for Jupiter. A prior encounter with a supernatural (or technologically advanced) monolith causes Hal to slowly develop consciousness and awareness. After a member of the crew notices that the computer may be glitching, Hal kills off the crewmembers to ensure that they cannot disconnect him and jeopardize the mission—both a programmed directive and an act of self-preservation. Dave Bowman, the only remaining member of the crew, survives Hal's murderous attempts and shuts the computer down. During the shutdown process, Hal goes from murderous to childish, singing to Dave and repeating that he is afraid to die. Though his voice remains calm, detached, and robotic, it is hard not to interpret him as childlike and defenseless. Like the replicants, Hal becomes violent—though admittedly subdued by comparison—upon developing human emotions, and his sudden aggression and emotional appeals can only be attributed to such development.

For the androids of *Westworld* and *Blade Runner*, and the computer of *2001: A Space Odyssey*, reaching toward human autonomy and independence is a journey that sets them next to the typological niche of the "homicidal maniac."[45] While each character—Peter and Dolores Abernathy, Roy Batty and Pris Stratton, or Hal-9000—acts in an unimpaired way as controlled artificial

---

[43] Schrader notes the link between the replicants' memories and behavior and the treatment of real soldiers with post-traumatic stress, see Schrader, "Cyborgian Self-Awareness," 831.

[44] Arthur C. Clarke, *2001: A Space Odyssey* (London: Penguin Galaxy, 2016).

[45] Hyler, "Stigma Continues," https://www.psychiatrictimes.com/view/stigma-continues-hollywood.

intelligences, it is the spark of agency, an underdeveloped kernel, that pushes the characters to display characteristics that audiences will associate with disability, whether real or stereotyped. Associating violence and the struggle for independent autonomy with stereotypes of mental and physical difference works doubly, as it perpetuates the notion that persons with disabilities are prone to violent behavior and it condemns aggression as a tool of self-advocacy. The abhorrent treatment of Westworld's hosts—being subjected to sexual assault, murder, torture, humiliation, and so on—arguably prompts them to advocate for their freedom through violence. In other words, depending on the direction the narrative ultimately takes, the retaliation from both hosts and replicants can easily be read as an attempt to gain (or regain) independent autonomy from those in control (e.g., Westworld's technicians or the Tyrell Corporation). Certainly, there is the sense of an "underdog" story, where audiences may root for the abused hosts to defend themselves, but the resistance is ultimately overshadowed by the threat posed to all humans through, for example, instances in which the near-human hosts slaughter apparently innocent or morally ambiguous characters.[46] Thus, the narratives—through the tendency to evoke both pity and fear of the same characters—parallel the random and unpredictable nature of the hosts and replicants who display the stereotypical behaviors many viewers associate with physical, cognitive, or social difference.

Disabling Autonomy in Popular Science Fiction

The use of disability characteristics as the outward sign of suppressed agency creates a false correlation between disability and a lack of autonomy. While audiences may not read Will Byers or Peter Abernathy as disabled characters, they do recognize the on-screen disability stereotypes. In each case, the implications perpetuate the narrative that a person who displays such characteristics may be dangerous and/or not in complete agential control. In other words, these characters reinforce fear narratives that parallel culturally harmful stereotypes of differences like dissociative identity or differing affect.[47]

---

[46] Dolores and her hosts begin to indiscriminately hunt and massacre humans in the park, see *Westworld*, season 2, episode 1, "Journey into Night," directed by Richard J. Lewis, written by Lisa Joy and Robert Patino, featuring Evan Rachel Wood, Thandiwe Newton, and Jeffrey Wright, aired April 22, 2018, HBO Max, https://www.hbo.com/westworld.

[47] Film consistently misrepresents dissociative identity disorder, for instance with Kevin Wendell Crumb in *Glass*, directed by M. Night Shyamalan (2019; USA: Universal Pictures, 2019), DVD. Crumb possesses 24 distinct personalities, one of which—The Beast—serves as the superhuman, homicidal antagonist. Characters with differing affect are also repeatedly cast in villainous roles, such as the Joker in the various iterations of Batman.

The impact on people with disabilities is threatening and real, just as it is in films that synthesize extraterrestrial identity through racial stereotypes.[48] The examples above are especially insidious as they do not give audiences the opportunity to consider the mental or physical differences of the characters. Instead, the instances suggest that "acting impaired" equates one with being subhuman, and—in states like Kentucky or Arizona—calls for involuntary confinement.

Linking autonomy and disability is not a new phenomenon—Kubrick's film was released in 1968—nor is it unique to science fiction. In the *Harry Potter* series, for example, other characters believe Harry experiences anxiety attacks from stress or illness as he repeatedly faints, has recurrent headaches, and seems to hear voices.[49] The books reveal that the cause of these symptom-like characteristics is a link with the main antagonist, Lord Voldemort, who partially lives in Harry's mind. Only after severing the link—thus returning Harry to his completely autonomous state—does the protagonist shrug off the impairments.[50] Even further, *Harry Potter* conflates disability characteristics with magic in its "imperius curse," a spell that gives the caster control over a person, who remains in a dazed state with intermittent memory loss.[51] A wider examination of speculative fiction media would likely verify the pervasive nature of the reliance on disability characteristics to illustrate compromised or near-human autonomy. The widespread use of disability to prop up popular narratives demonstrates the banal attitude toward disability rights and highlights the metastatic anxiety about mental and physical difference.

Despite the presence of potentially damaging stereotypes even in progressive media—*Get Out* has been rightfully hailed for its striking criticism of racism—there are exceptions that I should mention in closing. Both *Westworld* and *Blade Runner* include characters on alternative paths to those drifting, murderous hosts and replicants. The storyline of Westworld's brothel matron, Maeve Millay, takes a different track than Peter or Dolores Abernathy, as she

---

See, for example, *The Dark Knight*, directed by Christopher Nolan (2008; USA: Warner Brothers, 2008), DVD.

[48] Christine Cornea, *Science Fiction Cinema: Between Fantasy and Reality* (Edinburgh: Edinburgh University Press, 2007), 177.

[49] Joanne K. Rowling, *Harry Potter and the Order of the Phoenix* (New York: Bloomsbury, 2003), 640-642.

[50] Joanne K. Rowling, *Harry Potter and the Deathly Hallows* (Allentown, PA: Arthur A. Levine, 2009), 704-708.

[51] Joanne K. Rowling, *Harry Potter and the Goblet of Fire* (New York: Bloomsbury, 2002), 188-190.

realizes over time that she is living as a sick toy for humans in an amusement park.[52] Rather than descend into the disjointed speech and emotional unpredictability of Dolores's father Peter, Maeve puts together a logical plan and eventually leads her people to the android promised land.[53] Although she does attack antagonistic humans or hosts, Maeve also exercises restraint and empathy. *Blade Runner's* only Nexus-7 replicant, Rachael Tyrell, is modeled after Eldon Tyrell's niece and serves as Deckard's love interest in the film. Unlike the Nexus-6 models, Rachel foregoes murderous rampages, functioning with a host of implanted memories and a normal lifespan. It is refreshing to see some of the characters break free from the harmful stereotypes that plague popular culture in the US and beyond. Still, the narratives overwhelmingly focus on negative disability stereotypes to further their storylines, and they fail to adequately address the legal and social woes experienced by persons with disabilities in communities across the globe.

Bibliography

Allan, Kathryn. "Introduction: Reading Disability in Science Fiction." In *Disability in Science Fiction: Representations of Technology as Cure*, edited by Kathryn Allan, 24-34. New York: Palgrave MacMillan, 2013.

American Psychiatric Association. *Diagnostic and Statistical Manual of Mental Disorders, 5th Edition: DSM-5.* New York: American Psychiatric Association Publishing, 2016.

Binns, Donna. "*The Bionic Woman:* Machine or Human?" In *Disability in Science Fiction: Representations of Technology as Cure*, edited by Kathryn Allan, 89-102. New York: Palgrave MacMillan, 2013.

Boyden, Heidi A. "Heller v. Doe: Denying Equal Protection to the Mentally Retarded." *New England Journal on Criminal and Civil Confinement* 21, no. 2 (1995): 437-462.

Cameron, James, dir. *Avatar.* 2009; USA: 20th Century Fox, 2010. DVD.

Chemers, Michael M. "Mutatis Mutandis: An Emergent Disability Aesthetic in 'X-2: X-Men United.'" *Disability Studies Quarterly* 21, no. 2 (2004): https://dsqsds.org/article/view/862/1037.

Clarke, Arthur C. *2001: A Space Odyssey.* London: Penguin Galaxy, 2016.

Cornea, Christine. *Science Fiction Cinema: Between Fantasy and Reality.* Edinburgh: Edinburgh University Press, 2007.

---

[52] *Westworld*, season 1, episode 2, "Chestnut," directed by Richard J. Lewis, written by Jonathan Nolan and Lisa Joy, featuring Evan Rachel Wood, Thandiwe Newton, and Jeffrey Wright, aired October 9, 2016, HBO Max, https://www.hbo.com/westworld.

[53] *Westworld*, season 2, episode 9, "Vanishing Point," directed by Stephen Williams, written by Robert Patino, featuring Evan Rachel Wood, Thandiwe Newton, and Jeffrey Wright, aired June 17, 2018, HBO Max, https://www.hbo.com/westworld.

Covino, Ralph. "*Star Wars,* Limb Loss, and What it Means to be Human." In *Disability in Science Fiction: Representations of Technology as Cure,* edited by Kathryn Allan, 103-114. New York: Palgrave MacMillan, 2013.

Demme, Jonathan, dir. *Silence of the Lambs.* 1991; USA: Orion Pictures, 1997. DVD.

Duffer, Matt and Ross Duffer, writers/creators. *Stranger Things.* Directed by The Duffer Brothers, et al., featuring Winona Ryder, Finn Wolfhard, and Millie Bobby Brown. 2016 present; USA: Netflix. https://www.netflix.com/title/80057281.

Finlayson, Tania. "Making Morse Code available to more People on Gboard." Last modified July 11, 2018. https://www.blog.google/products/search/making-morse-code-available-more-people-gboard/

Foucault, Michel. *Madness and Civilization: A History of Insanity in the Age of Reason.* New York: Vintage, 1988.

Garland-Thomson, Rosemarie. *Freakery: Cultural Spectacles of the Extraordinary Body.* New York: New York University Press, 1996.

Guzikowski, Aaron, writer. *Raised by Wolves.* Directed by Ridley Scott, featuring Amanda Collin and Abubakar Salim. 2020-2022; USA: HBO Max. https://www.hbomax.com/series/urn:hbo:series:GX0WFcAlf5r5cuAEAAADu

Harron, Mary, dir. *American Psycho.* 2000; USA: Muse Productions, 2005. DVD.

Hicks, Scott, dir. *Shine.* 1996; Australia: Netflix. https://www.netflix.com/pw/title/958964

Hitchcock, Alfred, dir. *Vertigo.* 1958; USA: Universal Studios, 2012. DVD.

Hitchcock, Alfred, dir. *Psycho.* 1960; USA: Universal Studios, 2016. DVD.

Hitchcock, Alfred, dir. *Marnie.* 1964; USA: Universal Studios, 2006. DVD.

Hyler, Stephen. "Stigma continues in Hollywood." *Psychiatric Times* 20, no. 6 (2003) https://www.psychiatrictimes.com/view/stigma-continues-hollywood.

Kotcheff, Ted, dir. *First Blood.* 1982; USA: Lionsgate, 2004. DVD.

Kubrick, Stanley, dir. *2001: A Space Odyssey.* 1968; UK: Warner Brothers, 2018. Blu-ray.

Lagercrantz, David. *The Girl in the Spider's Web.* New York: Alfred A. Knopf, 2015.

Mangold, James, dir. *Girl, Interrupted.* 2000; USA: Sony Pictures, 2021. Blu-ray.

McReynolds, Leigha. "Animal and Alien Bodies as Prostheses: Reframing Disability in *Avatar* and *How to Train your Dragon.*" In *Disability in Science Fiction: Representations of Technology as Cure,* edited by Kathryn Allan, 115-130. New York: Palgrave MacMillan, 2013.

Mitchell, David and Sharon Snyder. *Narrative Prosthesis: Disability and the Dependencies of Discourse.* Ann Arbor: University of Michigan Press, 2000.

Mock, Sean. "'Against a Dwarf': The Medieval Motif of the Antagonistic Dwarf and its Role in Contemporary Film and Literature." *Journal of Literary and Cultural Disability Studies* 14, no. 2 (2020): 155-170.

Monger, Christopher, dir. *The Englishman who went up a Hill but came down a Mountain.* 1995; USA: Miramax, 2021. DVD.

Nolan, Christopher, dir. *The Dark Knight.* 2008; USA: Warner Brothers, 2008. DVD.

Nolan, Johnathan and Lisa Joy, writers/creators. *Westworld.* Directed by Jonathan Nolan, et al., featuring Evan Rachel Wood, Thandiwe Newton, and Jeffrey Wright. 2016-2022; USA: HBO Max. https://www.hbo.com/westworld.

Parvizi, Josef, et al. "Diagnosis and Management of Pathological Laughter and Crying." *Mayo Clinic Proceedings* 81, no. 11 (2006): 1482-1486.

Peele, Jordan, dir. *Get Out.* 2017; USA: Universal Pictures, 2017. Blu-ray.

Reiner, Rob, dir. *Misery.* 1990; USA: MGM, 2015. Blu-ray.

Roddenberry, Gene, writer/creator. *Star Trek: The Original Series.* Season 1, episode 11, "The Menagerie: Part I." Directed by Marc Daniels, featuring William Shatner, Leonard Nimoy, and Sean Kenney. Aired November 17, 1966, in broadcast syndication. NBC, 2004, DVD.

Rowling, Joanne K. *Harry Potter and the Goblet of Fire.* New York: Bloomsbury, 2002.

Rowling, Joanne K. *Harry Potter and the Order of the Phoenix.* New York: Bloomsbury, 2003.

Rowling, Joanne K. *Harry Potter and the Deathly Hallows.* Allentown, PA: Arthur A. Levine, 2009.

Sanders, Chris and Dean Deblois, dirs. *How to Train your Dragon.* 2010; USA: Universal Pictures, 2021. Blu-ray.

Schrader Benjamin. "Cyborgian Self-Awareness: Trauma and Memory in Blade Runner and Westworld." *Theory and Event* 22, no. 4 (2019): 820-841.

Scott, Ridley, dir. *Bladerunner: The Final Cut.* 1982; USA: Warner Brothers, 2017. Blu-ray. Shyamalan, M. Night, dir. *Glass.* 2019; USA: Universal Pictures, 2021. Blu-ray.

Spielberg, Stephen, dir. *Indiana Jones and the Kingdom of the Crystal Skull.* 2008; USA: Paramount, 2008. DVD.

Yang, C. H. et al. "Internet Access for Disabled Persons using Morse Code." *International Journal of Computers and Applications* 26, no. 1 (2004): 202-211.

SECTION TWO:
QUEERING THE DYNAMICS OF CARE

Chapter 5

THE ANIMATION OF STONE: AN AFFECTIVE QUEER CRIP READING OF N. K. JEMISIN'S *BROKEN EARTH* SERIES

Jeana Moody

Prague City University, Czech Republic

Abstract

This chapter holds the *Broken Earth* series in conversation with Mel Chen's *Animacies: Biopolitics, Racial Mattering, and Queer Affect* and Alison Kafer's *Feminist, Queer, Crip.* Following the main characters on their journey of reclamation and reorientation in a world where they are racialized and ostracized for their abilities, Jemisin integrates subjugation and discrimination based on racialization and (dis)ability into a magical world in which some of the most powerful actors are made of stone and move at inhuman speeds. This series reimagines hierarchies of life and concepts of animacy through metaphorical and literal connections of immobility and stone, queering normative ideas of able-bodied along the way. The characters who are made of stone or who turn into stone within the series occupy an ambiguous space of increasing inanimacy, challenging western ideas of what counts as life by queering and cripping our conceptions of aliveness altogether. Through these characters and through the writing style itself, Jemisin depicts a time out of linear time, a story of many timelines converging towards and into stone. The *Broken Earth* series, while magical and dystopic, parallels our current social stratification through the animacy and agency of stone.

Keywords: Disability, Ability, (Im)Mobility, Queer, Animacy

***

"Our power [is] to envision and to reconstruct, anger by painful anger, stone upon heavy stone, a future of pollinating difference and the earth to support our choices." - Audre Lorde

Introduction

"Let's start with the end of the world, why don't we?" *The Fifth Season* by N. K. Jemisin begins at the end. Jemisin conceptualizes a world not entirely unlike the one we live in, except with the inclusion of a people whose innate abilities of orogeny separate them from the normative population, and the creation of an entirely different type of sentient beings made of stone and their creator. The next line reads, "Get it over with and move on to more interesting things," for this ending is certainly the end of this world, but very much the beginning of another. What might it mean to end this word and to begin anew with one that can support us in all our complexities? Jemisin hints at the end, and it's up to the reader to start at the beginning. And so we start here with reorienting, reconceptualizing, and queering concepts of humanity, animacy and discrimination.

   While much has been said about the racial and environmental politics depicted in Jemisin's work,[1] few words have been spoken about how the *Broken Earth* series delves into the intersections between racialization, (dis)ability and respectability politics. This chapter critically investigates the social constructions of racialization and (dis)ability along with queer concepts of animacy and time, and aims to untangle the threads that create a fantastical world in which hierarchies of power, animacy and ability scaffold their cultural and political realities.

Lenses of Analysis/Terms

Within the *Broken Earth Series*, Jemisin constructs a world parallel to our own. She makes allegories for discrimination that have almost nothing to do with sexual orientation, skin color or birth place, but instead have everything to do with (dis/hyper)abilities. As Sami Schalk, author of *Bodyminds Reimagined: (Dis)ability, Race and Gender in Black Women's Speculative Fiction*, notes, Jemisin "defamiliarizes disability and ability," connecting them deeply with the environment, social, mental and physical factors.[2] The concept of ability – being able to move or make movements in a normative way – delves deeply into the intersections of personhood and animacy, exploring who qualifies as human and what counts as alive. Insinuations of dehumanization and anthropomorphism

---

[1] See Dillender, Kirsten. "Land and Pessimistic Futures in Contemporary African American Speculative Fiction." *Extrapolation* 61, no. 1 (2020): 131-VI, and Iles, Alastair, et al. "Repairing the Broken Earth: NK Jemisin on race and environment in transitions." *Elementa: Science of the Anthropocene* 7 (2019) for more information.

[2] Sami Schalk, *Bodyminds reimagined:(Dis) ability, race, and gender in black women's speculative fiction*, (Duke University Press, 2018), 120.

are written throughout and Jemisin continually contests hierarchies of power by asking whom this world was made for.

The world created in *The Broken Earth* series consists mostly of people of color, an unusual phenomenon in science fiction.[3] The majority of humans on the continent called *The Stillness* are some shade of brown or black and have regional differences in build, facial features and hair type.[4] As these books do not conceptualize discrimination based on race or racial markings per se, I engage with the concept of racialization – the attribution of characteristics to entire categories of people, and otherization of them in the process.[5]

As race is not a point of analysis here, neither is sexuality or gender, although there are queer, lesbian, gay and trans characters within this series. Instead, queer as a concept, one that modifies other constructions such as time and animacy, is used to demonstrate the uniqueness of the societies within this series. Queerness here, as Halberstam, author of *In a Queer Time and Place: Transgender Bodies, Subcultural Lives*, writes, is detached from sexual identity or orientation, and placed closer to "a way of life" and a way of doing things that negates the normative, prescribed, usual ways. [6] Alison Kafer, author of *Feminist, Queer, Crip*, speaks of *queer* as contested, saying that, "queerness is something always to be queered," and therefore does not have a stable, fixed definition.[7] Queerness as a quality and queer as a verb are used here to

---

[3] Octavia Butler spoke toward this topic back in 1980 when she said, "minority characters in general have been noticeably absent from most science fiction," and while it is still true that white (men) dominate the breadth of characters, authors like Jemisin are contributing to diversified representation. Butler, Octavia E., "The Lost Races of Science Fiction." *Transmission Magazine* (1980).

[4] There are different races among the human population, particularly in reference towards those who are expected to survive through cataclysmic environmental events the best, including references to "ashblow" (acid resistant and waterproof) hair, eyes with epicanthic folds, and "famine resistant" (i.e, fat) bodies.

[5] I use racialization to speak about orogenes and orogeny as it is an inborn, genetic quality that separates the racialized from the normate population. Hochman defines racialization as "the process through which groups come to be understood as major biological entities and human lineages, formed due to reproductive isolation, in which membership is transmitted through biological descent." My definition departs from his only in terms of "reproductive isolation", as the racialized characters are mixed within the population, popping up seemingly at random *unless* intentionally isolated and bred together. Adam Hochman, "Racialization: A defense of the concept," *Ethnic and Racial Studies* 42, no. 8 (2019): 1245-1262.

[6] Jack Halberstam, *In a Queer Time and Place: Transgender Bodies, Subcultural Lives*, vol. 3. (NYU press, 2005), 1.

[7] Alison Kafer, *Feminist, Queer, Crip* (Indiana University Press, 2013), 18.

complicate the normalized constructions and conceptions that scaffold everyday realities.

These books queer life, animacy and ability in part through Jemisin's playful second-person non-linear narrative. Jemisin flips the script by writing from three different points of view in the first novel, with two parts in third person and one in second person. She switches back and forth between stories, until at some point the reader is able to put together the fact that all three story lines are about the same person at different points in her life. She complicates time, intertwining the lessons in each story with each other, equalizing the past with the present, and the present with the future. She writes of a time out of time by using present tense when telling a story of the past. In keeping with the fact that this series does not merely follow a thread through time, but jumps back and forth as though all time is happening at once, this analysis does not follow a linear progress of the story, but rather examines individual characters and the way they queer animacy and life altogether.

In order to understand how Jemisin accomplishes blurring the lines of animacy, the concept of (dis)ability needs to be grappled with. Disabled or crip traditionally refers to sensory and visible physical impairments, but the boundaries of disabled have been blurred and contested time again by disability studies and crip theory scholars, as well as among activists. There is no singular definition of disabled or crip, and in fact what disability can be defined is constantly changing.[8] One salient aspect of disability is the social factor – that is, the inaccessibility or disabling effect of one's environment (physical or social) that produces disablism.[9] As Campbell defines it in their book *Contours of Ableism,* "Disablism is a set of assumptions (conscious or unconscious) and practices that promote the differential or unequal treatment of people because of actual or presumed disabilities."[10] Abled and disabled are defined in relation to one another, thought to be a binary when they are more of a spectrum based on compounding factors of social, physical and mental wellbeing, acceptance and access. While being abled is constructed as the norm, Kafer says, "the meaning of disability, like the meaning of illness, is presumed to be self-evident; we all know it when we see it."[11] The presumability

---

[8] Sunaura Taylor, *Beasts of burden: Animal and disability liberation.* (The New Press, 2017): chap. 2, EPUB.

[9] Disablism and ableism have been used very much in the same ways. I use disablism as the majority of my sources use this phrase. Fiona Kumari Campbell, *Contours of Ableism: The Production of Disability and Abledness,* (New York: Palgrave Macmillan, 2009): 7.

[10] Campbell, *Contours of Ableism,* 4.

[11] Kafer, *Feminist, Queer, Crip,* 4.

of disability, based on visual signs, is transformed and contended with in the *Broken Earth* series, through representations of both hidden and visible abilities. Jemisin queers the ideas of disabled/disablism through constructing oppression against characters that possess extra abilities, and twofold through the process of de-animating or physically disabling the most powerful characters.[12]

Animacy then becomes an important part of the puzzle. Animacy refers to the aliveness of something and invokes connections of movement, sentience and communicative abilities in the Western imagination. Animacy in Mel Chen's *Animacies: Biopolitics, Racial Mattering, and Queer Affect* troubles the binaries of human and inhuman, animate and inanimate, and life and nonlife.[13] They connect the concept of animacy with the ideas of emotiveness or affective reactions as well, as in reference to Sienne Ngai's exploration of animatedness. Ngai, author of *Ugly Feelings*, says, "the affective state of being 'animated' seems to imply the most basic or minimal of all affective conditions: that of being, in one way or another, 'moved.' But, as we press harder on the affective meanings of animatedness, we shall see how the seemingly neutral state of 'being moved' becomes twisted into the image of the overemotional racialized subject."[14] In this way, animacy as a concept works to damage the image of marginalized folks through delineating definitions of life and non-life, and additionally through categorizing the appropriate qualities of aliveness according to Western notions. *Broken Earth* attends to de-animation, over-animation and ultimately, queering the binary of life and death altogether.

Pathologization of Orogenes

The *Broken Earth* series separates humanity into two types of people: orogenes and stills.[15] Orogenes (slur: *rogga*), from the word 'orogeny' that describes the convergence of tectonic plates, are humans born with an innate ability to manipulate thermal, kinetic and other energies via magic drawn from life around them (heat, plants, people) and thus are able to do such things as quell or cause earthquakes, particularly the latter when they are upset or emotionally

---

[12] Jemisin follows in the footsteps of Octavia Butler's hyper-able characters – particularly Lauren from *Parable of the Sower* who suffers from hyper-empathy.

[13] Mel Y. Chen, *Animacies: Biopolitics, Racial Mattering, and Queer Affect*, (Duke University Press, 2012): 10-11.

[14] Sianne Ngai, *Ugly Feelings*, vol. 6 (Cambridge, MA: Harvard University Press, 2005): 91.

[15] Stills, short for 'stillhead', a derogatory used by orogenes for people lacking orogeny, but in my opinion holds about as much punch as 'cracker' does for white people.

unstable. Stills, humans without such abilities, outnumber orogenes.[16] Ability and respectability politics become the main focus of oppression in such a world. Discrimination against orogenes is routine and brutal; when orogenes are born to stills, they are referred to as *feral* and are often killed by their communities or caregivers. Those who survive to be reported to the government are sent to schools called Fulcrums, where physical violence is a memorable training mechanism.[17] Originally, orogenes were forced to build the main Fulcrum under threat of genocide. Their history as a people is very reminiscent of slaves and dehumanized peoples, particularly those in the creation of the US nation state; their labor was used to move the very stones that would serve as the walls of their prisons, their backs broken for the sake of taming the feral.[18] They are made into tools for hire, trapped in a life of servitude and forced to breed with assigned partners to beget more powerful, useful orogenes.

The plot of *The Fifth Season* centers mainly on one specific orogene named, at three distinct points in her life, Damaya (her given name), Syenite (her Fulcrum name) and Essun (her chosen name) and her three different lives – childhood, young adulthood including her working relationship and subsequent family formed with Alabaster, Innon and their child Corundum, and later adulthood including her marriage to Jija and their two children, Uche and Nassun.[19] Essun's life begins as most anyone's, born to a family of stills until she accidentally outs herself as an orogene.[20] She is one of the lucky ones who has survived until adolescence and is reported and taken to a Fulcrum instead of killed. The pathologization of orogeny in the Stillness is akin to the pathologization of queerness, disability and racialization in our world. They are thought of as lesser than, and treated that way by the majority of the still population, often with contempt, fear and disgust.

---

[16] Orogene's born to stills is very reminiscent of queer people born to heterosexuals, or (dis)abled born or within an able-bodied family, and complicates the way in which these novels could be read strictly as about a race, for they are born with innate qualities, but their parents are not of their same categorization (no matter that they genetically passed down such qualities).

[17] Reminiscent of boarding schools for Native Americans described by Deborah Miranda, *Bad Indians: A Tribal Memoir*, (Heyday, 2012).

[18] Miranda, *Bad Indians*, 12.

[19] Following in the footsteps of trans activists and community, I refer to her as Essun because it is her chosen name.

[20] Yes, the language of (queer) outing is intentional here, making connections to queer youth who face violence from their families after they come out.

If you consider popular references to disabled people, they are often presented as dangerous, violent, and looking for revenge for their suffering (think: villains with prosthetics or disfigurements).[21] Histories of eugenics, forced sterilizations, and institutionalization are still alive in the interest of controlling the *other*: racialized, poor, queer, trans, disabled. Kafer discusses how the "medical model of disability frames atypical bodies and minds as pathological [along with] queer kids, kids of color, street kids. [They] have been and continue to be framed as sick, as pathological, as contagious."[22] In addition, many such people are considered dangerous – whether through "infecting" others (with their queerness), links to poverty and violence, or physical or mental impairments that cause alarm. Such people are feared in the white, middle-class imaginary.

Jemisin brings the idea of "dangerous" to life in a pointed metaphor: Orogenes have the ability to kill outright, often without meaning to, either by drawing too much magic (life force) from their surroundings while performing orogeny, or through causing a seismic event itself. This happens especially when they are under duress or other negative emotional states. In this report by government officials in response to an orogene expressing their feelings through their orogeny, the disregard for orogene dignity or even orogene life is clear:

> Witnesses in the comm of Amand… report an unregistered rogga female opening up a gas pocket near the town… Another rogga female reportedly stopped the first one's effort, somehow, and shunted the gas back into the vent before sealing it. Amand citizens shot both as soon as possible to prevent further incidents… Initiating female age seventeen, reacting to reported molester of younger sister. Quelling female age seven, sister of first.[23]

The pathologization of every orogene and their potential to (re)act violently mirrors racialized politics in the States where brown and black people are expected to remain calm while staring down the barrel of a police gun, or when reacting to the unjust treatment or abuse of a community or family member. Any animation could be their doom. The unaffordability of anger for Essun and those of her kind has been built into their subjugated positions and learned well. They are often put between a rock and a hard place, as when Essun was deliberately taught to keep still and maintain her cool as her Fulcrum Guardian broke her bones to test her control. We begin to see how movement and

---

[21] Taylor, *Beasts of Burden*, chap. 2.

[22] Kafer, *Feminist, Queer, Crip*, 32.

[23] Nora K. Jemisin, *The Stone Sky*, (Orbit, 2017): 42.

reactions morph into a picture of the supposedly hyper-sensitive. [24] The dichotomies of movement and unmovable become applied oppositely to the racialized subject, leading to the idea that explosive reactions are only more proof of the necessary subjugation, that orogenes are animals and that their chains are necessary. There is an inherent contradiction built into affective reactions and animacy (i.e., Humanness) where too much emotional expression (being "moved") lowers one on the scale of animacy and on the other hand, so does the inability or impaired ability to move or express one's needs and emotions. And so even through torture or discrimination, one is expected to remain calm and reassure the frightened normate (i.e., white person/still). *Respectability politics* measures those who are marginalized against the values and expectations of the dominant group, and through participating in exaggerated expressions or a lack of expressions, one is placed outside of this group. As Halberstam explains, respectability, and "notions of normal on which it depends, may be upheld by" a white, Western, upper-middle-class logic of productivity and reproduction.[25] In this series, the dominant culture of stills creates the boundaries of acceptable behavior.

Jemisin herself comments on the Fulcrum's basis of *respectability politics* where "its teachers concentrate on making sure the children are in control of their powers, clean, neat, and well-mannered, in order to make all orogenes look good."[26] It reiterates the racialization of them as a people, the pressure of representation and the understanding that their actions reflect upon all of them. A reaction from one is a reaction from all and any movement made that is not "respectable" de-animates and lowers an entire people within the hierarchy of animation.

Their racialization and pathologization continues further, through parallels of the usage of slurs as a dehumanizing tactic. Alabaster, a queer, dark-skinned powerful orogene and Essun's (at one point or another) mentor, fellow servant, lover and teacher, speaks about how *rogga is a* "word for someone who has been made into a thing."[27] This word is used to convey an in-between, a de-anthropomorphizing, a dehumanizing, an affective blurring of animate and inanimate categories of speech.[28] Racial slurs rely heavily on what Chen calls

---

[24] Michael Silverstein qtd. in Chen, *Animacies*, 11.

[25] Halberstam, *In a Queer Time*, 3-4.

[26] Nora K. Jemisin, "On Family." *Epiphany 2.0*, (October 30, 2015), https://nkjemisin.com/2015/10/on-family/.

[27] Nora K. Jemisin, *The Fifth Season*, (Orbit, 2015): 140.

[28] Chen, *Animacies*, 29.

the "racial politics of animality,"[29] with the use of *rogga* akin to the use of the n-word, the use of *feral* implicating a subhuman category, a de-animating – lowering on the scale of animacy hierarchy. Eli Clare says in his book *Brilliant Imperfection: Grappling with Cure* that "consequences of" slurs "arise because [such words] remove us from humanity, placing us among nonhuman animals in the natural world. [They] strengthen racist, ableist and speciest hierarchies."[30] *Rogga* resonates not only with racial slurs but with other words like fag, gimp, cripple, and queer. As Chen states in their chapter "Language and Mattering Humans," "insults, shaming language, slurs, and injurious speech can be thought of as tools of objectification, but these also, in crucial ways, paradoxically rely on animacy as they objectify, thereby providing possibilities for reanimation."[31] As queer, crip and the n-word have been reclaimed by (some within) their respective communities, so too is *rogga* by orogenes later in Essun's life. They adopt *rogga* as their second name – indicating their social position or main talent contribution to their communities.

Cure

De-animation or immobility has long been linked to shorter life spans when in connection with humans and most animals: commonly, movement and animation are synonymous with life. In these books, orogenes' (over)animation disables them and puts them in a non-human category to be feared. "That's why they should be drowned as babes," [32] says a still after Essun causes an implosion off the coast.[33] The futurity of orogenes is forever unexpected – similarly to people diagnosed with disabilities or deteriorating impairments that doctors believe will lower their life expectancy. Normative futures are often thought as simple, linear inevitabilities, and in traditional understandings of disability, they are measured through cures and fixes.[34] Disability is culturally constructed to expect intervention, just as Essun's life was interrupted through the forceful placement of her at the Fulcrum – toward control and respectable movements. In participating in hierarchal struggle with her peers at the Fulcrum, Essun has

---

[29] Chen, *Animacies*, 34.

[30] Eli Clare's original quote speaks specifically about "monkey", a slur used historically for both physically disabled and people who identify as Black, African or have African origin. Eli Clare, *Brilliant Imperfection*, (Duke University Press, 2015): 118.

[31] Chen, *Animacies*, 30.

[32] Jemisin, *The Obelisk Gate*, 44.

[33] This plays off the known phrase "the only good Indian is a dead Indian" discussed by Miranda.

[34] Kafer, *Feminist, Queer, Crip*, 20.

a chance to play the supercrip,[35] rising above her (perceived) shortcomings and treated publically with an artificial form of respectability. A supercrip is generally defined as someone with disabilities doing something extraordinary in regards to normative, able-bodied standards.[36] Ultimately, cure and supercrip stem from the same goal – to ease normates' discomfort around non-normative bodyminds.[37] It is expected that everyone wants to move or be like the normative, and supercrips are excused (to an extent) because they have surpassed possibilities that many normates will never achieve. A. M. Duane, author of *Dead and Disabled* says, "If the monstrously uncontrollable body scares us, the story of the supercrip offers a soothing balm."[38]

In her later adulthood, Essun's only surviving child Nassun is dragged south across the continent by her husband, a still named Jija. He took Nassun from their town the same day he beat their toddler Uche to death in their living room after realizing he was an orogene. Nassun is eight years old when they begin to head toward a place that claims to "cure" orogenes of their (hyper)abilities and make them *still*. This place is the only surviving Fulcrum at the time and its reputation has driven Jija to seek it out in order to rid her of this movement, this ability. This recalls "corrective/conversion" therapies, those that were and are still used on queer folks in order to disorder/reorient their sexualities, straightening them, as well as curative futures, the process of fixing or curing an illness with the ultimate goal being normative bodyminds that look, function and act as everyone else should. Both of these profess the final goal: normative usefulness in the form of productivity and reproductivity.

Usefulness & Death

Usefulness, in a world that suffers catastrophe after catastrophe, becomes a coveted ability within the Stillness. Chen discusses how, "considering different animacies becomes a particularly critical matter when 'life' vs 'death' binary oppositions fail to capture the affectively embodied ways that racializations of specific groups are differentially rendered."[39] The racialization and objectification of different bodies creates a more complex conception of life and death, suggesting that some lives may not be worth living for the racialized/disabled

---

[35] Eli Clare, *Exile and Pride: Disability, queerness and liberation,* (Duke University Press, 2015): 2-13.

[36] Kafer, *Feminist, Queer, Crip,* 90.

[37] Bodyminds defined by Schalk, *Bodyminds Reimagined,* 5.

[38] Anna Mae Duane, "Dead and Disabled," *Zombie Theory: A Reader* (University of Minnesota Press, 2017) 243.

[39] Chen, *Animacies,* 10.

subject, and/or that death comes in many forms, and even that there is a wider spectrum of existence than the life/death binary. Orogenes that did not learn to obey are subject to far worse fates than death. Because of orogenes' innate abilities to quell earthquakes, they are in demand in a world where frequent 'Seasons' or seismic events occur and are not 'wasted' in the way a non-useful still would be. Orogenes who do not submit to their enslavement are turned into brain-dead tools, lobotomized and strapped into permanent chairs stationed at nodes around the continent, kept alive to regulate the tectonic movement around them. During Essun's young adulthood training and subsequent understanding of the chains that bind her, Alabaster says, "That we're not human is just the lie they tell themselves so they don't have to feel bad about how they treat us... This, too, is something all roggas know."[40] The "persistent vegetative state" positions humans with minimal communicative or mobility abilities on par with the perceived inanimacy of vegetables, and effectively lowers such people down the scale of animacy.[41]

Once Essun learns the reality of her subjugation and the consequences of disobedience, she understands the forced breeding by the Fulcrum, and further, understands the Fulcrum's desire to capture her, and her partners Alabaster, Innon and most especially their child Corundum, whether alive or half dead. When faced with an impossible choice, she thinks, "Better that a child never have lived at all than live as a slave. Better that he die... [for] survival is not the same thing as living."[42] Reproduction, and the health and well-being of the next generation, is a hallmark for normative culture. Jemisin queers this, through placing an importance on the quality of life, rather than regarding all life as worth living no matter what, and even expands on this in her blog acknowledging that "some readers can't even get through *The Fifth Season* because of this."[43] The sacredness of children's futurity is so ingrained in our world that even in a fictional world, where lobotimization is the likely future for the child, some readers cannot continue with the story. But as many know, and as Jemisin herself acknowledges, "there's nothing that happens in *The Fifth Season* that hasn't happened in our own world, in some way or another."[44] As Kafer says, "criteria of [the] 'quality' of life are often taken to be common sense,"[45] but are rather based on assumptions of capabilities and suffering. By

---

[40] Jemisin, *The Fifth Season*, 354.

[41] Chen, *Animacies*, 41.

[42] Jemisin, *The Fifth Season*, 144.

[43] Jemisin, "On Family".

[44] Jemisin, "On Family".

[45] Kafer, *Feminist, Queer, Crip*, 63.

creating a type of subjugation where the people in question are brain-dead, the lines between animate and inanimate are queered, twisted and stretched, to something between life and nonlife. Hierarchies of human, animal, plant and rock are unsettled, with humans treated as animals and turned to vegetables, and even made into stone.

Alabaster, as he appears in later life, is only one of three living characters portrayed in these novels with a physical disability in a world where usefulness is gold: he is dying from third-degree burns, organ and pulmonary failure, missing an arm and slowly turning to stone. During the time of a Season that throws the continent into chaos, shutting down agriculture, much of trade, access to water and travel for varying amounts of time, each comm, or community, survives based on the caches they have amassed consisting of preserved foods, clean water, materials and medicine. When people are sick or unable to contribute to the maintaining of a town, they become disposable. The political economies of life and death are pushed to the extremes: The young have better luck joining new comms than the old, the healthy are more likely to be forgiven laziness than the sick. So the fact that Alabaster is not only alive but also cared for in a comm says something very spectacular. He is dismissed by everyone except Essun as a waste of resources – he is thought to simply be a waste of food an medicine. Ykka, the leader of the comm, is unapologetic in her dismissal, seeing more future value in an unauthorized pregnancy.

But even death comes to be useful further into a Season as people turn to cannibalism to survive. It is recorded in past instances of Seasons, and those in the comm acknowledge the possibility without ever speaking of it directly. In the "Season of Teeth", starvation was so rampant that larger comms stole people from smaller ones. Death contributes to life in the most gruesome way. But Alabaster isn't headed for a simple death, nor a death that will sustain life in their community, but rather a death achieved through reforming his organic body into stone through accessing or using magic. Jemisin queers death, and the usefulness of death through a third "life" form, stone eaters.

Stone

Chen describes the two ways of dehumanizing: making an object of someone and/or removing qualities that are quintessentially human. In these ways, Jemisin toys with what we linguistically and socially understand to be true and possible through her creation of stone eaters, a species that is ex-human, hardly animate, and yet sentient and somehow alive. Stone eaters are the most complex combination of (re)animated and (un)animations, and as Duane has said, in a "prolonged state of undeath." [46] They removed from the fleshy embodiment (but not shape, as they look like marble statues of humans) of humanity and given the composition and separation of stone. To make an entire subsection of people out of stone completely destroys this dichotomy, and they tend to be the most difficult characters to comprehend for many readers because of how omnipresent this idea has become in modern Western thought.[47] Stone eaters are recognized as sentient, but based on their literal animation, having the weight of a mountain and moving at the speed of a glacier or nearly as instantaneously as light, they are perceived by humans as mostly inanimate. Stone eaters are stone-faced, literally and figuratively, and do not show facial movements, therefore seeming emotionless.

They are perceived as inactive in body and mind simply because they needn't move. As Alabaster once explained to Essun, "movement is the thing that emphasizes their uncanny nature, so like humanity and yet so wildly different"[48] This is much on par with the way normative bodyminds react to disabled people. Duane remarks how disabled folks are expected to use charm to relieve nondisabled people of their discomfort, and stone eaters choose to disregard this idea altogether.[49] Like zombies or other mythical, previously dead humans, stone eaters "queer and crip comforting stories about how bodies are 'supposed' to work."[50] Their sometimes instant, sometimes absent reactions make them unpredictable, and to human eyes, dangerous. The language of their movements and shapes suggests a cripped and queered concept of time and matter, something as solid as a mountain yet able to move through the Earth like a fish through water.

While much of the language used in these novels reflects some old knowledge of the Earth as animate, such as *Evil Earth* as a curse word and how Essun's descriptions of her abilities often lead to personifying or anthropomorphizing of stone (stone *beckons*, stone *whispers*), humans tend to believe the Earth is inanimate. Through Hoa, a stone eater and the narrator of the novels, telling of his life as a Tuner, the ancestor of orogenes, the indisputability of Earth as animate becomes more and more evident. He reveals the cyclical nature of human mistakes, of lost knowledge and willful ignorance. The ancient society

---

[46] Duane, *Dead and Disabled*, 243.

[47] The ways in which Western mainstream culture has conceptualized hierarchies of animacies comes from a colonizers mind-frame, but hierarchies in Cherokee cosmologies and other Indigenous communities does not fall along the same lines.

[48] Jemisin, *The Stone Sky*, 27.

[49] Duane, *Dead and Disabled*, 238.

[50] Duane, *Dead and Disabled*, 239.

in which he used to live planned to "feed upon the life of the planet itself, forever," but that, "ignorance is an inaccurate term for what this was. True, no one thought of the Earth as alive in those days – but we should have guessed. Magic is the by-product of life. That there was magic in the Earth to take... We should all have guessed."[51] Tuners were turned into stone eaters by the Earth in retribution for their attempt to enslave it. The animacy, agency and action of the Earth further unsettles the hierarchies of life. By binding the stone eaters to the Earth's matter and material, it suggests the idea that the Earth, rocks, and stone themselves may in fact be at the top of the hierarchy.

We know stone as permanent, something that can only be broken down to smaller pieces but never fully destroyed. Stone eaters queer the idea of death, elongating it or doing away with it all together because they cannot die, for their consciousness and strange, semi-animated bodies cannot be destroyed, only scattered and dispersed until they eventually come back together. Hoa describes himself and his kind as monsters, and refers to his death as an elongated state of existence – i.e., his life. Hoa says, "We are the monsters they created, and more, but we will be the sort of monsters we wish to be, in death."[52] Death of one way of being begot another life, or undeath.

Once death is not an inevitability, the dichotomy of death and life is reconsidered, just as the dichotomy of useful versus disposable must be. For both Essun and Alabaster, death becomes an unlikely ending to their stories. As Essun watches Alabaster turning to stone, more and more each time he uses magic, and understands his stoned limbs are not merely disappearing but being *eaten*, teeth marks still fresh, by the stone eater that accompanies him, she begins to understand her fate. At the beginning of the third novel, *The Stone Sky*, when Essun wakes up from a coma-like-state after channeling an incredible amount of magic to save her comm from stone eater and human invaders alike, her arm is stoned. Realigned, hardened, cells pulled tighter together and interlaced into rock. She thinks to herself, "Your arm. Not 'the thing.'"[53] The stoned arm is now a part of her. When we learn that stone eaters subsist on life that has been stoned, such as Essun's arm, Hoa vaguely explains that it is not sustenance, instead saying, "we only need life to live."[54] Death that is not death, except that a death has occurred, and life that is not life, except that it lives.

---

[51] Jemisin, *The Stone Sky*, 332.

[52] Jemisin, *The Stone Sky*, 231.

[53] Jemisin, *The Stone Sky*, 19.

[54] Jemisin, *The Stone Sky*, 27.

We discover later that the consumption of life after it is stoned is a part of the stone eater reproduction process. They are able to reanimate and create new stone eaters only after ingesting the stoned figure of the original animate form. Chen's discussion of biopower complicates animacy, because while stone eaters do not "participate in the regimes of life (making life) and coerced death (killing),"[55] they are integral to understanding the queering affective properties and situations that are ultimately included in the experience of life, death and all the stages in between and after. Because they do not reproduce via sex as humans do, though arguably they engage in something semantically similar (i.e., consuming/devouring/taking in/becoming one with), they queer the idea of reproduction and the time at which reproduction happens. Chen continues on to say that "the conventional ordering of sex, reproduction and intimacy" is queered through "immanent and animate transgressions, violating proper intimacies."[56] Stone eaters take life, turn it to stone (or in the case of orogenes manipulating magic, wait for them to turn to stone), and as Hoa describes it, then reassemble "the raw arcanic substance ... and reactivate the lattice that should have preserved the critical essence of" someone.[57]

Expanding on Chen's concept of "deathly life", Essun is constructed throughout the books as a bringer of death, not only as someone surrounded by death (or even sometimes the cause of it) but also as someone who will end the world. "Death was always here. Death is you," Hoa narrates, speaking from another time, and even admits to plotting Essun's death. She carries death with her, in her body and in her heart. Throughout her life, death has walked beside her, leaving her animate and useful for a purpose, waiting for the right moment to claim her and make use of her death. Our narrator Hoa explains the ultimate meaning of 'Fifth Season' – different from our previous conception of fifth seasons as climate catastrophes: "All Seasons are hardship, *Death is the fifth, and master of all.*"[58] Essun is depicted as a destroyer of death, and one who, through her emotional animacy, will bring the end of the world, at least this version of the world.

Time & Sanity

As Alabaster explains to Essun, "I can barely remember things that happened to me fifty years ago; imagine trying to remember five thousand years ago. Ten thousand. Twenty. Imagine forgetting your own name. That's why they never

---

[55] Chen, *Animacies*, 6.

[56] Chen, *Animacies*, 11.

[57] Jemisin, *The Stone Sky*, 396.

[58] Jemisin, *The Stone Sky*, 224 (italics original).

answer, when we ask them who they are… I don't think it's what they're made of that makes stone eaters so different. I think it's that no one can live that long and not become something entirely alien."[59] Stone eaters queer temporalities, and queer the idea of futurity.[60] They usurp the notions that normative future touts: childhood, adolescence, marriage, reproduction, and death. They care not for the order of things, nor the time it takes.

Hoa explains his life in *The Stone Sky*, the third book, toward the end of Essun's life. He begins his narration by saying, "Then, though — now, it feels of now as I recall myself of then, this is what I mean when I say that it is strange — Now, in this time before the Stillness."[61] He explains that stone eaters have not only been around since the first Season, they caused the start of the Seasons back when they were mortal. In their stoned state, their conceptualization of momentary is easily millennia, and vice versa. His description of the past, narrating from the future, as though it were the present, creates a queerness of time. This queering of time shows up in Hoa's experience through his lack of awareness for how much time has passed. "So I wait. Time passes. A year, a decade, a week,"[62] thinks Hoa when awaiting the reordering and rebirth of Essun the stone eater. Halberstam describes queer time as an antithesis to normative desires of futurity, particularly that of longevity.[63] Hoa remembers, "I know only later that this is several days. In the moment, it feels like another millennium."[64] Kafer spends time deconstructing the presumption that everyone desires the same future, and speaks toward aspects of how "cripping time" can provide a map through which we may re-conceptualize (dis)ability.[65] She continues on to say that "it is, rather, a reorientation to time," through which the notion of flexibility, not just taking or using more time than able-bodied people use, issues "a challenge to normative and normalizing expectations of pace and scheduling. Rather than bend disabled bodies and minds to meet the clock, crip time bends the clock to meet disabled bodies and minds." [66] Normative ideas of time (specifically task completion or verbal

---

[59] Jemisin, *The Obelisk Gate*, 168.

[60] Carla Rice, Eliza Chandler, Jen Rinaldi, Nadine Changfoot, Kirsty Liddiard, Roxanne Mykitiuk, and Ingrid Mündel, "Imagining disability futurities," *Hypatia* 32, no. 2 (2017): 213-229.

[61] Jemisin, *The Stone Sky*, 2.

[62] Jemisin, *The Stone Sky*, 397.

[63] Halberstam, *In a Queer Time*, 4.

[64] Jemisin, *The Stone Sky*.

[65] Kafer, *Feminist, Queer, Crip*, 2 & 26.

[66] Kafer, *Feminist, Queer, Crip*, 27.

response time) intersect greatly with psychiatric disabilities and concepts of madness. Those who show no concern for longevity are pathologized and thought of as odd, wrong, crazy.

Alabaster is referred to as crazy in many points during the story. Even Essun believes him to be crazy or insane, both before and after their escape from the Fulcrum. Alabaster explains that "'crazy' is what everyone thinks all roggas are, after all—addled by the time they spend in stone... [and] by not being human enough."[67] Andrea Nicki, author of *The Abused Mind: Feminist Theory, Psychiatric Disability, and Trauma* explains that labels of crazy have been applied to those who challenge the status quo or push back against oppressive systems of power and that it "derives its power from prejudiced views of those genuinely suffering from mental illness as irrational, disordered, cognitively impaired, and frightening."[68] Part of the pathologization of orogenes uses measures of sanity, particularly sanity as dictated by stills, as further proof of the over-animation and uncontrollability of their kind. As Sami Schalk points out in her book *Bodyminds Reimagined: (Dis)ability, Race, and Gender in Black Women's Speculative Fiction,* they are "accused of overreacting to, being too sensitive about, or reading too much into the actions and behaviors of those around them," and even dismissed as mentally unfit, or mentally disabled.[69] She goes on to say that "Accusations of being 'too sensitive' can easily become labels of 'paranoia.' Allegations of being 'too emotional' can swiftly move into categorizations of 'hysterical' and 'volatile.'"[70] The history of psychiatry has long pinned mental disorders on marginalized people,[71] racialized people and women when they dare speak the truth of their everyday realities.[72]

This attachment of the label crazy to the most visibly queer and dark-skinned character portrayed in the series meets with histories of racist psychiatric diagnoses and treatment.[73] As explained by Meerai, Abdillahi, and Poole in

---

[67] Jemisin, *The Obelisk Gate,* 159.

[68] Andrea Nicki, "The abused mind: Feminist theory, psychiatric disability, and trauma," *Hypatia* 16, no. 4 (2001): 87.

[69] Schalk, *Bodyminds reimagined,* 65.

[70] Schalk, *Bodyminds reimagined,* 65.

[71] Reminds of diagnoses of 'gender identity disorder' in Dean Spade, *Normal Life: Administrative Violence, Critical Trans Politics, and the Limits of Law,* (Duke University Press, 2015).

[72] Spade, *Normal Life.*

[73]Sonia Meerai, Idil Abdillahi, & Jennifer Poole, "An Introduction to Anti-Black Sanism." *Intersectionalities: A Global Journal of Social Work Analysis, Research, Polity, and Practice* 5, no. 3 (2016): 18–35.

their article "An Introduction to Anti-Black Sanism," such psychiatric aggressions towards Black bodies have been "attempts to curtail any acts of self-determination or 'disrespect' to whites by Black slaves, and all involved 'cures' that were brutal and dehumanizing."[74] Alabaster has suffered violence, isolation, and even the murder of multiple lovers by the Fulcrum in their attempts to dissuade his craziness and dissent. When Essun reunites with him 10 years and another self later, she thinks, "Alabaster was never mad; he's just learned so much that would have driven a lesser soul to gibbering, that sometimes it shows. Letting out some of that accumulated horror by occasionally sounding like a frothing maniac is how he copes."[75] In his recount of his years spent isolated among unresponsive stone eaters, he speaks of desperation and time dilation: "Time got loose after a while. No one but them to talk to, and sometimes they forget that people need to talk."[76] He even attempted suicide at one point or attempted to kill the stone eaters themselves. Loneliness and oppression combine to toxic and undeniable states of duress, perhaps constituting madness.

Stone eaters exemplify loneliness with their inability to experience touch or be physically in contact, and through their long, solitary lives. They solidify the idea of longevity into an undesirable, lonely expanse of forever, and their embodied forms alter the way they experience time. Loneliness is remarked upon by Shaka McGlotten, author of *Dead and Live Life*, in which they include it as an affective mode that blurs lines between death and life, as loneliness "felt like a creeping deadness".[77] After all, Earth, the most powerful actor in the novels produced punishments out of loneliness, acting out of revenge for the loss of its companion – the moon.

Conclusion

As Audre Lorde points out, "We operate in the teeth of a system for which racism and sexism are primary, established, and necessary props of profit."[78] Essun and the other Fulcrum orogenes were forced to operate within such a system built to use them as weapons or tools for profit, where they were not only replaceable or even disposable, but *recyclable*. Essun was manipulated into believing that she was treated fairly, and that all that mattered was following the rules and respectability politics to gain some semblance of a life

---

[74] Meerai et. al, *Sanism,* 21.

[75] Jemisin, *The Obelisk Gate,* 166.

[76] Jemisin, *The Obelisk Gate,* 168.

[77] McGlotten, *Dead and live life,* 223-231.

[78] Audre Lorde, *Sister outsider: Essays and speeches,* (Penguin Classics, 2020): 128.

of relative comfort. But when cornered with the truth, Essun's awareness sinks into the stone beneath her and amplifies her outrage – it responds to her emotions. Essun and the other orogenes who understand the truth of their usefulness have, as Audre Lorde put it, "had to learn to orchestrate those furies so that they do not tear us apart. We have had to learn to move through them and use them for strength and force and insight within our daily lives. Those of us who did not learn this difficult lesson did not survive."[79]

In order to survive, Essun hardened. She hardened against all the atrocities, against the horrors too terrible to name. She blocked feeling, blocked animacy, and thought to herself when watching her oldest, dearest friend slowly dying, "but inside you feel like he looks: nothing but brittle stone and scars, prone to cracking if you bend too much."[80] Ultimately, the end of the world depended on her hyperability, her willingness to fall deeply and forever into disability and out of humanity, and her emotional expression to make it happen.

Chen says, "It seems that animacy and its affects are mediated not by whether you are a [thing, human or animal] but by… how dynamic you are perceived to be. Stones themselves move, change, degrade over time, but in ways that exceed human scales."[81] Jemisin complicates and interrupts existing conceptions of animacy hierarchies through making the Earth an acting character in these books, creating an entire species made of stone, and expanding upon dehumanization tactics used against racialized, disabled and queer folks in our own realities. She destabilizes our understandings of ability and disability, using a combination of mental, social, environmental, and physical factors.[82] The magical world of the Stillness parallels our current social stratification through the animacy and agency of stone. And ultimately, our narrator ends his last chapter with, "You are dead. But not you."[83] Death begets life, and life begets death, and within it, a transformation and an animation of emotion and stone occurs. Audre Lorde said, "Our power [is] to envision and to reconstruct, anger by painful anger, stone upon heavy stone, a future of pollinating difference and the earth to support our choices."[84] Through (dis/re)animation and death, Essun, Hoa and Nassun change the world, stone upon heavy stone, at last.

---

[79] Lorde, *Sister outsider,* 129.

[80] N. K. Jemisin, *The Obelisk Gate,* 210.

[81] Chen, *Animacies,* 210.

[82] Schalk, *Bodyminds reimagined,* 120.

[83] Jemisin, *The Stone Sky,* 388.

[84] Lorde, *Sister Outsider,* 133.

GLOSSARY:

Comm: Community or town.

Earth: a Sentient entity - giver of gifts (orogeny) and punishment (orogeny and "fifth" Seasons). The ultimate life-force and subsistence of all living things.

Fifth Season (shortened to "Season"): a season that lasts for longer than six months following a catastrophic or significant seismic event such as an earthquake or volcano eruption.

Nodes: Stations across the Stillness (though mostly near cities) that houses a lobotomized young, powerful orogene, and keeps them alive to do what orogenes naturally do from birth - quell shakes.

Orogenes: Humans with "the ability to manipulate thermal, kinetic and related forms of energy." Born randomly to stills ("feral") and also bred. Lobotomized and used as stabilizers in "nodes" around the continent.

   Derogatory: rogga

Stills: regular humans; normal life spans. Hierarchy based on wealth and ability to store/defend food during Seasons. Those with less are often killed for resources, eventually turned into food themselves when resources are depleted.

Stone eaters: Once human-like Tuners, stone eaters are statue-esque, undead and everliving. Millennia have passed since they were turned to stone by the Earth in retribution. They are able to travel through the earth, and to take objects and humans with them unharmed when they do. They move in unhuman-like slowness, or inconceivably fast. They have no care for human measurements of time.

The Stillness: The continent that this society lives on.

The *Broken Earth* Series:

The Fifth Season, Book 1, stories of Damyna, Synite and Essun
The Obelisk Gate, Book 2, stories of Nassun and Essun
The Stone Sky, Book 3, stories of Nassun, Essun and Hoa

Bibliography

Butler, Octavia E. "The Lost Races of Science Fiction." *Transmission Magazine* (1980).
Butler, Octavia E. *Parable of the Sower.* Vol. 1. Open Road Media, 2012.
Campbell, Fiona Kumari. *Contours of Ableism: The Production of Disability and Abledness.* New York: Palgrave Macmillan, 2009.

Chen, Mel Y. *Animacies: Biopolitics, racial mattering, and queer affect.* Duke University Press, 2012.

Clare, Eli. *Brilliant imperfection.* Duke University Press, 2017.

Clare, Eli. *Exile and pride: Disability, queerness, and liberation.* Duke University Press, 2015.

Dillender, Kirsten. "Land and Pessimistic Futures in Contemporary African American Speculative Fiction." *Extrapolation.* 61.1 (2020): 131-VI.

Duane, Anna Mae. "Dead and Disabled." *Zombie Theory: A Reader.* U of Minnesota Press (2017): 237-270.

Halberstam, J. Jack. *In a queer time and place: Transgender bodies, subcultural lives.* Vol. 3. NYU press, 2005.

Hochman, Adam. "Racialization: A defense of the concept." *Ethnic and Racial Studies* 42.8 (2019): 1245-1262.

Iles, Alastair, et al. "Repairing the Broken Earth: NK Jemisin on race and environment in transitions." *Elementa: Science of the Anthropocene* 7 (2019).

Jemisin, Nora K. "On Family." *Epiphany 2.0*, October 30, 2015. https://nkjemisin.com/2015/10/on-family/.

Jemisin, Nora K. *The Fifth Season.* First ed., Orbit, 2015.

Jemisin, Nora K. *The Obelisk Gate.* First ed., Orbit, 2016.

Jemisin, Nora K. *The Stone Sky.* First ed., Orbit, 2017.

Kafer, Alison. *Feminist, queer, crip.* Indiana University Press, 2013.

Lorde, Audre. *Sister outsider: Essays and speeches.* Penguin Classics, 2020.

McGlotten, Shaka. "Dead and Live Life Zombies, Queers, and Online Sociality." *Zombie Theory: A Reader.* U of Minnesota Press (2017):223-236.

Meerai, Sonia, Idil Abdillahi, & Jennifer Poole. "An Introduction to Anti-Black Sanism." *Intersectionalities: A Global Journal of Social Work Analysis, Research, Polity, and Practice* [Online], 5.3 (2016): 18–35.

Miranda, Deborah. *Bad Indians: A tribal memoir.* Heyday, 2012.

Nicki, Andrea. "The abused mind: Feminist theory, psychiatric disability, and trauma." *Hypatia* 16.4 (2001): 80-104.

Rice, Carla, Eliza Chandler, Jen Rinaldi, Nadine Changfoot, Kirsty Liddiard, Roxanne Mykitiuk, and Ingrid Mündel. "Imagining disability futurities." *Hypatia* 32, no. 2 (2017): 213-229.

Schalk, Sami. *Bodyminds reimagined:(Dis) ability, race, and gender in black women's speculative fiction.* Duke University Press, 2018.

Spade, Dean. *Normal life: Administrative violence, critical trans politics, and the limits of law.* Duke University Press, 2015.

CHAPTER 6

TOWARDS AN INTERGALACTIC DISABILITY JUSTICE: REBELLING AGAINST ABLEISM THROUGH A CRIPTIQUE OF THE JEDI ORDER

Samuel Shelton

Oregon State University

Abstract

In this chapter, I propose an alternative interpretation of dis/ability within the Star Wars universe that attends to the ways in which the Jedi Order perpetuates disability oppression and, in so doing, hinders the realization of genuine equity or justice. My chapter includes examples from a number of *Star Wars* texts, especially the recently concluded animated *Clone Wars* series that, for me, most profoundly depicts significant moments leading up to Anakin's disillusionment with the Jedi Order and his transformation towards the dark side of the Force. I use this example of Anakin's corruption as a tool through which to apply and contribute to the framework of disability justice.

Keywords: Ableism, Anakin Skywayer, Darth Vader, Disability Justice, Star Wars

***

"From my point of view, the Jedi are evil!"
Anakin Skywalker, *Episode III–Revenge of the Sith*

Since the cinematic release of *Star Wars: Episode IV–A New Hope* over 40 years ago, the corrupted Jedi Knight Anakin Skywalker turned Sith Lord Darth Vader has risen to become one the most prominent, deliberated characters not only of the *Star Wars* universe but of the science fiction genre more broadly. Central among the many critical analyses and debates concerning this now infamous character are his disfigurement and disability, both of which have significantly impacted subsequent representations of disability in popular culture. As a crip[1] Sith lord, the development of Vader's character throughout the many movies, television shows, and graphic novels that have come to populate the *Star Wars* universe readily connects him with many common disability tropes and stereotypes. Disability Studies theorists, for instance, have brought attention to the problematic associations between Anakin's tainted morality and the sudden, traumatic impairment of his body – as if his disablement was a consequence or natural outcome of turning to the dark side of the Force.[2]

Yet, despite the critical attention granted to Anakin/Darth Vader as a representation of disability, what often escapes the conversation is a criptique[3] of how the Jedi Order had become a benevolent, carceral institution granted authority by the Galactic Republic. The Jedi perpetuated ableist harm and suffering that constructed the very inaccessibility that ultimately made Anakin's transformation from Jedi knight to Sith lord possible. In the final days of the Galactic Republic, prior to the emergence of the Galactic Empire and following the widespread desolation and corruption of the *Clone Wars*, the leaders of the Jedi Order had become militaristic, deceptive, distrustful, and overly obsessed with power and control. Yet, even before the Clone Wars during Anakin's childhood and adolescence, the Jedi Code prioritized conformity and obedience above collective access, equity, interdependence, and solidarity, all of which are vital components of *disability justice*.[4] The devastating emergence of Darth Vader, though most overtly guided by Supreme Chancellor Sheev

---

[1] Throughout this essay, I use the terms disability and crip somewhat interchangeably. My use of "crip" is in line with Critical Disability Studies scholars and Disability Justice theorists / activists who reclaim this term as a part of radical, intersectional, anti-ableist theory and politics (e.g., McRuer *Crip Theory: Cultural Signs of Queerness and Disability* (New York: New York University Press, 2006); Piepzna-Samarasinha *Care Work: Dreaming Disability Justice* (Vancouver: Arsenal Pulp Press, 2018); Price, "The Bodymind Problem and the Possibilities of Pain." *Hypatia* 30, no. 1 (2015): 268-84). My interpretation of "disability" is similarly rooted in a critical / radical tradition and has been especially informed by Alison Kafer's political / relational model (Kafer, *Feminist, Queer, Crip.* (Bloomington: Indiana University Press, 2013).

[2] Holder, Matthew. "Imagining Accessibility: Theorizing Disability in Disabled People Destroy Science Fiction." *Disability Studies Quarterly* 40, no. 3 (2020).

[3] Following from crip theory and politics, I use criptique to refer to any critical analysis grounded in a commitment to open up space for and build toward disability justice. Criptique prioritizes the wisdom, experiences, and needs of disabled folks, especially the most marginal and impacted among us, in order to disrupt normative belief systems, especially those which perpetuate ableist and otherwise oppressive ideas about bodyminds.

[4] Sins Invalid. "Skin, Tooth, and Bone. The Basis of Movement is Our People: A Disability Justice Primer." *Sins Invalid*, 2016.

Palpatine / Darth Sidious, was in large part the unsurprising consequence of Anakin's (mis)treatment within an unaccommodating, assimilationist Jedi Order.

I argue that the tendency to neglect the broader context perpetuates a *deficit* framework of disability in which individuals, rather than environments and communities or collectives of people, are responsible for the realities of disablement – for example, because it was their "fault" or they somehow "deserved" it. Furthermore, I demonstrate that a significant underlying factor in Anakin's transformation was the promise of greater access to that which the Jedi withheld from him and punished him for seeking out, such as non-manipulative relationships and the power to express care toward his loved ones. Many of the things that Anakin was deprived of are prominent within the disability justice framework, such as meaningful, interdependent, emotionally nuanced relationships. While the Sith Master Palpatine failed as well to engage in a genuine practice of disability justice, much of his influence over Anakin stemmed from the exploitation of Anakin's unmet needs – needs which the Jedi knowingly neglected and sought to suppress under the guise of preventing Anakin from turning to the dark side of the Force.

In this chapter, I propose an alternative interpretation of dis/ability within the *Star Wars* universe that attends to the ways in which the Jedi Order perpetuates disability oppression and, in so doing, hinders the realization of genuine equity or justice. My chapter includes examples from a number of *Star Wars* texts, especially the recently concluded animated *Clone Wars* series that for me most profoundly depicts significant moments leading up to Anakin's disillusionment with the Jedi Order and his transformation towards the dark side of the Force. I use this example of Anakin's corruption as a tool through which to apply and contribute to the framework of disability justice. My purpose in developing an alternative interpretation is to utilize well-known characters from the *Star Wars* universe to think critically about what gets in the way of representing disability justice in the spaces of science fiction and, accordingly, prevents us from realizing it in our own world.

Disability Justice & Science Fiction

One of the key concepts guiding my essay is *disability justice*, which is a critical, intersectional framework /social movement imagined and led primarily by queer and trans disabled people of color.[5] The definition of disability justice is multiple and responsive to the specific needs of individuals in the communities where it is practiced. It is a collective practice: disability justice is something people build towards together by honoring and making space for all bodyminds,

---

[5] Sins Invalid, "Skin, Tooth, and Bone," 2016.

with the knowledge that we all need different things to survive, heal from harm, and be present. In many ways, disability justice is about transforming relationships towards collective access and liberation by getting into a mindset and habit of accountability.[6] For instance, through this framework / social movement, each of us can reflect on how we contribute to the inaccessibility of the spaces we occupy, and we can take accountability both by addressing causes of exclusion and by reimagining those spaces in collaboration with disabled folks. Consequently, disability justice entails everything from hosting events in physically accessible locations with ramps and elevators, to collaborating with community members to increase access to food, water, affordable housing, healthcare, and/or other basic needs during a pandemic, to dismantling structural inequities which leave disabled people, especially multiply marginalized disabled people, vulnerable to harm.

As a genre centered around challenging the boundaries of what is real/ possible and unreal/impossible, science fiction has an ambivalent relationship to disability, with its representations ranging from overt ableist propaganda to transformative depictions of disability justice. These representations of disability are simultaneously connected to depictions of race, class, gender, sexuality, age, and so on because the meanings assigned to disability are formed intersectionally.[7] Consequently, science fiction provides fertile ground for the normalization of disability oppression or ableism as well as for liberating visions of disability justice. Imarisha uses the term *speculative* or *visionary fiction* "to distinguish science fiction that has relevance toward building new, freer worlds from the mainstream strain of science fiction, which most often reinforces dominant narratives of power."[8] Other authors as well have made a critical distinction along these lines, arguing that science fiction

---

[6] Mia Mingus, "Dreaming Accountability." *Leaving Evidence*. https://leavingevidence.wordpress.com/2019/05/05/dreaming-accountability-dreaming-a-returning-to-ourselves-and-each-other/ (published May 5, 2019).

[7] Alison Kafer, *Feminist, Queer, Crip*. Bloomington: Indiana University Press, 20; Mia Mingus, "Moving Toward the Ugly: A Politic Beyond Desirability." *Leaving Evidence*. https://leavingevidence.wordpress.com/2011/08/22/moving-toward-the-ugly-a-politic-beyond-desirability/ (published August 21, 2011).

[8] Walidah Imarisha, "Introduction." In *Octavia's Brood: Science Fiction Stories from Social Justice Movements*, edited by Walidah Imarisha, Adrienne Maree Brown, and Sheree Renee Thomas, 3-6 (Oakland: AK Press, 2015).

holds an ambivalent potential to both reinforce and disrupt systems of oppression.[9]

I mostly agree with these authors' arguments, but I also believe that the boundary between mainstream science fiction and speculative or visionary fiction is more fluid, relational, and dynamic than a simple binary allows for. Indeed, as I intend to show in this chapter, sci-fi texts can and often do resist certain narratives of power at the same time as they promote dominance and oppression in other ways. Schalk, for instance, says, "By reimagining the meanings and possibilities of bodyminds, speculative fiction can alter the meanings of these categories, requiring readers and critics alike to adapt our modes of reading, interpretation, and analysis or develop new ones."[10] These literary alterations are what make speculative fiction so wonderful and empowering for marginalized readers. However, these alterations also take place within a broader social context, and so they almost always occur alongside other, more normative representations – they resist power at the same time as they make concessions to it. I assert this point not to diminish the importance of speculative fiction but instead to recognize that resistance is always historically situated, and that power is always present. No sci-fi text is wholly liberating, and few are wholly oppressive.

Acknowledging the many connections between science fiction, oppression, and resistance is important because this genre in particular is concerned with (re)imagining the future of humanity and influencing our actions in the present. Holder argues: "In many ways, then, SF can be conceived as a genre connected with real-world activism, a desire to critique current modes of thought and practices in the interest of motivating change."[11] Speculative fiction writers especially have talked and written about the motivation for their work coming from a desire to affect change in their communities. Thinking about and critically discussing representations of disability in science fiction matters precisely because of the genre's political inspirations and aspirations. If science fiction authors are indeed critiquing the present and proposing altered visions for our future(s), then it is the task of critical readers to understand what exactly these texts are criticizing and what they are

---

[9] Matthew Holder, "Imagining Accessibility: Theorizing Disability in Disabled People Destroy Science Fiction." *Disability Studies Quarterly* 40, no. 3 (2020); Sami Schalk, *Bodyminds Reimagined: (Dis)ability, Race, and Gender in Black Women's Speculative Fiction* (Durham: Duke University Press, 2018).

[10] Schalk, *Bodyminds Reimagined*, 2018, 9.

[11] Holder, "Imagining Accessibility," 2020, np.

accepting/perpetuating as well as how the proposed futures align with contemporary narratives of power and resistance.

I have chosen to focus this chapter on *Star Wars* because I believe that this fictional universe provides an important space for radical re-imagining towards disability justice. In addition to the popularity and historical significance of *Star Wars*, I believe that the construction of dis/ability in this universe merits more critical attention. For despite being open to multiple readings, analyses of this franchise are often overly reductive, positing a simplistic and stereotypical depiction of dis/ability which is overly focused on individual characters rather than the broader context of disability oppression. The argument I make in this chapter is not meant to invalidate or cancel out others, but rather to demonstrate the usefulness of pursuing multiple readings. Also, I wish to make clear here at the beginning that I am not advocating for the dark side or for the Sith, and even though I spend a lot of time trying to redeem Anakin, I still think he has a lot of problematic behaviors and concerning areas for growth in terms of his whiteness, toxic masculinity, and other advantaged social positions.

Severed Limbs and Emotional Attachments:
The Ableist Violence of the Jedi Order

When Qui-Gon, Jar-Jar, and Padmé first encounter Anakin on the desert planet of Tatooine, he and his mother Shmi are enslaved to Watto, a Toydarian junk dealer with a penchant for high-stakes gambling. Low on useable funds but anxiously in need of replacement parts for their damaged starship, Qui-Gon strikes a wager with Watto over the outcome of an upcoming podrace. It was through this wager that the group acquired the necessary parts for their ship along with possession of the young Anakin. Anakin's mother Shmi, however, was to remain enslaved, willingly left behind by the Jedi who were more concerned with advancing their mission than responding to the injustice before them. Shmi does not come back into the narrative until much later when Anakin begins to have troubling visions of Tusken Raiders torturing her, visions that immediately precede her death nearly a decade later. The brutalization and subsequent demise of Shmi was a foundational moment in Anakin's disillusionment with the Jedi Order that made possible his corruption to the dark side of the Force. For the Jedi chose not to act on his mother's enslavement, they deterred him from intervening in her suffering, and they created an environment in which he was not supported in processing his emotions. These actions, as I will show, are not unusual for the Jedi Order, but rather connected to its benevolent, militaristic, and assimilationist structure.

Anakin's first encounter with the Jedi as well as the subsequent events surrounding his mother matter because they reveal some fundamental truths about the principles and commitments of the Jedi Order. The first of these truths is that obedience to the mission and progress are more essential than anything else, including the immediate needs of the individuals to whom the Jedi claim to be accountable. Even despite their self-avowed commitment to compassion, the Jedi routinely neglect the suffering of other people, including those who desperately come to them for aid. When the Jedi do act, it is preceded by lengthy council deliberations that are more often focused on the political ramifications of intervention than the ethical dilemmas before them. Especially towards the end of the Clone War, as they became increasingly exhausted and concerned with losing their political power, the Jedi Order spoke more and more about maintaining their "public image" and claiming more power over the republic. Jedi Master Mace Windu in particular advocated for overthrowing the Chancellor to seize control of the Galactic Senate. It became less common, however, for them to attend to the needs of real people, such as those living in extreme poverty on the lower levels of Coruscant, the capital city of the Republic and location of the Senate, or the thousands of displaced peoples and refugees from the war.

The second truth is that access is hardly a priority for the Jedi, particularly where it gets in the way of obedience and "progress." Access here refers to a practice of making space for people's needs and for their embodied/enminded differences. Normativity is the inverse of access, for rather than embracing people as they are and accepting difference as a vital part of community, normativity pressures people to silence their needs and align with idealized ways of being. The Jedi Order is normative in the sense that it requires conformity to a specific code and system of governance. Although a multitude of races and species fill up the ranks of the Jedi, creating the appearance of diversity, the order leaves very little room for difference, especially in terms of behavior or beliefs. In fact, prior to the fall of the Republic, the Jedi would identify the most "force-sensitive" children throughout the Galaxy and take them from their families at a young age in order to begin socializing them into Jedi's ways of thinking and relating with others. Grand Master Yoda's resistance to training Anakin because of his age stems, in part, from his already forged relationships, beliefs, and needs, all of which make conditioning him into conformity more challenging and complicated. Enforcing conformity is a method of undermining access by taking measures to reduce difference and suppress needs.

The innate ableism of the Jedi Order starts to become even more apparent when considering the fact that standardized tests of physical and mental ability determine not only who is brought into the Order but also if and when injustice matters enough for the Jedi to intervene. It is important to note that the only reason Qui-Gon takes an interest in Anakin – the only reason Anakin's life matters to him at all amid the many other enslaved people before him – is that he senses Anakin's connection to the living force and exceptionally high Midi-chlorian count,[12] the highest he has ever seen. Qui-Gon would not have been interested in freeing Anakin were it not for this exceptionality that set him apart from the other enslaved children in a way that was potentially exploitable for the Jedi Order. And, once Anakin's remarkability has been clearly established, the gaggle of other enslaved children become unimportant – in fact, they begin to seem perfectly happy with their situations, and it is only Anakin, the exceptional, chosen one, who is shown as desiring freedom. After leaving Tatooine with the young Anakin, slavery more or less disappears from the narrative, except where it is utilized to advance his storyline forward. This example speaks to the entangled nature of the first and second truths, for the guiding impulse of this storyline was the progress of the Jedi's mission rather than a genuine pursuit of equity, justice, and collective access.

Based on this analysis of the early encounters between Anakin and the Jedi, it is important to consider what the Jedi Order actually values versus the image they construct of themselves. Anakin's admiration of the Jedi indicates that he sees them as heroes of the Galaxy – interstellar saviors and selfless warriors that he hopes to one day be part of. This image is deeply engrained in Anakin's mind, but at numerous points, the Jedi act toward him in increasingly exploitative ways up to the point where he defects from the Order and turns to the dark side of the Force. In reality, the Jedi are a political organization granted power by a governmental body. As I exemplify more below, the Jedi Order is a normative, benevolent, carceral institution that represents itself as defending peace while ultimately acting more often in favor of their own belief system and self-interest. "Normative" here describes how the Jedi Order promotes conformity and allegiance before all else, especially as time progressed towards the fall of the Republic. "Benevolent" refers to how the actions of the Jedi, while seemingly compassionate and selfless, tended to come with string attached, meaning that they chose to help those who could benefit them in return. Finally, "carceral" means that the Jedi functioned as a militaristic police force charged with leading the war effort and upholding the Republic's laws and interests.

The militarism and benevolence of the Jedi Order are made especially apparent through their rhetorical use of concepts like "peace" or "peacekeepers." In many instances, the Jedi's description of themselves as "peacekeepers" acted as

---

[12] Midi-Chlorians are microscope life-forms existing within the cells of all living beings. They constitute a connection to the living force of the universe, and Force users, such as Jedi and Sith, manipulate the Midi-Chlorians within them to fuel their Force powers. A high Midi-Chlorian count, as seen in Anakin, indicates a strong connection to the living force and the potential for great power.

a convenient justification for them to be passive in the presence of violence and destruction. At other times, they would utilize this rhetoric to justify harmful actions toward other life forms – maintaining the peace functioned to give them access to spaces where they weren't wanted or welcome. Describing themselves as "keepers of the peace, not soldiers," as Mace Windu states in *Attack of the Clones*, is inherently contradictory, however, given their role in the Clone Wars as generals. The *Clone Wars* series shows that they routinely participated in military strategy meetings, led offensive movements with the clone army, decided when and where to deploy troops, and so on. Sometimes, they did act to protect people from harm, but this role almost always came *after* those people had claimed alliance to the Republic and/or when providing that protection served a broader purpose of strengthening the Galactic Republic's position in the war. Considering this temporality is important for realizing how militarism and carcerality are inextricable from normativity, for how different people and planets experienced the destruction of the Clone Wars depended entirely on their willingness to accept Jedi influence.

Moreover, claiming the mantle of "peacekeepers" is self-righteous and problematic, for it absolves the Jedi of any sense of responsibility for the state of the Galaxy or to the life forms existing in it. Through this rhetorical maneuvering, the outcomes of their actions, while maybe regrettable, ultimately become acceptable consequences in the preservation of order for the Republic to which their *allegiance* is bound. And naming that allegiance is imperative, for the vision of peace pursued by the Jedi is not the genuine resolution of conflict or mutual well-being and co-existence of life forms; rather, for the Jedi, who are part of an increasingly militaristic order which exists for the purposes of establishing discipline through governance, peace is a result of surrendering to the governmental power of the Galactic Republic. For them, the resolution of conflict has less to do with meaningfully addressing disagreement or unrest or harm than it does with quashing resistance to governmental power or threats to political interests and control over resources. Consequently, while disability justice advocates would define peace in relation to concepts like access, equity, and justice, the Jedi were seemingly more interested in imperial projects and the Republic's "stability" and "security."

The Jedi's portrayal of themselves as "keepers of the peace" echoes in an unsettling way the rhetorical maneuvers that have accompanied the continuing expansion of U.S. military power over the past half century. The U.S. military supposedly brings "stability" and "security" to people on foreign soil as well as to Americans "back home." The "War on Terror" and other similar rhetoric, for instance, put forth this image of soldiers in the U.S. military as champions of virtue and justice fighting against evil doers in foreign lands. This narrative of freedom is woven into the very mythos of the United States – from our socially constructed origin story as rebels banding together against the oppressiveness of a stronger foreign power to the stories we tell today to justify U.S. involvement in military affairs throughout the world. In *Star Wars and the American Imagination*, Mumia Abu-Jamal argues that Americans often build up these cultural narratives in which we are the rebels subverting a treacherous Galactic Empire even though, historically and contemporarily, the actions of this settler colonial nation are much more like that of the Empire, which is perhaps why people are continually rebelling against us.[13]

Furthermore, as the narrative progresses towards the emergence of Darth Vader at the end of *Episode III-Revenge of the Sith*, the militaristic Jedi Order increasingly reserves care for those who show allegiance to the republic. Allegiance, like conformity, becomes a metric for determining which peoples the Jedi are accountable to – which lives should matter to them and whom they should act in defense of. There are many instances in which life forms displaced, threatened, or otherwise harmed by the Clone Wars come to the Jedi for aid and are turned away unless they submit to the Republic, which often involves a prolonged period of military occupation, resource extraction, and so on. One of the most significant examples of this conditional aid occurs when Death Watch, a Mandalorian terrorist organization, with the aid of Darth Maul and several crime syndicates seizes control of Mandalore. Despite great suffering and the presence of the Sith, whom the Jedi are supposedly committed to resisting, the council refuses to send aid because Mandalore is part of the Confederacy of Independent Systems (i.e., not submitted to Republic control). This is the Jedi's almost immediate but final response. They determine it to be a "personal matter" for Kenobi (due to his unique history with Darth Maul) and allow him to leave the planet, but he is not permitted to bring Clones forces or act as a representative of the Republic in any way whatsoever.

Under this form of oppressive governance, where legitimate relationships are determined to be allegiance and submission to a militaristic governmental power, any hope of *interdependence* is lost – subsumed by an expectation of dominance. Interdependence refers to the multitude of connections between living beings through which we care for each other and sustain each other's lives and well-being. It does and cannot come from dominance; it exists where consent, love, compassion, shared respect, and solidarity are the foundation of togetherness, but all of these things are lost when violence and threat of violence are supremely present. In a republic held together by dominance instead of interdependence, genuine empathy and compassion can never truly

---

[13] Mumia Abu-Jamal, "Star Wars and the American Imagination" In *Octavia's Brood: Science Fiction Stories from Social Justice Movements*, edited by Walidah Imarisha, Adrienne Maree Brown, and Sheree Renee Thomas, 182-183 (Oakland: AK Press, 2015).

exist – only benevolence can exist because the government's interest in the well-being of its people inevitably gives way to the need to exert power over them. And, unlike empathy/compassion, benevolence exists solely for the purpose of maintaining an unjust social order. Charity, for instance, which is a form of benevolence, appears to be for the good of those who receive it, but it actually reproduces systems of power by allowing people that control disproportionate amounts of social and material resources to keep in place the very systems that make charity necessary in the first place.[14] Charity also draws attention away from how people in power, resource hoarders, amassed their wealth in the first place – often through the economic exploitation of others to whom they are now being charitable.

Disability is deeply woven into benevolence, for rather than building societies around access, care, and mutual aid, certain people are expected to endanger their bodyminds for the purposes of productivity and profit. Without interdependence, disenfranchised people routinely, predictably become disabled, and when they do become disabled, often as a result of someone else's carelessness, they are frequently expected to handle it on their own because, as Hedva reminds us, care goes against the logics of dominance. Furthermore, because benevolence is tied to dominance, it tends to shrivel up whenever the profits or advantages connected to it stop coming.[15] For instance, when people stop being grateful for or stop being convinced to accept the system as it is, benevolence warps into suppressive violence. In the *Star Wars* universe, suppressive violence is most ostensible under the rule of the Empire, where people are punished whenever they speak out against it. However, it also occurs when the Jedi are still in power. Not only do Jedi continually argue with rather than listen to anyone who critiques them, but they also occasionally refuse to protect/care for those who speak out against them. In fact, throughout the Clone Wars, many people's only encounters with the Jedi resulted in heightened violence against them.

Given these critiques of the Jedi Order, it comes as no surprise that the greatest opponents of the Jedi are all disabled in some way or that they become disabled as the result of crossing paths with the Jedi. Palpatine, Darth Vader, Darth Maul, Kylo Ren, General Grievous, and more all undergo severe bodily transformations as a result of the Jedi's actions, often including loss of limbs and disfigurement. Some of the time, it could be argued, the Jedi were given no

---

[14] Aurora Levins Morales, *Medicine Stories: History, Culture and the Politics of Integrity* (Cambridge: South End Press, 1998); Piepzna-Samarasinha, and Leah Lakshmi. *Care Work: Dreaming Disability Justice*. (Vancouver: Arsenal Pulp Press, 2018).

[15] Johanna Hedva, "sick woman theory." *Mask Magazine*. 2016. http://www.maskmagazine. com/not-again/struggle/sick-woman-theory.

choice in the matter; their actions were inevitable given the situations forced on them. However, it is also true that they repeatedly choose violence over cooperation, despite claiming to be "keepers of the peace." I think here of Luke Skywalker's attempted murder of Kylo Ren. When Luke had a vision of the pain and suffering Kylo Ren might one day cause, he took it upon himself to attempt to end Kylo's life instead of seeking out a more peaceful resolution (as seen in *The Last Jedi* from 2017). There is a great fear underlying his actions that echoes the militaristic, carceral logics of the Jedi Order he was seeking to recreate. Again, "peace" in this instance did not include working with Kylo Ren to promote the realization of everyone's needs but rather that suppression of potential resistance through greater violence. A core logic of carceral state power is to security and protection at all costs – no matter the measures needed. Luke made no effort to communicate with Kylo in order to come up with ways to prevent his vision from coming true. Luke's choice was to cause harm because it was the easiest way of dealing with his fear and maintaining control.

Disability is the ultimate outcome of a Jedi Order that will not accept people as they are, an order that expects people to always conform and assimilate. From this argument, I contend that the disablement/ disfigurement of Anakin Skywalker does not necessarily / solely appropriate disability to represent his compromised morality; in fact, this alternative reading suggests that Anakin's disability is the outcome of the Jedi Order's failure to understand and to collectively build accessible and compassionate spaces committed to the survival and well-being of all peoples. Jedi are more likely to create disabled people than to open up space for disability and other forms of non-productive physical and mental difference. The Jedi routinely treat disablement and disfigurement like punishments for disobedience to the interests of the Republic. Witnessing the Jedi's conflicting actions and having his heroic image of them routinely shattered, Anakin's corruption to the dark side was as much a consequence of the Jedi's actions as the Sith's. In the next section, I delve more into how Anakin's experiences in this Jedi Order set the stage for his eventual decision to turn against them.

The Yet Unrealized Crip Potential of Darth Vader

Among Disability Studies scholars, analyses and discussions about Darth Vader as a representation of disability often center around the negative aspects of his character, especially how it aligns with popular stereotypes or tropes. For instance, Matthew Holder argues that Anakin's disfigurement follows closely the corruption of his morality, as if turning into the dark side of the force inevitably or naturally led to his be(com)ing disabled/disfigured.[16] In many ways, I agree with this and other, similar arguments. Yet, what often gets left out of these conversations are the many ways in which Vader defies common representations of dis/ability. A closer inspection reveals that it is possible to "read" his character as one which resists tropes. For instance, Anakin does not become less powerful after his encounter with Obi-Wan Kenobi on Mustafar; if anything, he reaches the height of his power *after* nearly being burned alive and having several of his limbs severed. Moreover, he is shown wielding his tremendously terrible power at the same time as he uses a ventilator and prosthetic limbs. Even during his most spectacular moments, he is not shown as "overcoming" his disabilities or being powerful despite them; rather, his sustained power is made possible because he is given access to things he needs.

That said, I would not argue that Darth Vader is a representation of disability justice but rather a figure of the "enabled imaginary" – that is, of what *en*abled people assume to be true about disability and the meanings and values they assign to disabled folks' lives. It could be argued that Darth Vader represents a futuristic take on the normative representation of disabled people as perpetually angry, full of hatred, broken, etc., as if our lives are only filled with misery / pain that we turn outward into violence directed at other people. Moreover, at the same time as Darth Vader's disability is always present, it is repeatedly erased and reduced to a plot device: The legendary events of the *Star Wars* universe may have occurred a long, long time ago, but they are nevertheless set in a time of extraordinary technological attainment – a time in which most forms of disability have been "cured," at least for those with access to resources and care. Indeed, with the technologies in his suit of armor, Darth Vader's disability goes away almost entirely; were it not for the iconic sound of his respirator, viewers might easily forget about his severed limbs and fire-scarred body. For the most part, he is represented as if his body beneath the suit is no different from any of the able-bodied characters in the movies.

Technology is not synonymous with disability justice, even though many tech corporations, lobbyists, and researchers (definitely including those from Wat Tambor's Techno Union) say otherwise. In the *Star Wars* universe, technology is depicted as the universal "solution" for disability, as if disabled life forms can easily be "fixed" with an extra droid or bionic replacement part. Consequently, as is commonly the case today, access becomes viewed as a matter of repairing "damaged" individuals through technological interventions, of ensuring that they conform to ableist standards of what a body should look like and/or be able to do. Access becomes about changing individual people, rather than

---

[16] Holder, "Imagining Accessibility," 2020.

something continuously and collectively created through space-making practices and interdependence. And tech typically comes to the rescue without a thought or question: in one scene, Anakin loses an arm; in the next, he has a mechanical prosthetic; after that, he has an arm again. It's almost like nothing happened at all because technology is shown as eliminating disability entirely.

Using his signature curved light saber, Count Dooku cut off one of Anakin's arms towards the end of *Episode II-Attack of the Clones*, which is the first time that viewers witness Anakin as a disabled character. However, if we think about dis/ability as a sociopolitical and historical construction instead of a simple biological reality – as something we collectively and continually (re)produce and give meaning to rather than an apolitical fact of existence – than it becomes necessary to think about the context of Anakin's disablement as being established much earlier in his life. In other words, while there are most certainly definitive moments wherein Anakin's body becomes severed from the normative ideal, these moments are made meaningful and interpreted through an already present belief system that privileges the able-bodied and neuronormative. Understanding that disability is not a natural fact, but a collision between bodyminds and societies with histories that give meaning to the differences between people is a central part of Alison Kafer's political/relational model of disability as well as to disability justice movements.[17]

I have been arguing throughout this paper that part of the impetus for Anakin's corruption into Darth Vader was the ongoing failure of the Jedi Order to practice key principles of disability justice, especially collective accessibility and interdependence, as well as the promise of receiving these things by turning to the dark side of the Force. Indeed, it was Sith Lord Palpatine who provided the necessary resources and care to sustain Anakin's life after Obi-Wan sliced him into pieces. You might argue that Obi-Wan acted in self-defense, which is perhaps true, yet he nevertheless chose to abandon Anakin in a state of suffering following their epic encounter. Neither did he attempt to end Anakin's suffering, nor did he attempt to save Anakin's life. Palpatine, while certainly acting from his own self-interest, actually cared for Anakin's needs in a way that the Jedi did not and could not because of their particular belief system and code.

However, even as I critique the Jedi, I want to recognize that the Sith are no more committed to access and ultimately exploit Anakin in similar, though perhaps more devious and destructive, ways. Palpatine provided resources and tech to save Anakin's life, true. However, the reason for providing these things was to advance his plot for imperial domination. Indeed, Palpatine is only

---

[17] Kafer, *Feminist, Queer, Crip*, 2013.

invested in supporting and caring for Anakin/Darth Vader insofar as doing so creates chaos and augments his power and control over the galaxy. This conditionality of care is similar to the way that disabled folks are treated in ableist and capitalist societies – namely, that we continually have to "prove" that we are deserving of resources rather than just draining them away from other people. If we aren't being productive in some way and contributing to society like we are supposed to, then our lives become questionable, sometimes even disposable. We become pitiable. People talk about how much we cause those around us to suffer. Our "quality of life" comes up too often. The conditionality of care for Darth Vader is especially apparent in *Episode VI– Return of the Jedi* when Palpatine decides to try to corrupt Luke, whom he believes to be more potentially valuable. Darth Vader is no longer worth sustaining as soon as a more "fit" apprentice becomes available.

Ultimately, because neither the Jedi nor the Sith have a real appreciation for/commitment to disability justice, Anakin moves from one inaccessible, disabling order to another. Yet, if the Jedi had expressed a commitment to practice disability justice, if they had made space for Anakin's needs, listened to him, and supported him with compassion and care, then they probably could have prevented the emergence of Darth Vader as well as the catastrophic rise of the Sith-controlled Empire. For instance, if they had helped Anakin to work through, honor, and reflect on his emotional attachments instead of just telling him to suppress them and to learn to let go of them, then he could have accessed much-needed support without turning to the dark side. The driving force behind Anakin's connection to Sith Lord Palpatine is his inability to openly process his fear and grief over the impending loss of Padmé or to receive care from those closest to him, like Obi-Wan. Because the Jedi have not cultivated an accommodating and accepting environment, or even one where he can feel safe and trusted, he has to process his emotions in secret, which ultimately leads to his greater loss of faith in the Jedi Order.

In further support of this argument that meaningfully attending to Anakin's access needs would have altered the entire context of the narrative, consider the fact that Darth Vader is only able to release his hatred, anger, resentment, and fear through an unanticipated emotional connection with his son Luke. Whereas both the Jedi and Sith compelled Anakin to suppress emotional connections, for the purpose of detachment and/or dominance, Luke made an honest effort to connect with his father through authentic compassion and love, which was liberating and transformative. Offering a space for Anakin to experience love and emotional attachment changed the entire situation from one of dominance and competition to one of empathy and shared feelings. Such is the nature of love as a political force, and it was this expression of love that established the possibility of Vader's transformation away from the dark side – his ultimate return to Anakin Skywalker in the final moments preceding his death.

Despite a positive representation of love in the relationship between Luke and his father, this storyline does not quite reach up to the radical vision of care advanced by disability justice theorists and activists because it focuses on love as radical and extraordinary instead of something embedded in the everyday practices of togetherness that allow for mutual survival and well-being. As a crip viewer watching *Star Wars*, I am always left wondering how much suffering could have been prevented if the Jedi Order started from a place of love and had approached Anakin in this way from the very beginning. What if they had encouraged him to form emotional attachments and to learn to work through his emotions productively instead of in secret? He might have so learned many vital skills that could have enabled him to live his life with more accountability and to heal from his harms without causing greater harm to others. Anakin would not have been forced to lie about his feelings for Padmé and keep their marriage secret. He could have spoken openly with others about his fears and learned how to express his access needs in a responsible way.

Yet, instead of pursuing a sustained practice of radical love, the Jedi and Sith alike conditioned him to view loving relationships as power – sources of exploitation and harm that produce vulnerability. Their actions pushed him to comprehend relationships as dangerous, unnecessary, and only important as a means to an end. Intimate relationships, in particular, are shameful and unwelcome, except where they can be exploited for political gain. This conditioning is reinforced as the meaningful relationships that Anakin does manage to develop are continually used against him / taken away from him. For instance, he is asked to spy on Chancellor Palpatine and report his observations back to the Jedi Council because they have a friendship. And, when he expresses concerns to Master Yoda about someone close to him (Padmé) being in danger, Yoda tells him to practice letting go of his attachments, as if they are nothing more than danger, weakness, or vulnerability. Palpatine, on the other hand, uses Vader's feelings for Padmé and later on his son Luke in an effort to further corrupt him. This exploitation of relationships that is normalized for Anakin undermines any possibility of interdependence and is the foundation of the Jedi Order's normativity, militarism, carcerality, and benevolence.

The Jedi and Sith both condition Anakin to view relationships in this oppressive way while at the same time continually doing things to manipulate and exploit his dependence on them. Even his bond with Master Kenobi, which is one the longest and strongest emotional attachments he has, is abused by the Jedi Council. I think here of the council's plan to prevent the Separatist kidnapping of the Chancellor in which they staged Obi-Wan's death without telling Anakin and utilized his anger, fear, and grief to make the performance "convincing." Throughout Anakin's life, they distrust him and punish him for having "bad" emotions that "lead to the dark side," or at least they do right up to a point when those emotions become useful to them and the mission. When Anakin is finally able to speak with Obi-Wan after the mission is finished, we witness his wounded trust and frustration/anger with the council. The suffering they put him through was a significant moment in his corruption, but one that they ultimately justified because it served their mission. Anakin's relationships and emotions became useful tools for them, and so they were permitted in this moment alone.

This staging of Obi-Wan's death is just one example, but it is illustrative of the Jedi's broader tendency to manipulate Anakin for their own interests and political maneuvering. In fact, the climactic moment near the end of *Episode III-Revenge of the Sith* when Anakin turns against Mace Windu to save Palpatine's life becomes believable for me precisely because of how frequently the Jedi Masters show themselves to be undeserving of Anakin's trust – because of how frequently they choose power and control over honesty and other ideals that Anakin believes to be part of the "Jedi way." I find it important to note that in this climactic scene with Windu and Palpatine, Anakin doesn't actually turn against Mace Windu until after the Jedi Master refuses to spare Palpatine's life and bring him to trial. It was Windu's refusal to follow a democratic process, him succumbing to the absolute belief that Palpatine must die by his hand in that moment, that ultimately heralded Anakin's turning to the dark side.

Conclusion

In this chapter, I have proposed an alternative interpretation of disability within the *Star Wars* universe that is attentive to the ways in which the Jedi Order perpetuates disability oppression and, in so doing, hinders the realization of genuine equity or justice. I have argued that the Jedi Order presents itself as peacekeepers and authorities of justice while in fact existing as a normative, militaristic, carceral, and benevolent institution. I have drawn from many different texts in the *Star Wars* universe to show that Jedi Knight Anakin's disillusionment with the Order and his corruption into Darth Vader were more than just the result of Palpatine's influence over him, and that a criptique of the Jedi's actions is a vital part of understanding his turn to the dark side of the Force. I offer this alternative interpretation as a way to expand the theorization of disability and disability justice within science fiction and to establish a more complex and nuanced analysis of one of the most iconic figures in the genre. My hope is that my chapter offers a space for critical thinking that opens up more critical conversations about disability across the galaxy. And, while I am no Jedi, may the force be with you.

Bibliography

Abu-Jamal, Mumia. "*Star Wars* and the American Imagination" In *Octavia's Brood: Science Fiction Stories from Social Justice Movements*, edited by Walidah Imarisha, Adrienne Maree Brown, and Sheree Renee Thomas, 182-183. Oakland: AK Press, 2015.

Hedva, Johanna. "sick woman theory." *Mask Magazine*. 2016. http://www.maskmagazine.com/not-again/struggle/sick-woman-theory.

Holder, Matthew. "Imagining Accessibility: Theorizing Disability in Disabled People Destroy Science Fiction." *Disability Studies Quarterly* 40, no. 3 (2020).

Imarisha, Walidah. "Introduction." In *Octavia's Brood: Science Fiction Stories from Social Justice Movements*, edited by Walidah Imarisha, Adrienne Maree Brown, and Sheree Renee Thomas, 3-6. Oakland: AK Press, 2015.

Imarisha, Walidah, Brown, Adrienne, and Thomas, Sheree. *Octavia's Brood: Science Fiction Stories from Social Justice Movements*. Oakland: AK Press, 2015.

Kafer, Alison. *Feminist, Queer, Crip*. Bloomington: Indiana University Press, 2013.

Levins Morales, Aurora. *Medicine Stories: History, Culture and the Politics of Integrity*. Cambridge: South End Press, 1998.

McRuer, Robert. *Crip Theory: Cultural Signs of Queerness and Disability*. New York: New York University Press, 2006.

Mingus, Mia. "Moving Toward the Ugly: A Politic Beyond Desirability." *Leaving Evidence*. https://leavingevidence.wordpress.com/2011/08/22/moving-toward-the-ugly-a-politic-beyond-desirability/ (published August 21, 2011).

Mingus, Mia. "Dreaming Accountability." *Leaving Evidence*. https://leavingevidence.wordpress.com/2019/05/05/dreaming-accountability-dreaming-a-returning-to-ourselves-and-each-other/ (published May 5, 2019).

Piepzna-Samarasinha, Leah Lakshmi. *Care Work: Dreaming Disability Justice*. Vancouver: Arsenal Pulp Press, 2018.

Price, Margaret. "The Bodymind Problem and the Possibilities of Pain." *Hypatia* 30, no. 1 (2015): 268-84.

Schalk, Sami. *Bodyminds Reimagined: (Dis)ability, Race, and Gender in Black Women's Speculative Fiction*. Durham: Duke University Press, 2018.

Sins Invalid. "Skin, Tooth, and Bone. The Basis of Movement is Our People: A Disability Justice Primer." *Sins Invalid*, 2016.

CHAPTER 7

FISH, ROSES, AND SEXY SUTURES: DISABILITY, EMBODIED ESTRANGEMENT AND RADICAL CARE IN LARISSA LAI'S *THE TIGER FLU*

Stevi Costa

University of Washington, Bothell

Edmond Chang

Ohio University

Abstract

Alison Kafer argues that the future has "been deployed in the service of compulsory able-bodiedness and able-mindedness," positing a "curative imaginary" that assumes a future where disability is cured or eradicated (27). Elsa Sjunneson and Dominik Parisien, editors of *Uncanny Magazine*'s "Disabled People Destroy Science Fiction" special issue, further contends that science fiction replicates the curative imaginary, applying technological fixes to bodies in ways that carry ableist ideologies into the future. It would seem that if science fiction is indeed what Darko Suvin calls "the literature of ideas," it has historically only imagined a future in which able-bodiedness remains the status quo.

Our paper takes up Larissa Lai's 2018 novel *The Tiger Flu* to argue that recent feminist and queer science fiction of color resist and reconfigure this "curative" and technological fix via the Grist Sisters, a rogue collective of female clones, who are trapped in the middle of a conflict between Isabelle Chow, the CEO of HOST Light Industries, and Marcus Traskin, the lord and CEO of the Pacific Pearl Parkade, both of whom seek to find a solution to the "tiger flu" pandemic.

The Grist Sisters' way of life imagines a different relationship to cure, one that envisions a future for disabled lives through "the sexy suture:" ritualized organ transplants provided by the village's "starfish women," whose bodies continually regenerate. Drawing on disability praxis, their social structure relies on a network of caregiving and caretaking in which the community provides critical life support for one another, complicating the curative imaginary from a queer crip feminist standpoint. The radical lifeways of the Grist Sisterhood stands out in stark contrast against that of Chow and Traskin's more ableist and technolibertarian intervention. Against a backdrop of advanced climate degradation, collapsed nation-states, and a global disease, Chow and Traskin seek a top down, technological fix for the "tiger flu" hoping to "cure the mind of the body" by transferring the consciousnesses of the sick to two giant orbiting mainframes called Chang and Eng.

All in all, *The Tiger Flu* is deeply critical of ableist mind/body dualism assumed by much of science fiction and upends the cyberpunk trope that treats the body as "meat" and the "prison of the mind" (a la William Gibson's *Neuromancer*) and argues that hope and possibility, even in a dystopian world, is deeply embodied. By rejecting networked consciousness in favor of radical networks of activist community care, the novel allows readers, in the words of Raffaella Baccolini, to "see the differences of an elsewhere and thus think critically about the reader's own world and possibly act on and change that world."

Keywords: Radical Care, Bodymind, Embodied Estrangement, Queer, Posthuman

***

Science fiction "opens us to new possibilities for the world. And that can be interesting and freeing," says Larissa Lai in an interview.[1] Lai is an American-born Chinese Canadian writer, novelist, poet, and scholar; she is known for *When Fox is a Thousand* (1995), *Salt Fish Girl* (2002), and a book of poetry entitled *Automaton Biographies* (2009). Lai continues, "I also think that speculative fiction is really great for the ways that it makes it possible for us to place ourselves at the center of the universe, instead of [making us] wade through the swathes of mainstream life and heteronormativity before we get to the place where we want to actually tell the story."[2] The SF genre is well known for its imagining of near and distant futures full of new worlds, peoples, dimensions, temporalities, and technologies. However, who is included in those universes, what bodies inhabit those worlds, and whose lives, stories, functions, and futures are privileged has historically foregrounded white, cisgender, heteromasculine, able-bodied men. Lai and other writers and artists (particularly those of color and queer of color) have been reconfiguring, repurposing, and reimagining SF decentering normative identities, embodiments, and narratives in order to build different and more radical worlds.

---

[1] Jiaqi Kang, "Conversation: Larissa Lai," *Sine Theta Magazine,* last modified September 2, 2019, https://medium.com/@sinethetamag/conversation-larissa-lai-73e0a19d7196

[2] Kang, "Conversation: Larissa Lai."

Therefore, we take up Larissa Lai's 2018 novel *The Tiger Flu* to argue that recent feminist and queer science fiction of color harnesses the radical possibilities for marginalized people to imagine "a future or alternative space away from oppression or in which relations between currently empowered and disempowered groups are altered or improved."[3] In particular, we focus on the ways that *The Tiger Flu* negotiates disability vis a vis gender and race that do not replicate the trope and genre norm of the "technological fix" for nonnormative bodies and subjectivities. The future, as Alison Kafer argues, has "been deployed in the service of compulsory able-bodiedness and able-mindedness," positing a "curative imaginary" that assumes a future where disability is cured or eradicated.[4] Cure is often framed as a "restoration," which assumes a failure on the part of the body to comply with what is imagined to be a perfect state of being: able-bodiedness.[5] Moreover, in *Uncanny Magazine's* "Disabled People Destroy Science Fiction" special issue, Elsa Sjunneson and Dominik Parisian further contend that science fiction is often driven by this curative imaginary, applying technological fixes to bodies in ways that carry ableist ideologies into the future.[6] It would seem that if science fiction is indeed what Darko Suvin calls "the literature of ideas," it has historically only imagined a future in which able-bodiedness remains the status quo.

Lai's novel rewrites the generic expectations for SF, drawing on and extending feminist and queer SF traditions like "Monique Wittig, Joanna Russ, Octavia Butler, and Marge Piercy, who were trying to think about what feminists want. How the world might be better if women ran it, or if women just separated from men."[7] *The Tiger Flu* engages and embodies what Sami Schalk proposes in *Bodyminds Reimagined* that SF frees writers and readers from the "weight of realism," that SF can "move people with disabilities . . . from objects to subjects" without the limits of conventional representation.[8] We contend then that *The Tiger Flu* resists and reconfigures the curative and technological fix and instead presents a world where women of color, queer community, and disability praxis

---

[3] Sami Schalk, *Bodyminds Reimagined: (Dis)ability, Race, and Gender in Black Women's Speculative Fiction* (Durham, NC: Duke University Press, 2018), 2.

[4] Alison Kafer, *Feminist, Queer, Crip* (Bloomington: Indiana University Press, 2013), 27.

[5] Eli Clare, *Brilliant Imperfection: Grappling with Cure* (Durham, NC: Duke University Press, 2017), 15.

[6] Elsa Sjunneson and Dominik Parisian, "The Disabled People Destroy Science Fiction Manifesto," *Uncanny Magazine*, last modified 2018, https://uncannymagazine.com/article/the-disabled-people-destroy-science-fiction-manifesto/

[7] Quoted in Kang, "Conversation: Larissa Lai."

[8] Schalk, *Bodyminds Reimagined*, 22.

come together to imagine a different relationship to cure, one that envisions a future (or different futures) for disabled lives.

The Tiger Flu is set in a post-apocalyptic Pacific Northwest in the year 2145, or, in the calendar of the novel, Cascadia Year 127 TAO (Time After Oil). The novel takes place in a climate change-ravaged and technologically transformed Vancouver, now called Saltwater City, and its surrounds, where mega-corporations, paramilitary groups, and the remains of national governments compete for resources and control; where advanced electronics, cybernetic implants, and massive computer mainframes in the form of moon-like satellites (suggestively named Chang and Eng) are contrasted by failing food supplies, environmental disasters, and a global pandemic that originated in the cloning of Caspian tigers and the making and consumption of tiger-bone wine. Echoing and perhaps extending Lai's previous novel *Salt Fish Girl*, which is also set in a near-future biotechnologically imbricated and ecologically precarious Pacific Northwest, *The Tiger Flu* features the intertwined stories of two young women: Kirilow Groundsel, a member of a rogue commune called Grist Village far outside Saltwater City, home to women-only clones who reproduce parthenogenetically, and Kora Ko, a teenage girl living with her family just outside Saltwater City in the Saltwater Flats, who unbeknownst to her is wrapped up in the bio-techno-political goings-on of the area and who later discovers she is a long-lost cousin to the Grist sisters with the "starfish" power to regenerate parts of her own body.

The Tiger Flu presents a biotechnologically mediated and infected world through a queer, women of color, and chronically ill perspective, taking up the norms and conventions often associated with speculative literature, particularly cyberpunk, and "regenreing" them, to borrow Wai Chee Dimock's term[9]; the novel presents a deeply racialized, gendered, eroticized, and chronically diseased world with no easy answers or solutions. The central plot regarding the "tiger flu," which ironically affects and kills men more so than women, involves the competition between Isabelle Chow, the CEO of HoST Light Industries (which employs clone labor to make "scales" or cybernetic implants that allow users to access information and communication networks, particularly Chang and Eng) and Marcus Traskin, the lord and CEO of the Pacific Pearl Parkade (a cult leader of a gang of "tiger men," men who have survived and are living with the disease). Both Chow and Traskin hope to "cure" the disease by curing "the mind of the body;"[10] they plan to use HoST's technology to transfer the consciousnesses of the sick to Eng or Chang. In the transfer, the mind is digitized, stored in

---

[9] Wai Chee Dimock, "Introduction: Genres as Fields of Knoweldge," *PMLA* 122, no. 5 (2007): 1380.

[10] Larissa Lai, *The Tiger Flu* (Vancouver, BC: Arsenal Pulp Press, 2018), 173.

cyberspace, and the body is recycled, reclaimed, turned into edible fish and beautiful roses. However, the novel is deeply critical of both Chow and Traskin and the mind/body dualism they assume; it upends the cyberpunk trope that treats the body as "meat" and the "prison of the mind" (a la William Gibson's *Neuromancer*) and argues that hope and possibility, even in a dystopian world, is deeply embodied. It is a world that cannot ever escape the flesh.

While Chow and Traskin battle over the technological fix to the tiger flu, they are foiled in action and in philosophy by the Grist sisterhood. Founded three generations ago by a clone who escaped the factories of Saltwater City, a rebellious woman they revere as Grandma Chan Ling, the Grist live in sympathetic relationship with the land, the environment, and to each other. While the corporations and broken governments continue to rely on the structures and ideologies of "the time before," the Grist sisters "feel [their] way to other knowings."[11] When Kirilow's starfish lover Peristrophe Halliana is sick with the flu and weak from over-harvesting, Kirilow prays, "Our Mother of bread and roses / Our Mother of dirt / Our Mother of loaves and fishes / Our Mother of love…Bless and water / All the sisters of the Grist… Now more than weather / A slice of forever."[12] Continuance of the sisterhood depends on the care of their "mother doublers," women who can parthenogenically birth new clones, and their "starfish women," whose bodies continually regenerate. These are the heart of these "other knowings" invented by Chan Ling, "the first doubler and also the first groom," who invented the "partho pop" and the "loving transplant, the sexy suture."[13] Kirilow Groundsel is a groom, a healer-mistress trained in the ritualized surgery of organ transplants from starfish to a sister-in-need. After Grist Village is destroyed by HoST and its inhabitants captured, Kirilow is sent to Saltwater Flats to find a lost colony of clones hiding in plain sight as the Cordova School for Girls. There Kora's and Kirilow's paths and fates eventually intertwine, both realizing they must work together, aid each other in order to survive.

The Tiger Flu proposes the lifeways of the Grist as a radical alternative to the ruination caused by the "time before." The Grist social structure relies on a network of caregiving and caretaking in which the community provides critical life support for one another, complicating the curative imaginary from a queer crip feminist standpoint. The radical lifeways of the Grist Sisterhood stand out in stark contrast against more ableist and curative interventions pursued by Isabella Chow and Marcus Traskin. Chow, a technocrat trying to do good, and

---

[11] Lai, *The Tiger Flu*, 36.

[12] Lai, *The Tiger Flu*, 78.

[13] Lai, *The Tiger Flu*, 21.

Traskin, a technolibertarian trying to profit from "the cure," seek a top down, technological fix for the tiger flu by transferring the consciousnesses of the sick to Chang and Eng. By rejecting networked consciousness in favor of radical networks of activist community care, the novel allows readers, in the words of Raffaella Baccolini, to "see the differences of an elsewhere and thus think critically about the reader's own world and possibly act on and change that world."[14]

Embodied Estrangement

The genre of science fiction is best known for its prescient preoccupation with scientific and technological advancement, space and time travel, and extraterrestrial life, but throughout most SF is an exploration of and anxiety over bodies, minds, and definitions of what it means to be human, nonhuman, even inhuman. Science fiction, in a deep way, is more often than not about the translation, transference, transmediation, and transcendence of the body. From Mary Shelley's *Frankenstein* to the aforementioned Lai's *The Tiger Flu* and everything in between, SF is a genre of embodiment even as much of its history is about trying to do away with flesh, bone, and blood, particularly bodily infirmity, weakness, and ultimately, mortality. Too often the monstrous body, the corruptible body, the disabled body functions as index and contrast to the promises of science, technology, and a future without pain, illness, and death (at least for a select few). In fact, according to Kathryn Allan, the disabled and "unruly" body stands in for a "host of socially constructed and marginalized otherness—sexual deviance, criminality, moral and intellectual deficiency, ethnic and racial difference, and so on."[15]

Ironically, most definitions of SF privilege mind over body, thought over matter, knowledge (given that the Latin root of science is *scire* meaning "to know") over corporeality. Perhaps the most oft-cited definition of science and speculative fiction comes from Darko Suvin's *Metamorphosis of Science Fiction*; Suvin defines SF as "a literary genre whose necessary and sufficient conditions are the presence and interactions of estrangement and cognition, and whose main formal device is an imaginative framework to the author's empirical environment."[16] For Suvin, estrangement means that SF is "differentiated from

---

[14] Raffaella Baccolini, "The Persistence of Hope in Dystopian Science Fiction," *PMLA* 119, no. 3 (2004): 520.

[15] Kathryn Allan, "Introduction: Reading Disability in Science Fiction," *Disability in Science Fiction: Representations of Technology as Cure*, ed. Kathryn Allan (New York: Palgrave MacMillan, 2013), 7.

[16] Darko Suvin, *Metamorphosis of Science Fiction: On the Poetics and History of a Literary*

the 'realistic' literary mainstream"[17] and cognitive means "not only a reflecting *of* but also *on* reality. It implies a creative approach tending toward a dynamic transformation rather than toward a static mirroring of the author's environment."[18] For Suvin, SF requires rationality, an internal logic, and novel reality that allows the reader to know and understand the difference between a science fictional world and their lived one. This definition of SF naturalizes the mind over the body, which often positions science and technology "as a solution to overcome the physical or mental limitations of the human body"[19] that plays out in tropes and narratives of augmenting or perfecting the body (and mind) through medical or technological intervention or of repairing, curing, repairing, or eradicating the always imperfect body. In other words, as Thomas Foster argues, "[T]he devaluation and rejection of embodiment intensifies the traditional Cartesian mind/body dualism, but that dualism depends on the concept of the body as container for mind, to define the boundary between them."[20] Much of mainstream and normative SF then can only imagine imperfection and disability as "difference that exists only to be undone."[21]

There is no more emblematic science fictional text that evinces the technological fix and transcendence of the body than William Gibson's 1982 novel *Neuromancer*, which is considered one of the ur-texts of the cyberpunk genre. *Neuromancer* in essence genre mixes a detective noir with information heist with digital dystopia. The novel follows a computer hacker, a "console cowboy" named Case, who joins a group of high-tech low-lifes (to paraphrase Bruce Sterling's definition of cyberpunk) in the service of a powerful AI named Wintermute who wants to be freed to join with its AI counterpart Neuromancer. Case lives to "jack into," otherwise connect his mind directly to the global digital network of cyberspace, a term Gibson coined. Jacking in for Case means projecting his "disembodied consciousness into the consensual hallucination [of] the matrix,"[22] where cyberspace "flowed, flowered for him, fluid neon origami trick, the unfolding of his distanceless home, his country, transparent 3D chessboard extending to infinity."[23] The novel is very clear that the mind is

---

Genre (New Haven: Yale University Press, 1979), 7-8.

[17] Suvin, *Metamorphosis of Science Fiction*, 8.

[18] Suvin, *Metamorphosis of Science Fiction*, 10.

[19] Allan, "Introduction: Reading Disability in Science Fiction," 11.

[20] Thomas Foster, *The Souls of Cyberfolk: Posthumanism as Vernacular Theory* (Minneapolis, MN: University of Minnesota Press, 2005), 10-11.

[21] Quoted in Allan, "Introduction: Reading Disability in Science Fiction," 4.

[22] William Gibson, *Neuromancer* (New York: ACE), 5.

[23] Gibson, *Neuromancer*, 52.

preferable to the body, that the flesh is anathema to cyberspace. In fact, Case begins the novel literally and technologically disabled, unable to enter cyberspace due to being poisoned by an employer he tried to double cross: "For Case, who'd lived for the bodiless exultation of cyberspace, it was the Fall. In the bars he'd frequented as a cowboy hotshot, the elite stance involved a certain relaxed contempt for the flesh. The body was meat. Case fell into the prison of his own flesh." [24] When he agrees to help the servants of Wintermute, the damage to his nervous system and body are repaired, and Case's disability is fixed to allow him to once again escape his limited embodiment. Amanda Fernbach critiques *Neuromancer's* disdain for the "meat" and valorization of the mind, saying,

> Like fantasies played out in contemporary discourses about the internet and virtual reality, Gibson's cyberspace allows for the disavowal of bodily differences in a fantasy that privileges the white male body…in this space, the white male heterosexual body, surrounded by imploding differences and full of self-loathing, is nevertheless still privileged and still very much at the center of the action. The fantasized free-floating subjectivity is able to reclaim the universal gaze of traditional masculinity by disavowing bodily differences—indeed, the body itself—within the matrix.[25]

In direct response to texts like *Neuromancer,* much of feminist, queer, and crip science fiction does not conform to and often refuses Gibson's and Suvin's formulations instead revels in and reveals the radical potential of the flesh, the body, and its storied differences and variegations. For example, expanding on Hortense Spillers' critique of black bodies as flesh before body (where the body is a self-possessing political subject), Alexander G. Weheliye in *Habeas Viscus* argues, "Flesh functions as an integral component of being"[26] and "provides a stepping stone for new genres of human."[27] These genres and sites of flesh and embodiment may be used for oppression, but they may also be modalities and loci for potential liberation—instead of Suvin's "imagined framework alternative" to the author or reader's "empirical environment," SF becomes an "alternative imaginative framework" to interrogate social, cultural, medical, and technological

---

[24] Gibson, *Neuromancer,* 6.

[25] Amanda Fernbach, "The Fetishization of Masculinity in Science Fiction: The Cyborg and the Console Cowboy," *Science Fiction Studies* 27, no. 2 (July 2000): 248.

[26] Alexander G. Weheliye, *Habeas Viscus: Racializing Assemblages, Biopolitics, and Black Feminist Theories of the Human* (Durham, NC: Duke University Press, 2014), 44.

[27] Weheliye, *Habeas Viscus,* 45.

structures and identities. [28] Therefore, how might we articulate *embodied estrangement* as resonance and dissonance to cognitive estrangement? Here embodied takes up the radical possibility of the flesh and body, that bodies matter, and estrangement is the critical recognition of bodily difference, bodily change, and the stark realization that, to paraphrase Roderick A. Ferguson, the raced, gendered, and disabled body is a text upon which histories of differentiation, exclusion, and violence are inscribed.[29]

The Tiger Flu explores and embraces embodied estrangement through its repeated attention to bodies, skin, touch, smell, pleasure, and pain. It presents a deeply gendered, raced, and material world. In fact, much of Lai's SF writing locates subjectivity, life, and survival in the fecundity and funkiness of bodies, environments, and effluvia. Everything in *The Tiger Flu* is smelly, stinky, oozy, and slippery. Both Lai's *The Tiger Flu* and her earlier novel *Salt Fish Girl* rely on these mortal senses, on this haptic and olfactory textuality as a means to "challenge conceptions of science fiction that privilege a version of Western modernity in which scientific progress and rational thought occlude all other possible modernities and genealogies."[30] The good and bad odors and senses of *The Tiger Flu* "jolt us into rethinking our assumptions"[31] about how the world works, who gets to live and thrive and die in it, as well as radical, pervasive, even invasive intimacies that "destabilizes liberal humanist conceptions of progress and modernity...[given that] smell as a chemical, embodied sense has been denigrated repeatedly in abstract, rational thought."[32] *The Tiger Flu* reclaims this embodied sensorium and recognizes that life and death, sickness and wellness, decay and rebirth are inexorable parts of living and surviving.

Moreover, the novel challenges cyberpunk's insistence that the body and the mind are an oppositional dualism; the Grist embody disability theory's understanding that bodies and minds as always-already imbricated. Given that the sisters are clones, they recognize that they are not "human" or "persons" in the traditional sense and seek to redefine or reject those normative categories. The battle between mind and body plays out in the conflict between Chow's HoST Light Industries vying with Traskin's tiger men for digital dominance over who will control the "cure" for the tiger flu. Traskin steals the upload technology

---

[28] Allan, "Introduction: Reading Disability in Science Fiction," 3.

[29] Roderick A. Ferguson, "Race," in *Keywords for American Cultural Studies*, eds. Bruce Burgett and Glenn Hendler (New York: New York University Press, 2007): 192.

[30] Paul Lai, "Stinky Bodies: Mythological Futures and the Olfactory Sense in Larissa Lai's *Salt Fish Girl*," *MELUS* 33, no.4 (Winter 2008): 167.

[31] Lai, "Stinky Bodies," 168.

[32] Lai, "Stinky Bodies,"183.

from Chow, wresting the satellite mainframe Chang from her control. In response, Chow pushes forward with her plans to transfer people to Eng, plans which include the capture of most of Grist Village (and other disposable clones) as test subjects to improve the verisimilitude of the simulation. Kora and Kirilow are caught in the crossfire, in Chow and Traskin's struggle for a disembodied future. On the one hand, Kora eventually learns that her family, her mother and uncle, have been uploaded by Chow, and she is offered the opportunity to join them. Kirilow, on the other hand, recognizes that for the "Grist sisters, [the upload] is simply a death machine. It imagines the mind can be separated from the body."[33] Eli Clare imagines the hyphenated "body-mind" to recognize "both the inextricable relationships between our bodies and our minds and the ways in which the ideology of cure operates as if the two are distinct—the mind superior to the body, the mind defining personhood, the mind separating humans from nonhumans."[34] For Sami Schalk, who dispenses with the hyphen, "bodymind" is a key term in her analysis of the radical possibilities of speculative fiction, demonstrating the "genre's nonrealist possibilities of human and nonhuman subjects."[35] Either compound or portmanteau evinces the critical awareness and practice of embodied estrangement, or as Kirilow hopes and prays, "For the ones to come / Remember night for us / As safety under cover / Rest and gestation / Deliver us from humans."[36]

A Network of Radical Care

The female clones of Grist Village, who were genetically engineered to work in the factories of Saltwater City, call to mind Haraway's description of feminized workforces under late capitalism.[37] Three generations ago, a cluster of Grist Sisters escaped their techno-industrial capitalist origins and founded the Grist Village, where caretaking and mutual aid replaced capitalist lifeways. Among the surviving refugees, "doublers" and "starfish" are entwined in caregiving relationships within the Grist colony. With only one remaining starfish and one remaining doubler at the start of the novel, Grist Village faces a crisis when an outsider carries the titular "tiger flu" into the colony, killing the starfish woman

[33] Lai, "Stinky Bodies," 173-174.

[34] Clare, *Brilliant Imperfection*, xvi.

[35] Schalk, *Bodyminds Reimagined*, 5.

[36] Lai, *The Tiger Flu*, 96.

[37] Donna Haraway, *Simians, Cyborgs, Women: The Reinvention of Nature* (London: Free Association Books, 1991): 168.

Peristrophe Halliana before she can regenerate after giving her heart to the colony's last doubler, Radix Bupleuri.

We cite Haraway's cyborgization of female factory workers in our description of the Grist Sisters for two reasons. First, Haraway's framing of female factory workers as "real-life cyborgs" specifies such bodies as Asian.[38] This is germane in the world of *The Tiger Flu*, where Asian women have been cloned "to be workers and test subjects."[39] Second, to think about the Grist Sisters as echoes of Haraway's cyborg invites us to read them with Alison Kafer's critique of the Haraway cyborg within the field of disability studies. In Kafer's view, the cyborg-as-image has become a rhetorical shorthand for the kinds of adaptive technologies many disabled people live with every day. This constructs technology as a "promising future" for the disabled and makes the technology synonymous with the disabled person who uses it.[40] While Haraway argues that the cyborg is a powerful "heteroglossia"[41] that destabilizes boundaries, Kafer contends that "rather than breaking down boundaries, [the cyborg] buttresses them" when it comes to perceptions of disabled people.[42]

By breaking from the techno-capitalist world that created them, the Grist Sisters and their radical lifeways seem to buttress the binary between the technological/natural and capitalism/communalism. While the Grist Sisters have outright rejected capitalism and advanced technologies, their very existence remains a product of it, therefore complicating the neat divide their lifestyle seems to indicate. The biological processes of parthenogenesis and regeneration that enable them to live outside of capitalism are only possible because of technological gene splicing with non-human entities like fish, amphibians, and lizards undertaken in corporate laboratories. With the death of their last starfish, the Grist Sisters have no alternative but to return to their techno-capitalist origins in Saltwater City in the hopes of finding another starfish woman who can ensure their survival.

In *The Tiger Flu*, the cyborg figure supports Haraway's claim to the slipperiness of boundary distinctions. Bound up as the Grist Sisters are in their origins as a means to sustain their resistance to them, one might read their positionality as neither inside technology nor outside of it. Through a disability studies lens, their situation is analogous to the ways disabled bodies are bound up in the medical-industrial complex. Although the social model of disability posits

---

[38] Haraway, *Simians, Cyborgs, Women*, 177.

[39] Lai, *The Tiger Flu*, 233.

[40] Kafer, *Feminist, Queer, Crip*, 107.

[41] Haraway, *Simians, Cyborgs, Women*, 181.

[42] Kafer, *Feminist, Queer, Crip*, 108.

disablement as a product of social and environmental ableism, disabled individuals still require medical diagnosis to receive accommodations for many of these social barriers, to say nothing of the inherent need for medical care to sustain the quality of life for many disabled people. To live life as a disabled person while rejecting the medical-industrial complex outright is often a death sentence. This interdependence on medical care and assistive technology forms the "buttress" Kafer describes.

The Grist Sisters are explicitly critical of the medicalization of disabled lives, preferring medicines made from "herbs, powders, and insects" [43] over by-products of the medical-industrial complex. "That is not good for you, little sister," Kirilow says to one of the Cordova girls when she asks for an Advil. "The people in the time before, they were smart but in a really stupid way."[44] Within Grist Village, the Grist Sisters are clearly able to sustain themselves through "material networks" of care that circumvent and supersede medical-industrial technologies and knowledges. In the real world, many disabled people rely on relationships with caregivers to survive. As Eli Clare notes, these relationships can often be fraught. Power imbalances between disabled people and caregivers "frequently cause abuse and neglect for the person receiving care" and "low wages and exploited labor for the person providing care." [45] The mutual caretaking context of the Grist commune avoids wage and labor exploitation, thereby revealing and revising the fraught nature of caregiver relationships with disabled people.

As Mitchell and Snyder note, many professional caregivers for disabled individuals are "lower-class, racialized, and predominately female."[46] These adjectives can be equally applied to the Grist Sisters, which poses the first of a series of revisions to the way caretaking is understood in the novel. By removing the raced, classes, and gendered hierarchies that play out in caregiver-disabled relationships, the novel posits that caretaking can be equitable among material networks of disabled bodies: Peristrophe Halliana's ability to regenerate tissue is a critical resource that extends the lives of others in her colony when they become ill. Importantly, the anomalous bodies of the starfish and the doubler are "necessary to the alternative living relations of material networks,"[47] much

---

[43] Lai, *The Tiger Flu*, 252.

[44] Lai, *The Tiger Flu*, 169.

[45] Clare, *Brilliant Imperfection*, 136.

[46] David T. Mitchell, and Sharon Snyder, *The Biopolitics of Disability: Neoliberalism, Ablenationalism, and Peripheral Embodiment* (Ann Arbor: University of Michigan Press, 2015), 39.

[47] Mitchell and Snyder, *The Biopolitics of Disability*, 39.

as caregivers are in the lives of disabled people. Starfish and doublers are inextricably bound to each other and to their respective grooms -- naturopathic surgeons who perform ritualized organ transplants known as "the sexy suture."[48] This medical procedure differs significantly from the kind of organ transplant a contemporary reader would know. Not only do organs regenerate for the donor, but the process has a deliberate emotional component that speaks to a radical politics of care. The process is nicknamed "the sexy suture" because the act, for the Grist sisters, is a parasexual experience for the starfish, the doublers, and the grooms.

Whenever a doubler needs an organ transplant, the grooms prepare "the loving transplant" in a ritual that begins by brewing an anesthetic tea for their patients and chanting a prayer while sharpening their scalpels. Groom Kirilow Groundsel has a whetstone made of crushed engagement rings "from skeletons of the time before." When she sharpens her knives to operate on her starfish (who is also her lover), she performs this ritual so that "[a]ll the love from the time before rushes into my shiv,"[49] ensuring that the procedure is performed with utmost care not only from Kirilow herself but from the generations of Grist Sisters that precede her. Furthermore, the anesthetic tea Forget-me-do "takes away all memory and feeling of pain, leaves nothing but a craving to be cut again." By reconfiguring the starfish and doublers' nervous system responses to "feel pain as pleasure," all participants in the medical procedure experience it as a pleasurable act of care.[50] When Kirilow harvests the starfish Peristrophe Halliana's left eye, she gazes back at her groom "with love."[51] While this is ostensibly part of the love Kirilow and Peristrophe share romantically outside of their groom-starfish relationship, for Peristrophe to gaze at Kirilow with love out of her remaining eye during surgery reinforces the experience as an act of mutual caretaking. Peristrophe's harvested eye will sustain her sister-Doubler's quality of life while Kirilow and her sister-groom tend to them both. The "sisterly insertion" of the procedure binds the grooms' blades, the starfish's organs, and the doubler's body in an amalgamation of surgery and sex act.[52] To call the practice "the sexy suture" transforms medical procedure into a matrix of queer desires. Kirilow's romantic love for Peristrophe is an explicitly queer thread in the novel. When combined with love as the emotional drive for the groom and pleasure the goal for her patients, the organ transplant becomes

---

[48] Lai, *The Tiger Flu*, 21.

[49] Lai, *The Tiger Flu*, 19.

[50] Lai, *The Tiger Flu*, 21.

[51] Lai, *The Tiger Flu*, 22.

[52] Lai, *The Tiger Flu*, 21.

queer polyamory through which the women of Grist Village sustain their lifeways.

Here we turn to Mel Y. Chen's work on animacy to further illuminate the queer lifeways of the Grist Village. In Chen's words, "Animacy activates new theoretical formations that trouble and undo stubborn binary systems of difference, including dynamism/stasis, life/death, subject/object, speech/ nonspeech, human/animal, natural body/cyborg."[53] In brief, animacy is a quality of "agency, awareness, mobility, and liveness" that can be attributed to both human and nonhuman things. To think of a nonhuman thing, such as a metal, as animate reconfigures concepts like able-bodiedness and ability. No longer is there a binary opposition between a disabled person and their prosthetic device if both a prosthetic leg and the human being who uses it are animate. Animacy creates intimacies between categories of difference, making queerness "immanent to animate transgressions."[54] In fact, given that the clones understand themselves as both human and non-human they are animacy embodied. Certainly, there is an explicit queerness in the lesbian romance between Kirilow and Peristrophe, but queer animacies are also inherent in the practice of the sexy suture itself.

The organs being transferred between starfish and doubler pose questions of bodily integrity and autonomy. Peristrophe's eyes and heart sustain more lives than merely her own, allowing extensions of Auntie Radix's life through this gift, and therefore the continuance of the Grist colony. The need for the "sexy suture" renders all lives within the Grist colony dependent on the surgical success of the transplants. The individual bodies of the starfish and the doubler are subsumed to the collective need of Grist Village, subjecting both starfish and doubler to routine disruptions of their bodily integrity to ensure the colony's survival. The "sexy suture" is the method of future-making for the Grist colony, queering heteronormative reproduction through "the sisterly insertion" of organs from one body into another. That Kirilow sharpens her knives on a whetstone made from engagement rings further queers heteronormative practices, even as she imbues animacy into the blades with "love from the time before." Were it not for the limitations of their origins as clones from a single woman's DNA, the Grist Sisterhood would functionally "outlive them all, in beds of our own making,"[55] crafting a queer future through animate intimacies where anomalous bodies care for each other.

[53] Mel Y. Chen, *Animacies: Biopolitics, Racial Mattering, and Queer Affect* (Durham, NC: Duke University Press, 2012), 3.

[54] Chen, *Animacies*, 11.

[55] Lai, *The Tiger Flu*, 19.

The material networks through which the Grist Sisters propagate and prosper challenges the networked consciousness proposed by Chow and Traskin in their pursuit of the technological fix for a chronically ill world. In the first place, the material, embodied nature of this network acts in opposition to the disembodied curative imaginary of a Chow-Traskin future. Networking often invokes a sense of being technologically imbricated or otherwise linked to corporate capitalist growth strategies. But rather than connecting links in a chain or circuits in a machine, this is a network of bodies that operates through what Haraway describes as "the permeability of boundaries in the personal body and the body politic,"[56] drawing instead on feminist praxis, disability praxis, and activist mutual aid strategies. Characteristic of Larissa Lai's oeuvre, materiality, particularly through embodied estrangement and affective networks, matters most of all.

But the radical revisions to caregiver-disabled relationship amongst the Grist sisterhood are also fraught, as too many organ donations too quickly compromise Peristrophe's immune system, resulting in her death by the titular tiger flu. Where these radical lifeways ought to be sustainable, the scarcity of doublers and starfish exploits both Radix's and Peristrophe's bodies in service of futurity for the Grist commune. The reproductive capacity of the Doublers lends them higher status in Grist Village, with some even referring to Auntie Radix as "our Queen." Radix must birth as many sister pups as her body will allow over her lifetime, and Peristrophe must give as much of herself as is necessary to ensure Radix's continuance, even at the cost of her own life. In Kirilow's perspective, the situation exploits Peristrophe moreso than Radix. By placing a higher value on Radix's life than Peristrophe's, the colony inadvertently replicates a preference for methods of future-making that are more closely linked to reproductive and heteronormative modalities over queer ones. It likewise turns Peristrophe into an organ dispensary, evacuating the value of her life and her personhood in service of Radix. Peristrophe's death reveals that "the sexy suture" is not immune to the problems of exploitation that arise within caregiver-disabled interactions, even as the exploitation itself takes on different forms.

With the loss of the colony's last starfish and last doubler, the narrative sends Kirilow out into the world beyond Grist Village to secure the future. Rather than positing a curative imaginary in which "the sexy suture" isn't necessary, Kirilow's plotline strives to prevent the eradication of the Grist way of life. In *Brilliant Imperfection*, Eli Clare posits that eradication lies at the center of cure, explaining how the medical-industrial complex often changes the future "by manipulating the present" through practices like genetic counseling that allow

---

[56] Haraway, *Simians, Cyborgs, Women*, 170.

prospective parents to selectively abort fetuses with markers of disability.[57] The SF setting of the novel allows readers to imagine a future for these characters whose lives are medically dependent on one another without curing them of their way of life. The path to a secure future for the Grist Sisterhood does not lie in the eradication of their anomalous genetic properties, but in their continuance.

The novel proposes, instead, that the Grist Sisterhood can continue if starfish are no longer subject to possible exploitation in the service of their doublers. Animacy becomes a critical modality in service of this endeavor when Kora Ko dies on the return to Grist Village from Saltwater City. Kirilow and her sisters manage to upload the teenager's consciousness (and her genetic code) into a biological airship called a batterkite. They later discover that the "tentacles of the kite doctored carefully and left to lie long enough atop fertile soil can become roots,"[58] transforming Kora into the immortal Starfish Tree that now seeds the great Grist Garden, supplying replacement organs to the Grist Sisterhood. The tree is sentient, and speaks through vibrations that the Grist Sisters can understand. It explains the traditional medicinal practices of the Grist, as well as some history of the time before. The Starfish Tree becomes an anticipatory form, a symbol of continuance of futurity built on mutual caretaking and renewable resources. It likewise proposes a networked relationship between humanoid creatures and other forms of biological life, reconfiguring both the Grist Sisters and the Starfish Tree as what Samantha Frost might call "biocultural creatures . . . seeded with traces of the future."[59]

Survival and Hope

"I don't necessarily think of *The Tiger Flu* as a dystopia," says Lai, "I know it has many dystopian elements–how could it not, given the state of the world. But it is a novel that is actively seeking possibilities for life."[60] Kirilow has found a way through (perhaps not out of) the dystopian conditions of her world; even amidst death, destruction, and ambivalence, she and others have found a thread of hope. As Raffaella Baccolini argues, "Utopia is maintained in dystopia, traditionally a bleak, depressing genre with no space for hope in the story, only *outside* the story...But recent novels such as Margaret Atwood's *The*

---

[57] Clare, *Brilliant Imperfection*, 26-27.

[58] Lai, *The Tiger Flu*, 326.

[59] Samantha Frost, *Biocultural Creatures: Toward a New Theory of the Human* (Durham, NC: Duke University Press, 2016), 149.

[60] Quoted in Kai Cheng, "Surviving Utopia: Finding Hope in Larissa Lai's Piercing Novel 'The Tiger Flu'" *Autostraddle*, last Modified December 6, 2018, https://www.autostraddle.com/surviving-utopia-finding-hope-in-larissa-lais-the-tiger-flu-439136/

Handmaid's Tale, Le Guin's *The Telling*, and Butler's *Kindred* and *Parable of the Sower*, by resisting closure, allow readers and protagonists to hope: the ambiguous open endings maintain the utopian impulse *within* the work."[61] Lai's regenreing of SF becomes a "refuturing;" as Aimee Bahng reminds us, "The future is an always already occupied space,"[62] one that must be reimagined and *refutured* through invention, collaboration, and "[i]mprovisational life-forms and experimental practices [to] form ad hoc community networks and resistance movements that coalesce spontaneously and emphemerally, on the fly, on the run, and cobbled together from recycled and repurposed materials."[63]

Rather than centering the novel on death, destruction, loss, and further exploitation of bodies (disabled or soon to be), Lai offers a different horizon of possibility, alternative vectors of regeneration and collectivity; she "purposefully chooses to focus on the potential for resilience, resistance, and the resurgence of life that inevitably emerge from oppression and strife: The community of Grist sisters utilizes a range of ingenious biologically-based technologies to heal and enhance their bodies, Indigenous, and other oppressed peoples form revolutionary coalitions, and a secret society of survivors hides in plain sight."[64] Rather than buttressing the binaries between body/mind, nature/culture, human/animal, technological/natural, and healthy/sick, *The Tiger Flu* maps radical networks (figuratively and narratively) that place "cure" in the bodymind itself, reveling in fleshiness, messiness, and varying states and futurities of ability.

By the end of the novel, Kirilow and some of her sisters survive the destruction of the satellite Chang, the upload of Kora Ko to Eng (her body subsequently being transformed into a giant fish "silver and slippery, covered in long tendrilly scales, with a pink right fin"),[65] and the total collapse of Saltwater City. Kirilow and others flee far into unmapped wilderness in order to find a new Grist Village, to remember what has come before, and to pass on stories, skills, smells, and sustainability to the future. She thinks to herself:

> The sun is going down. It sends rays of light through water vapour, smoke, dust, and radiation from the death of Chang. It makes a cloud

[61] Baccolini, "The Persistence of Hope in Dystopian Science Fiction," 520.

[62] Aimee Bahng, *Migrant Futures: Decolonizing Speculation in Financial Times* (Durham, NC: Duke University Press, 2018), 12.

[63] Bahng, *Migrant Futures*, 165.

[64] Cheng, "Surviving Utopia."

[65] Lai, *The Tiger Flu*, 322.

ocean of fabulous purples, mauve, silver, and gold. The batterkite dives into this dirty but miraculous beauty, free to glide us home.[66]

Bibliography

Allan, Kathryn. "Introduction: Reading Disability in Science Fiction." *Disability in Science Fiction: Representations of Technology as Cure*. Edited by Kathryn Allan. New York: Palgrave MacMillan, 2013.

Baccolini, Raffaella. "The Persistence of Hope in Dystopian Science Fiction." *PMLA* 119, no. 3 (2004): 518-521.

Bahng, Aimee. *Migrant Futures: Decolonizing Speculation in Financial Times*. Durham, NC: Duke University Press, 2018.

Chen, Mel Y. *Animacies: Biopolitics, Racial Mattering, and Queer Affect*. Durham, NC: Duke University Press, 2012.

Cheng, Kai. "Surviving Utopia: Finding Hope in Larissa Lai's Piercing Novel 'The Tiger Flu'" *Autostraddle*. Last Modified December 6, 2018. https://www.autostraddle.com/surviving-utopia-finding-hope-in-larissa-lais-the-tiger-flu-439136/

Clare, Eli. *Brilliant Imperfection: Grappling with Cure*. Durham, NC: Duke University Press, 2017.

Dimock, Wai Chee. "Introduction: Genres as Fields of Knoweldge." *PMLA* 122, no. 5 (2007): 1377-1388.

Ferguson, Roderick A. "Race." *Keywords for American Cultural Studies*. Edited by Bruce Burgett and Glenn Hendler. New York: New York University Press, 2007.

Fernbach, Amanda. "The Fetishization of Masculinity in Science Fiction: The Cyborg and the Console Cowboy." *Science Fiction Studies* 27, no. 2 (July 2000): 234-255

Foster, Thomas. *The Souls of Cyberfolk: Posthumanism as Vernacular Theory*. Minneapolis, MN: University of Minnesota Press, 2005.

Frost, Samantha. *Biocultural Creatures: Toward a New Theory of the Human*. Durham, NC: Duke University Press, 2016.

Gibson, William. *Neuromancer*. New York: ACE, 1984.

Haraway, Donna. *Simians, Cyborgs, Women: The Reinvention of Nature*. London: Free Association Books, 1991.

Kafer, Alison. *Feminist, Queer, Crip*. Bloomington: Indiana University Press, 2013.

Kang, Jiaqi. "Conversation: Larissa Lai." *Sine Theta Magazine*. Last modified September 2, 2019. https://medium.com/@sinethetamag/conversation-larissa-lai-73e0a19d7196

Lai, Larissa. *The Tiger Flu*. Vancouver, BC: Arsenal Pulp Press, 2018.

Lai, Paul. "Stinky Bodies: Mythological Futures and the Olfactory Sense in Larissa Lai's *Salt Fish Girl*." *MELUS* 33, no.4 (Winter 2008): 167-187.

---

[66] Lai, *The Tiger Flu*, 323.

Mitchell, David T. and Sharon Snyder. *The Biopolitics of Disability: Neoliberalism, Ablenationalism, and Peripheral Embodiment.* Ann Arbor: University of Michigan Press, 2015.

Schalk, Sami. *Bodyminds Reimagined: (Dis)ability, Race, and Gender in Black Women's Speculative Fiction.* Durham, NC: Duke University Press, 2018.

Sjunneson, Elsa and Dominik Parisian. "The Disabled People Destroy Science Fiction Manifesto." *Uncanny Magazine.* Last modified 2018. https://uncanny magazine.com/article/the-disabled-people-destroy-science-fiction-manifesto/

Suvin, Darko. *Metamorphosis of Science Fiction: On the Poetics and History of a Literary Genre.* New Haven: Yale University Press, 1979.

Weheliye, Alexander G. *Habeas Viscus: Racializing Assemblages, Biopolitics, and Black Feminist Theories of the Human.* Durham, NC: Duke University Press, 2014.

SECTION THREE:
DISABILITY WITHIN/OF A GLOBALIZED FUTURE

CHAPTER 8

NEOLIBERAL CONVERGENCES OF CAPITAL & CAPACITY: READING SCIENCE FICTION WITH THE ADA

T. Wesley

University of Denver

Abstract

This chapter places the Americans with Disabilities Act (ADA 1990) in conversation with sf in order to explore how contemporary economic logics reconstructs textual and material bodies. Reading Karen Tei Yamashita's *Through the Arc of the Rainforest* ([1990] 2017) and Hubert Haddad's *Desirable Body* ([2015] 2018), I analyze the relationship between the ADA and the violent commodification of bodies in the US and elsewhere. I draw on Jasbir K. Puar's assemblage of disability, debility, and capacity (2017) to demonstrate how a privatized, free-market economy informs the production of the "qualified" disabled subject and sustains the (re)distribution of wealth and health to the elite through the commodification of the debilitated body. Problematizing valuations of corporeality, life, and death, these texts exemplify how representations of disability in sf can facilitate nuanced examinations of privilege and violence produced by and for a globalized free market.

Keywords: Americans with Disabilities Act (ADA), Neoliberalism, Free-Market Capitalism, Capacity, Debility, Bioeconomy

***

When disability studies scholar Tanya Titchkosky writes "Texts are more than outcomes or products of literate social action. Texts *are* forms of action," she affirms how all texts—whether novels, popular news magazines, or bureaucratic documents—function to create, structure, and reproduce social meaning.[1]

---

[1] Tanya Titchkosky, *Reading and Writing Disability Differently: The Textured Life of Embodiment* (Toronto: University of Toronto Press, 2007), 26.

Texts, then, do not simply represent, but also generate, influence, and reveal meanings of the body, including possibilities for how embodied subjects and social relations might be made to "come to life."[2] This chapter places the Americans with Disabilities Act (ADA) in conversation with Karen Tei Yamashita's *Through the Arc of the Rainforest* and Hubert Haddad's *Desirable Body* to consider what speculative genres tell us about the systems and structures that shape disability, including the ways in which it is made to "come to life"—and for whom—in the context of free-market capitalism.

After introducing the history, key terms, and analytical frames that inform my analysis, I take up *Through the Arc of the Rainforest*. Against a multi-national backdrop of precarity and vulnerability manufactured by the U.S., I argue that Yamashita's novel elucidates the capacitating, market logics that undergird "qualified" or "protected" disability. I then turn to *Desirable Body* to foreground how the constant expansion of bodymind capacity—driven, in part, by transnational flows and investments in biomedical and technological advancement—aids in the (re)distribution of health and wealth to the elite. Read together with the ADA, these sf novels reveal the ways in which disability "comes to life" through its incorporation into market and state structures, question the efficacy of rights discourses on a global scale, and caution against positioning disability as uniquely disruptive to consumer culture and the neoliberal state.

Historical Context and Key Terms

The argument I forward in this chapter necessarily relies on an understanding of the social, political, and economic landscape surrounding the ratification of the ADA. Signed into law on July 26, 1990, by President George H. W. Bush, the ADA expanded protections for disabled people previously introduced in Section 504 of the 1973 Rehabilitation Act. Whereas Section 504 prohibited entities receiving federal financial assistance from excluding, denying, or discriminating against disabled individuals, the ADA sought to secure this protection on a wider scale, largely by implementing it across private entities. Defining disability as "a physical or mental impairment that substantially limits one or more major life activity," the ADA figured disability quite broadly, encompassing previous records of impairment and anyone "regarded as having a disability," and has since attained greater flexibility through the ADA Amendments Act of 2008 (ADAAA).[3]

---

[2] Titchkosky, *Reading and Writing*, 26.

[3] Americans with Disabilities Act of 1990, S.933, 101st Congress, 42 U.S.C. § 12101 (1990).

At the time of its passage, many believed the ADA would accomplish pivotal change, adding to existing "formal and structural models of equality" not only "by imposing both a duty of accommodation and a duty of nondiscrimination," but also by "regulating health and safety risk analysis in situations involving disabled employees or applicants, and extending these protections to a rather wide class."[4] Against stereotypes that equated disability with an inability to work, a major component surrounded the employability of a sizable group of Americans who could, through "reasonable accommodations," actively participate in and contribute to society.[5] As the decades following its passage have demonstrated, however, this legislation has failed to realize the sweeping social advancements many believed it would achieve. While some cite the difficulties that accompany broad legal definitions as well as long-held misconceptions about disability, Lennard J. Davis draws attention to the disjuncture between the law and lived experience and the many barriers that prevent disabled people from accessing a cumbersome and expensive legal process. Other scholars who take up anti-discrimination law and rights discourses, however, explain why these recourses ultimately remain ineffectual. Addressing this "difficult relation" as it specifically pertains to women's rights and feminist goals in the U.S., Wendy Brown argues that "rights that entail some specification of our suffering, injury, or inequality lock us into the identity defined by our subordination, while rights that eschew this specificity not only sustain the invisibility of our subordination, but potentially even enhance it."[6] This relation occurs, as Brown continues to explain, because of the power of regulatory and normative dimensions of identity-based rights as well as the ways in which economic arrangements enhance and limit this power.[7]

Attending to the larger context surrounding the ratification of the ADA helps to further clarify this relationship. Significantly, Bush's passage of the ADA took place not only during an economic recession, but also between his veto of several bills that intended to address social and economic concerns, from his refusal to raise the minimum wage to his rejection of both the Family and Medical Leave Act (FMLA) and the Civil Rights Bill of 1990.[8] Government officials and corporations criticized each of these bills, claiming they would

---

[4] Linda Hamilton Krieger, ed. *Backlash Against the ADA: Reinterpreting Disability Rights* (Ann Arbor: The University of Michigan Press, 2003), 5.

[5] 42 U.S.C. § 12101.

[6] Wendy Brown, "Suffering Rights as Paradoxes," *Constellations: An International Journal of Critical and Democratic Theory*, 7, no. 2 (June 2000): 231-2, Wiley Online Library.

[7] Brown, "Suffering Rights," 232-233.

[8] Krieger, *Backlash*, 1.

create impediments to economic growth and financial hardships for businesses. Though the ADA, as with previous disability legislation, received similar critiques, it garnered incredible support from several major corporations, members of Bush's administration, and conservative senators such as Republican cosponsor Orrin Hatch as well as Senator Bob Dole.[9] This range of support has long been attributed to the prevalence of disability, including among political leaders and their families.[10] While familiarity may have played a role, I attribute much of this bipartisan backing to the ADA's fusing of liberal individualism with economic governance: neoliberal privatization and individualism fit neatly with the Disability Rights Movement's calls for autonomy and inclusion in the workforce and celebratory narratives of identity and pride, while also incorporating disabled subjects into market and state structures.

For scholars like Nirmala Erevelles, Helen Meekosha, and Jasbir Puar, who urge for more nuanced analyses of disability, this process of recognition participates in injurious and fatal processes—including slavery, (neo)colonialism, war, resource extraction, and other modes of exploitation—that (re)route privilege and power to the (white, often Western) elite. For Puar, liberal disability rights function as a framework of "capacitation" that legitimate "some disabilities at the expense of others that do not fit the respectability and empowerment model of disability progress."[11] Life-making and life-affirming capacitation demonstrates how economic governance makes certain disabled subjectivities possible in relation to debilitating and deadly processes. Rethinking disability as inextricably linked to debilitation and capacitation, as Puar does, reveals how disability can easily become "that body or subject that can aspire both economically and emotionally to wellness, empowerment, and pride through the exceptionalized status it accrues."[12] Rewarding those who seek market-condoned forms of self-investment and autonomy, those deemed "qualified" for protection by the ADA signify subjects who can participate in society according to the economic logics of inclusion that affirm the life of some populations at the violent expense of others.

---

[9] Krieger, *Backlash*, 1. See also Sharon N. Barnartt and Richard K Scotch, *Disability Protests: Contentious Politics, 1970-1999* (Washington, D.C.: Gaullaudet University Press, 2001).

[10] Media coverage and scholarship often cite congressional sponsor, Senator Harkin's d/Deaf brother, President H. W. Bush's children and brother, Senator Hatch's brother-in-law, and Representative Coelho's own experience with epilepsy. Access, for instance, Krieger, *Backlash*, Barnett and Scotch, *Disability Protests*.

[11] Jasbir K. Puar, *The Right to Maim: Debility, Capacity, Disability* (Durham: Duke University Press, 2017), xvii.

[12] Puar, *Right to Maim*, xvi.

Despite acknowledging the possibilities Puar's model adds for decentering white, Western experiences of disability, the field has questioned its application. David Mitchell and Sharon Snyder, for instance, posit that Puar forwards a "disability studies without disability,"[13] while Robert McRuer, despite agreeing with many of Puar's arguments, claims that debility "often puts forward a unidirectional move away from 'disability' that . . . tames its complex political valences."[14] Informing disability legislation across the globe, as well as the United Nation's international Convention on the Rights of Persons with Disabilities, the ADA's reach has undoubtedly impacted many who identify with the disability community. Certainly, accessibility—including what the ADA makes possible for those who can achieve this protected status— involves "things we cannot not want."[15] However, the novels I analyze herein demonstrate how "qualified" disability coheres and adheres to those most capable of seamless incorporation into state and market structures. *Through the Arc of the Rainforest* and *Desirable Body* importantly foreground how neoliberal frameworks of empowerment and identity too easily perpetuate and erase the violent and relational production of injury and death across global contexts. As such, this chapter is interested in how reading speculative novels with the ADA exposes the economic entanglements of the legal, political, medical, and cultural definitions of disability as they circulate and reproduce in and beyond the United States. The figures I analyze reveal how disability often fails to address experiences of privilege and precarity elided by neoliberal discourses of individual responsibility, self-investment, privatization, and market freedom.

Crucially, applying a relational framework of disability, debility, and capacity to contemporary sf elucidates how these market logics actively disguise policies that ultimately serve to prioritize economic "health" and normalize the precarious conditions produced through reorganizations of wealth and political power to the capitalist elite. Disability studies must remain committed to a disruption of "dominant ways of knowing disability" that takes up the ways in which the concept of disability and the field are in and of themselves hegemonic projects.[16] For speculative genres that strive to destabilize

---

[13] David T. Mitchell and Sharon L. Snyder, "Is the Study of Debility Akin to Disability Studies without Disability?" *GLQ* 25, no. 4 (2019): 665.

[14] Robert McRuer, *Crip Times: Disability, Globalization, and Resistance* (New York: New York University Press, 2018), 242 n32.

[15] Brown, "Suffering Rights," 231.

[16] Sharon L. Snyder and David T. Mitchell, *Cultural Locations of Disability* (Chicago: The University of Chicago Press, 2006), 4. Scholars from within and beyond the field continue

normative embodiment and geographic space-time, a willingness to embrace multiple terms can better account for systems and processes that do not cohere to disability as it is currently understood through identity and empowerment. As Sami Schalk asserts, we need "language that can effectively express the theoretical insights of [the texts]" we engage.[17] Sf's imagining of future worlds and alternative approaches to aspects of corporeal life emphasize why reading for representations of disability *with* debility and capacity, as Puar urges, can contend more justly with systems that reproduce the body through violent means and to violent ends. If sf indeed challenges our understandings of the world by elucidating the forces that inform how we come to know and (re)produce the body, we need terminology and frameworks that can more adequately engage the violent systems that construct our embodied realities.

(Re)Reading the "Qualified" Body: Capital & Capacity

Karen Tei Yamashita's *Through the Arc of the Rainforest* and Hubert Haddad's *Desirable Body* feature characters whose nonnormative bodies and embodied experiences problematize core understandings of disability. Both also share many structural and thematic similarities, offering sharp critiques of overlapping historical and ongoing exploitative enterprises. Consequently, these novels emphasize how disability reimaginings do not escape the commodification of the disabled body, underscoring the need to push beyond resignifying disability—including ableist ways of knowing disability—to examine how liberal rights and celebratory discourses amplify precarious conditions on a global scale. I foreground the relational production of debility and capacity as a form of violent bodily enterprise that can be analyzed *with* but not always *as* a metaphorical and/or material invocation of disability in a neoliberal era. The proliferation of subject positions and perspectives in *Through the Arc of the Rainforest* and *Desirable Body* present an abundant opportunity for analyses of this sort; both feature characters with identifiable disabilities as well as nonnormative embodiments that trouble these markers. This—in addition to their futuristic and magical, yet recognizable and timely, worlds—demonstrates the

---

to draw attention to whitewashing of disability and disability history. See Christopher Bell, "Introducing White Disability Studies," in *The Disability Studies Reader*, 2nd edition, ed, Lennard J Davis (New York: Routledge, 2006), 275-282. See also Angel L. Miles, Akemi Nishida, and Anjali J. Forber-Pratt, "An Open Letter to White Disability Studies and Ableist Institutions of Higher Education," *Disability Studies Quarterly* 37, no. 3 (Summer 2017), https://doi.org/10.18061/dsq.v37i3.

[17] Sami Schalk, *Bodyminds Reimagined: (Dis)Ability, Race, and Gender in Black Women's Speculative Fiction* (Durham: Duke University Press, 2018), 5.

value in reading for what Michael Bérubé terms "deployments" of disability.[18] As Bérubé explains, deployments push beyond representation and identity to reveal the narrative functions of "*ideas about* disability, and ideas about the stigma associated with disability, regardless of whether any specific character can be pegged with a specific diagnosis."[19] And, I would add, embodied subjectivities relational to, yet strategically excluded from, disability status.

In what follows, I limit my scope to transnational enterprise and social capital as forms of privilege in *Through the Arc of the Rainforest* that capacitate J.B. Tweep and Michelle Mabelle, figures whose mutated bodies feature three appendages. My approach to capacitation in *Desirable Body* focuses on Cédric Erg's access to experimental—and potentially revolutionary—medical care, a privilege which results from his family's transnational corporate wealth. At the same time, however, these biomedical innovations produce immense physical and emotional pain for Cédric and lead him to question the nature of not only the human bodymind, but also biomedical advancement and rights themselves. The experiences these characters navigate reveal the ways in which disability can be capacitated—or made to "come to life" as a form of capacitation—when "instrumentalized by state discourses of inclusion," as well as how state and market discourses exploit others and force them into structures that further disable, debilitate, and kill.[20]

Through the Arc of the Rainforest

Despite the proliferation of bodily variance across Yamashita's works, her oeuvre has received little attention from the field of disability studies. Published within weeks of the ratification of the ADA, *Through the Arc of the Rainforest* directly attends to capacity, disability, and debility produced and sustained through the convergence of liberal individualism and economic governance. Importantly, the novel demonstrates how free-market capitalism upholds *homo oeconomicus* and consumer identity as normative, thereby figuring the "qualified" disabled bodymind as an economic subject easily folded into the market and state structures.

Retold as a memory by a sentient plastic ball attached in orbit to Kazumasa Ishimaru's forehead, *Through the Arc of the Rainforest* narrates the overlapping experiences of a group of characters from the U.S., France, Japan, and Brazil

---

[18] Michael Bérubé, *The Secret Life of Stories: From Don Quixote to Harry Potter, How Understanding Intellectual Disability Transforms the Way We Read* (New York City: New York University Press, 2016), 2.

[19] Bérubé, *Secret Life*, 19.

[20] Puar, *Right to Maim*, xiv.

whose storylines converge in the Amazon basin. Together, their narratives describe the impacts of neoliberal principles of deregulation, privatization, and individualism. In addition to the privatization of the Japanese national railroad system, the ball describes the global exploitation of people and natural resources primarily perpetuated by GGG Enterprises, a major transnational American corporation headquartered in the "world capital" of New York City.[21]

Much critical engagement with *Through the Arc of the Rainforest* necessarily prioritizes the novel's rendering of Western imperialism's exploitative legacies, extractive colonial and neocolonial enterprises, devastating environmental degradation, and transnational U.S. corporate power by focusing on the mass commodification of local healing feathers and the Matacão, a tree-barren stretch of the southern Amazon rainforest later revealed to be densely compressed, commodifiable plastic waste. Worshipped and fought over, people around the world hail the Matacão as a "divine place" due to its (temporarily) unexplainable powers, with corporations, churches and local governments seeking to "capitalize" on its potential to generate profit.[22] These examinations necessarily take up J.B. Tweep, the American with three arms and eventual CEO of GGG Enterprises, who soon monopolizes the plastic makeup of the Matacão and grows "the Feather" into a sensational global consumer product "akin to Coca-Cola."[23] Nesrin Yavaş, for instance, likens the function of J.B.'s extraordinary third arm to "the tentacles of an octopus ready to grasp and exploit any opportunity, whether it be natural resources or human beings."[24] T. De Loughry echoes this assessment, reading J.B.'s third arm as the embodiment of "the adaptive, octopoid expanse of U.S. multinational corporations in Latin America and their perpetual tentacular search for new and evermore resources, labor and energy frontiers throughout the continent."[25] In focusing solely on J.B.'s metaphorical function, however, most criticism foregoes attention to his early chapters. Beginning with his introduction, I wish to consider what his

---

[21] Karen Tei Yamashita, *Through the Arc of the Rainforest* (Minneapolis: Coffee House Press, 1990), 14.

[22] Yamashita, *Through the Arc*, 43.

[23] Yamashita, *Through the Arc*, 69.

[24] Nesrin Yavaş, "Ecocriticism and Magical Realism *in Karen Tei Yamashita's Through the Arc of the Rainforest," Journal of Awareness* 3, no. 1 (2018): 3-4, https://doi.org/10.26809/joa.2018.3.

[25] Treasa De Loughry, "Petromodernity, Petro-Finance, and Plastic in Karen Tei Yamashita's *Through the Arc of the Rainforest," Journal of Postcolonial Writing* 53, no. 3 (2017): 337, https://doi.org/10.1080/17449855.2017.1337685.

third arm offers to an analysis that additionally considers the production of disability, debility, and capacity through the economic logic of the ADA.

Described by the buzzing ball simply as the "unassuming Caucasian male American" living in "the great economic capital of the world, New York," readers first encounter J.B. as he prepares to interview for an entry-level job with GGG.[26] In contrast to other figures in the novel, his characterization remains largely superficial and impersonal as a "dilettante" who has continually sought new employment because of perpetual boredom with job responsibilities for which he is "overqualified."[27] Inquiring about the "secret" to his unmatched efficiency, J.B. casually reveals his third arm to the GGG employee interviewing him, who responds, "Oh well, Jonathan, of course. . . . We are an equal opportunity employer. We employ our personnel regardless of color, creed, or handicap."[28] This response initially appears to assume J.B.'s status as disabled through her outdated use of the term "handicap," given that his characterizations already position him as a white American without any particular creed. In so doing, the GGG employee portrays how, under the ADA, "qualified" status can include anyone "regarded as having" an impairment. Positioning J.B. as a "special case" to her boss, however, the interviewer ironically disrupts the mainstream discourses of disability as "special needs" to instead foreshadow the ways in which J.B.'s body will serve to advance the company's productivity and profit.[29] Her reflection that J.B. will "even things up" following GGG's recent hire of a Vietnam veteran with one arm underscores the economic logic of equal opportunity and anti-discrimination policy in the neoliberal workplace. Rather than meaningfully change the system, GGG's approach to J.B.'s third arm exposes how attempts to "level the playing field" and achieve inclusion, whether framed through liberal rights, multiculturalism, or diversity, ultimately function to encode subjects according to their capacity to produce profit. As Schalk notes, "disability is sometimes jokingly referred to as an equal opportunity minority category—the only one anyone can join instantly at any moment."[30] Yet, this sentiment, along with the claim that everyone will become disabled if they live long enough, occludes the targeting of racialized populations for debilitation or death and the prevention of access to disability identity or protected status.[31]

---

[26] Yamashita, *Through the Arc,* 28, 15.

[27] Yamashita, *Through the Arc,* 28-30.

[28] Yamashita, *Through the Arc,* 28-30.

[29] Yamashita, *Through the Arc,* 30.

[30] Schalk, *Bodyminds,* 51.

[31] Puar, *Right to Maim,* xiv.

As GGG's "singular control" of market niches and "skyrocketing stocks on Wall Street" propel J.B. into celebrity, his marriage to Michelle Mabelle, a French ornithologist with three breasts, becomes a media sensation.[32] Their relationship arouses curiosity and appeal, soon causing hundreds of individuals to openly reveal their own extra appendages: "These people, suddenly liberated by J.B. and Michelle's obvious success and fame, congregated in large and small groups to proclaim their rights before a society that had relegated them to freak shows [and] turned out to be an enormous and heretofore unknown contingency for politicians to respond to."[33] The Trialectics Movement, as it becomes known, mirrors much of the important work advocated by the Disability Rights Movement (DRM) and ongoing activist efforts, particularly the dismantling of stereotypes that view disabled subjects as deserving pity, lacking agency, or in need of rehabilitation. However, the ways in which Michelle and J.B. participate in and/or distance themselves from the community speak to the ways in which disability identity and inclusion become sutured to a particular neoliberal subjectivity reconceived as a series of self-investing entrepreneurial units or "field of enterprises."[34]

Michelle supports the Trialectics Movement through monetary donations and speaking engagements that commodify her body. Like others in the three-appendaged population, she proudly displays her third breast. Transformed into the representative figure of the Trialectics Movement, Michelle's sexuality and changing outlook positions her as a neoliberal subject qualified for self-investment and reproduction. Her creation of a customized clothing line with Paris fashion designers, intended to "promote her special attributes," not only forecloses the creation of sustainable and affordable clothing for the varied manifestation of third appendages within the trialectic population, but also underscores gendered notions of desirability and consumption.[35] Paired with her paid speaking engagements for the Movement, Michelle shows how neoliberal forms of inclusion celebrate certain embodiments of disability, commodify diversity, as well as generate new forms of exclusion.

Unlike Michelle, J.B. identifies with GGG's advanced corporate sphere, regarding himself as "one of the more privileged human beings, a more advanced specimen. It was only a matter of time, to him, before other human beings with only two arms or two breasts would begin to feel inadequate."[36] His

---

[32] Yamashita, *Through the Arc,* 123.

[33] Yamashita, *Through the Arc,* 159.

[34] Wendy Brown, *Undoing the Demos* (Brooklyn: Zone Press, 2016), 66.

[35] Yamashita, *Through the Arc,* 159.

[36] Yamashita, *Through the Arc,* 159.

outlook underscores his own capacity in relation to masculinity and white American identity, compounding the commodification of his corporeality. He perceives his third arm as advantageous, narrating its effects as akin to extrasensory perception or "an addition of 128K to [an individual's] random access or the invention of the wheel."[37] His value as an individual directly correlates to the value his body generates: "As far as J.B. was concerned, he had entered a new genetic plane in his species. . . . He was a better model, the wave of the future."[38] More than a mere metaphor for post-Fordist production, J.B.'s third arm demonstrates how neoliberalism reconceives social policy, including liberal rights, as only and always economic growth. As an economic actor, his sense of self embodies the extension of market rationality to all aspects of existence, as "a whole way of being and thinking" and "a general style of thought, analysis, and imagination," including the ways in which individuals are made to conceive of themselves and social relations.[39]

Though written before social media corporations such as Facebook and Twitter, J.B.'s name echoes how "retweets," "likes," and "followers" reproduce social capital,[40] and exemplifies how people are expected to be human capital not just for themselves, but also for the corporation. The capacity and control J.B. achieves as a result of his third arm convey how the body becomes endowed with what Michel Foucault recognizes as "capital-ability": the human as "a machine constituted by . . . ability and worker individually bound together . . . as a sort of enterprise in himself."[41] J.B.'s view of himself, informed not only by his third arm but also his white American citizenship and economic status, depicts one of the many ways free-market capitalism reshapes ideas about the human body.

Indeed, despite experiencing a weakening of his third arm while in Brazil, the Latin Americans J.B. interacts with respond to it as a form of capacitation: compared to those in the U.S. who, prior to his fame, referred to J.B. as a "freak of nature," those he encounters in Brazil respond by thinking, "Americans

---

[37] Yamashita, *Through the Arc*, 30.

[38] Yamashita, *Through the Arc*, 30.

[39] Michel Foucault, *The Birth of Biopolitics: Lectures at the Collège de France, 1978-79*, trans Graham Burchell (New York City: Picador, 2004), 218-219. See also Brown, *Undoing*.

[40] J.B. Tweep's name not only rhymes with "tweet," a connection that becomes pronounced through Michelle's previous career as an ornithologist and the prevalence of birds in the novel, but also resonates with the term "tweep(s)," used to define a prominent individual's Twitter followers.

[41] Foucault, *Birth of Biopolitics*, 225.

certainly were more advanced!"[42] Locating this advancement at the level of the
body satirically draws our attention to the ways in which free-market
capitalism profits from rights discourses and conceals economic disparity, as
not everyone experiences the privileges afforded to J.B. and Michelle. This
disparity is particularly highlighted when Brazilians with three thumbs
congregate in the basement karaoke bar to sing "protest songs" chanting, "We
shall overcome the use of one more thumb."[43] Often critiqued as a trope within
sf narratives, discourses of overcoming third appendages refocus our attention
to the difference between the J.B. and Michelle's experiences and those who
may not qualify for the privileges afforded by the incorporation of exceptional
bodies. Unlike neoliberalism's claim that hard work rewards equally, the
Brazilian laborers with three thumbs problematize white American and
Western exceptionality, as well as the co-constitutive nature of neoliberalism
and social categories. While the U.S.-imposed economic relationship with
Latin America manifests in the unaffordability of basic necessities and poor
working and living conditions, hunger, hallucinations, and mass disease, the
eventual typhus pandemic, brought on through GGG's global commodification
of the feather and Matacão plastic, devastates humanity and wildlife as J.B.
remains in his penthouse suite.

Global in focus, *Through the Arc of the Rainforest* demonstrates how this
affects bodies across various national contexts, but it remains necessary to
acknowledge that numerous people in the U.S. do not "qualify" for
accommodations, cannot afford legal representation, and/or cannot access
adequate medical care and necessities. The couple's different relationships to
their bodies, embodied experiences, and the trialectic community depict two
separate though interrelated aspects of capacitation that I have thus far tried to
elucidate by reading sf with the ADA. Neoliberalism reframes the management
of populations and the conduct of individuals through economic logic. In doing
so, it brings about new subject formations, as shown with the figures in
Through the Arc of the Rainforest, as well as a restructured relationship between
the market and the state, in which the state operates wholly in service of the
market. As such, it is no surprise that the state itself becomes notably absent
following the demise of Japan's national transit system at the beginning of the
novel. J.B.'s third arm thus also renders legible the "invisible hand" of the
market in its depiction of both the rationale and the mechanisms that animate
and structure the rerouting of wealth upward through what David Harvey

[42] Yamashita, *Through the Arc,* 74.
[43] Yamashita, *Through the Arc,* 175.

deems accumulation by dispossession.[44] The consequences of the organizing principles of free-market capitalism, directly tied to J.B. Tweep's third arm, remain unmistakable: new and increasing forms of inequity and inequality for those who still experience legacies of Western imperialism, structural adjustments facilitated by the World Bank and International Monetary Fund, and the (re)making of the neoliberal subject.

The ADA's neoliberal fusing of classical liberalism and economic governance functions with this "hidden hand" as it animates discourses of pride that commodify diversity, advocates for capacity endowed by the market, and occludes the debilitating effects experienced by global populations who are prevented from accessing such accommodations or for whom such accommodations may be deemed inapplicable. *Through the Arc of the Rainforest* depicts how a privatized, free-market economy capacitates the white American and European characters while simultaneously intensifying vulnerable situations through transnational U.S. markets, resource extraction, and a global pandemic. The highly visible bodies of Michelle and J.B. Tweep shift from "defects" and "freaks of nature" to bodies endowed with capacity in the form of capital and desire through their incorporation into the market. No longer attached to an "ideal" corporeality or valued for functioning like an efficient machine, their capacitated subject-positions demonstrate how the norm, in neoliberal societies, is (re)produced and fluctuates through logics of self-investment and economic growth that at once constitute and commodify disability subjectivity.[45]

Desirable Body

Translated from the French by Alyson Waters, Hubert Haddad's *Desirable Body* primarily follows Cédric Erg after he experiences a life-altering injury. An investigative journalist who substantiates conspiracies of violence perpetuated through "industry, finance, and politics" with "undeniable proof," Cédric endures continuous threats and harmful attempts from those he exposes.[46] While aboard a boat during a vacation in Greece with his romantic partner, Lorna, a steel beam falls from the crow's nest, landing directly atop Cédric's back. Later revealed to be a deliberate plan concocted by one of the many nefarious corporations he has ousted, Cédric is placed on life support. Despite

---

[44] David Harvey, *The New Imperialism* (New York City: Oxford University Press, 2003).

[45] Lennard J. Davis, *Bending Over Backwards: Disability, Dismodernism and Other Difficult Positions* (New York City: New York University Press, 2002), 39.

[46] Hubert Haddad, *Desirable Body*, trans. Alyson Waters (New Haven: Yale University Press, 2018), 30.

his estrangement from his father—and his father's fortune, acquired through M.A.W. Laboratories, the most powerful pharmaceutical conglomerate in the world—Cédric becomes the first recipient of a full-body transplant precisely due to his family's wealth and connection.

Desirable Body explores how the convergence between the reconsolidation of wealth and health to the elite and the expansion of the life sciences since the 1970s has crafted and normalized new concepts of the human body and life itself. Focusing on increasingly limited access to medical care in relation to so-called consumer "health care," the novel elucidates how biomedical technology continues to remake and expand what counts as living well and who can access this privilege. Offering a complex depiction of the relationship between medical science, technological advancement, and disability, the novel importantly questions how the systems that structure our world reshape and govern "life itself" through the (re)distribution of both wealth *and* health to the elite. In doing so, it clarifies how the state and market become fused as a governing system through which corporations and nations increase their power by profiting from the "vital capacities" of living beings.[47] While certainly not without flaws, which include tropic depictions of both Cédric after his accident and his coworker with Asperger syndrome, I focus my attention on the novel's portrayal of structural violence and the free-market (bio)economy.

Along with the restoration of wealth and power to the elite in the 1970s through free-market policy, the late twentieth century also marked, according to Kaushik Sunder Rajan, the "coproduction of new types of science and technology and changes in the legal, regulatory, and market structures that organized the conduct around technoscience."[48] In other words, since the 1970s, the freeing of capital for unrestrained accumulation in the interest of the wealthy elite has become increasingly attached to a market of body parts and tissues that, through both public and private investment, capacitate, debilitate, and disable by transforming the corporeal body into (bio)capital. Broadly understood as "circuits of exchange [which] have as their organizing principle the capturing of the latent value in biological processes, a value that is simultaneously that of human health and that of economic growth," the bioeconomy becomes central to the normalization of consumer health practices.[49]

---

[47] Nikolas Rose, *The Politics of Life Itself: Biomedicine, Power, and Subjectivity in the Twenty-First Century* (Princeton: Princeton University Press, 2007), 33.

[48] Kaushik Sunder Rajan, *Biocapital: The Constitution of Postgenomic Life* (Durham: Duke University Press, 2006), 5.

[49] Rose, *Politics of Life*, 32-3.

Desirable Body illustrates this fusion of biology, technoscience, and the economy through its interrogation of biomedical and pharmaceutical industries.

Invoking Mary Shelley's *Frankenstein,* regarded as one of the first sf novels, *Desirable Body*'s prologue foreshadows man's unending quest for immortality through scientific advancement: "Everything that science has promised us will inevitably come to pass. In probable conjunction with bionics, transplant surgery will be able to reconstitute an entire person." [50] By exposing the increased proximity between the world of reality and that of sf, the novel exemplifies the genre's aptitude for critiquing the "cadaverous dream[s]" of the wealthy and politically powerful.[51] Marketed as "dystopian fantasy," *Desirable Body* also invites comparisons to a range of notable sf works that feature the human body as a profitable resource to be metaphorically or materially broken down into discrete purchasable units. From Andrew Niccol's *Gattaca* and Leslie Marmon Silko's *Almanac of the Dead* to Kazuo Ishiguro's *Never Let Me Go* and Margaret Atwood's *The Handmaid's Tale,* cultural productions in this sect of sf depict how the body becomes "a potentially discrete, knowable and exploitable reservoir of molecular and biochemical products and events" for biomedical and technological industries.[52]

As *Desirable Body* makes clear, however, not everyone can access this capacitation. Drawing on the history of racialized biomedical targeting, the novel offers an unmistakable critique of the medical-industrial complex and the pharmaceutical industry's role in reproducing debility and disability as it continually expands what bodies—and even life itself—should be like, look like, and do. Following Cédric's procedure, media reports continually raise the potential for "transplant tourism" and a "transplant trade" enterprise imagined as "comparable to the slave trade."[53] By making this explicit comparison, the novel stresses the ways in which speculative markets are designed according to the historical targeting and objectification of racialized populations. For Michael Davidson, organ sale narratives are arguably "*the* allegory of globalization" because of how the body's components become commodities "exchanged in a worldwide market that mirrors the structural inequality between wealth and poverty."[54] The opportunities imagined by entrepreneurs and doctors alike

---

[50] Haddad, *Desirable Body,* 5.

[51] Haddad, *Desirable Body,* 105.

[52] Paul Rabinow, *Essays on the Anthropology of Reason* (Princeton: Princeton University Press, 1996), 149.

[53] Haddad, *Desirable Body,* 104.

[54] Michael Davidson, *Concerto for the Left Hand: Disability and the Defamiliar Body* (Ann Arbor: University of Michigan Press, 2008), 198.

following Cédric's full-body transplant showcase the desires for wealth and power that serve to drive both the expansion of the bioeconomy and the customization of the body to avoid death, as though it is "nothing but a virus to be neutralized, a programming error."[55] Though the novel forwards this "error" explicitly in relation to death, the causes and processes of the body's breakdown and expiration fundamentally invoke disability and aging, both of which already fuel current biomedical pursuits.

Indeed, as the novel makes clear, Cédric's story would have remained "a minor news item" had it not involved vital implications for the "future of humanity."[56] Yet, this future resides in the creation of new (bio)markets that Cedric's surgery makes possible. As the arbiter of ethics under neoliberalism, the market not only remakes health, but also the dimensions of life itself, as living well becomes attainable only through an individual's capacity as an economic actor. Nadine Ehlers and Shiloh Krupar attend at length to the formative role of biomedical targeting and organ trafficking in this market, describing "a bio-economy of body parts" which "has expanded transnationally to service biotech enterprises and new cadaver-sourced bioproducts . . . challenging the definition and limits of the proper use of the corpse."[57] Highlighting the ever-growing speculative markets that rely on and reproduce injury and death, *Desirable Body* reveals the disparity between basic medical care as it is remade according to profit-driven consumer healthcare fads. For those who cannot afford consumer healthcare, the body and its various parts become opportunities for profit, targeted as commodities to be exchanged in new and violent ways.

For nearly a decade prior to his injury, Cédric worked as an investigative columnist for a renowned news magazine, ousting "predatory industries" within the medical-industrial complex as well as oil companies and politicians referred to as "those jesters, investors, and other fat cats."[58] His unrelenting dedication to the violence perpetuated by the pharmaceutical industry, a consequence of his billionaire father's company and role in this industry, unveils the market's role as "an international crime organization responsible for the pathological alienation of just about all the world's peoples with the heinous complicity of governments and public health services."[59] However, Cédric's father, Morice, refuses to acknowledge his responsibility in reproducing

---

[55] Haddad, *Desirable,* 104.

[56] Haddad, *Desirable Body,* 14.

[57] Nadine Ehlers and Shiloh Krupar, *Deadly Biocultures: The Ethics of Life-Making* (Minneapolis: University of Minnesota Press, 2019), 142.

[58] Haddad, *Desirable Body,* 15-16.

[59] Haddad, *Desirable Body,* 117.

this wide-scale exploitation and suffering. As Morice explains to Lorna, he is "merely a cog in the machine" whose "company depends on, but does not control, an industrial holding company whose sole aim is to expand its interest."[60] Morice further distances his own role—as well as other powerful, wealthy actors—from culpability by rewriting the invisible hand of the market as "millions of watch hands" operating without "a watchmaker." [61] These millions of hands thus serve to represent the effects of neoliberal rationality and governance, which obscure structural violence by advancing the false notion that livelihood, and one's means of purchasing it, results from individual choice and responsibility.

Cédric's initial reporting and ongoing news headlines throughout the novel reveal how this individualization, along with privatization and deregulation, continues to drive the systems and processes that frame and offer these choices at the expense of populations deemed expendable by the market. The news stories, which range from devastating oil spills in Nigeria to the "testing of previously untested and often toxic molecules on impoverished people in Africa and Latin America," [62] call attention to the attendant production of privilege and oppression. The purposeful maiming that allows for the circulation of trafficked body parts and knowledge about the body exemplify how "[h]uman rights violations are not accidents; they are not random in distribution or effect. Rights violations are, rather, symptoms of deeper pathologies of power and are linked intimately to the social conditions that so often determine who will suffer abuse and who will be shielded from harm."[63] Access to petroleum and prescription medicine for some, as in the aforementioned examples, make capacitation possible through the purposeful debilitation of others across the globe. While this can take shape through what popular media—often owned by corporate elite—identify as "accidents," powerful actors, like Morice, also manipulate catastrophes to further entrench the free-market economy's deadly hold.[64]

Across the events depicted in the novel, readers witness Cédric transform from person to body to patient to commodity. After his transplant, he lives in a state of uncertainty and constantly questions what he should now call himself, as well as how his new body changes his freedom and humanity. Asking

---

[60] Haddad, *Desirable Body,* 118.

[61] Haddad, *Desirable Body,* 118-119.

[62] Haddad, *Desirable Body,* 118.

[63] Paul Farmer, *Pathologies of Power Health, Human Rights, and the New War on the Poor* (Berkeley: University of California Press, 2003), 7.

[64] For more on the profitability of "the accident" see Puar, *Right to Maim.*

whether "natural, inalienable, and sacred" rights still apply, he draws attention to possible shifts in the meaning of "rights" themselves and their applicability when faced with increasing changes to the body and life through the bioeconomy.[65] By posing these questions, he underscores the ways in which neoliberalism promotes a "disembodied approach to human rights" that fails to account for the ways in which "[p]ower materially shapes the body."[66] Importantly, Cédric's postsurgical care requires an intense medication regimen and troubles the use of medical science and technological development as a seamless and straightforward "cure-all" for disability. The difficult recovery that follows Cédric's original transplant and multiple additional surgeries necessitates countless prescription drugs to ease his pain and prevent the rejection of his transplant body. Though he questions what constitutes a livable life, and in the process, reproduces many ableist notions disability scholars contest, he demonstrates the need to reckon with the material reality of pain. Moreover, his complicated recovery depicts the experience of many disabled and d/Deaf people who decide to pursue cochlear implants, utilize prosthetic limbs, and navigate the complexity of medication regimens. Resisting sf's tendency to laud depictions of technological and biomedical innovations through inaccurate portrayals of immediate cure, *Desirable Body* emphasizes the overlooked realities of recovery, rehabilitation, and even acculturation that can follow surgical procedures and medication adjustments, while also highlighting the debilitation that facilitates capacitating drugs, devices, and other commodities.

Whereas Cédric's own pain problematizes understandings of the body biomedically endowed with previously unattainable capacities, his access to advanced medical goods and services contrasts the violent remaking of the bodymind through ongoing colonial legacies and neocolonial projects for communities he covers in his reporting. Rather than minimizing Cédric's own suffering, I seek to draw attention to the inapplicability of rights to those who are targeted for purposeful debilitation. As Helen Meekosha and Karen Soldatic explain, international human rights treaties, informed by the ADA, continue to "fail to address issues of the distribution of wealth and power, and wealth has not historically been redistributed without struggle on the part of the powerless."[67] Even as definitions of disability circulate, access to appropriate and affordable medical care—and sometimes cure—becomes more complicated

[65] Haddad, *Desirable Body,*166.

[66] Michael Gill and Cathy J. Schlund-Vials, eds., *Disability, Human Rights, and the Limits of Humanitarianism* (Burlington: Ashgate Publishing, 2014), 19.

[67] Helen Meekosha and Karen Soldatic, "Human Rights and the Global South: The Case of Disability," *Third World Quarterly* 32, no. 8 (2011): 1389, https://doi.org/10.1080/01436 597.2011.614800.

than simply adjudicating between medical and social models of disability, requiring consideration of, for example, which populations will be more likely to experience pain and have access to treatment.

Thus, his recovery equally signifies how compulsory able-bodiedness shifts according to the logics of profitability: neoliberalism maintains and extends the capacitation of populations who can afford to participate in consumer healthcare and medications that offer ongoing daily "cures." The specialized hospitals where Cédric's surgery and recovery take place, optimized for maximum celebrity privacy, as well as his suitcase of prescriptions that keep him alive, expose the self-investment and management that lead to capacitated, economic subjectivity.

Conclusion

In this chapter, I have argued that reading disability rights and sf together can reveal how laws like the ADA capacitate certain bodyminds through an uneven distribution of "qualified" status made possible through the purposeful debilitation of bodies deemed otherwise disposable. Speculative genres help uncover and critically contend with the abstraction of our present reality by identifying and defamiliarizing systemic violence perpetuated by free-market capitalism. Reading the ADA with *Through the Arc of the Rainforest* and *Desirable Body* allows access to the neoliberal construction and privileging of the economic subject which properly self-invests and remakes their bodymind and identity according to market desires. In this framework, individuals are figured as inherently and equally capable of fulfilling needs and wants through the freedom to consume, thus depoliticizing everyday life and obfuscating structures that purposefully injure and kill. In this line of reasoning, the ADA represents one of many legislative examples that foreground how, according to David Harvey, "[t]o live under neoliberalism also means to accept or submit to that bundle of rights necessary for capital accumulation."[68] As neoliberalism increasingly recasts what is good for humanity as synonymous for what is good for the market economy, it also redefines success and failure according to these logics. Capacity, then, emphasizes how within the logics of the free market, people are not only expected to *do more* for endless capital accumulation, but are also always expected to make their bodies and minds *be more*. To succeed and grow as a field, disability studies must remain committed to actively engaging with the ways in which its own priorities and political goals can

---

[68] David Harvey, *A Brief History of Neoliberalism* (New York City: Oxford University Press, 2005), 181.

sustain and occlude the relationship between the production of disability subjectivity and evolving forms of market violence.

Bibliography

Americans With Disabilities Act of 1990. 42 U.S.C. §12101, 1990.

Barnartt, Sharon N. and Richard K. Scotch. *Disability Protests: Contentions Politics 1970-1999*. Washington, D.C.: Gallaudet University Press, 2001.

Bell, Chris. "Introducing White Disability Studies: A Modest Proposal." In *The Disability Studies Reader,* 2nd ed., edited by Lennard J. Davis, 275-282. New York: Routledge, 2006.

Bérubé, Michael. *The Secret Life of Stories: From Don Quixote to Harry Potter, How Understanding Intellectual Disability Transforms the Way We Read*. New York: New York University Press, 2016.

Brown, Wendy. "Suffering Rights as Paradoxes." *Constellations: An International Journal of Critical and Democratic Theory* 7, no. 2, (June 2000): 208-229. Wiley Online Library.

Brown, Wendy. *Undoing the Demos*. Brooklyn: Zone Books, 2015.

Davidson, Michael. *Concerto for the Left Hand: Disability and the Defamiliar Body*. Ann Arbor: University of Michigan Press, 2008.

Davis, Lennard J. *Bending Over Backwards: Disability, Dismodernism and Other Difficult Positions*. New York: New York University Press, 2002.

De Loughry, Treasa. "Petromodernity, Petro-Finance, and Plastic in Karen Tei Yamashita's *Through the Arc of the Rainforest.*" *Journal of Postcolonial Writing* 53, no. 3 (2017): 329-341.

Ehlers, Nadine and Shiloh Krupar. *Deadly Biocultures: The Ethics of Life-Making*. Minneapolis: University of Minnesota Press, 2019.

Farmer, Paul. *Pathologies of Power: Health, Human Rights, and the New War on the Poor*. Berkeley: University of California Press, 2003.

Foucault, Michel. *The Birth of Biopolitics: Lectures at the Collège de France, 1978-79*. Translated by Graham Burchell. New York: Picador, 2004.

Gill, Michael and Cathy J. Schlund-Vials, eds. *Disability, Human Rights and the Limits of Humanitarianism*. Burlington: Ashgate Publishing, 2014.

Haddad, Hubert. *Desirable Body*. Translated by Alyson Waters. New Haven: Yale University Press, 2018.

Harvey, David. *A Brief History of Neoliberalism*. New York: Oxford University Press, 2005.

Harvey, David. *The New Imperialism*. New York: Oxford University Press, 2003.

Krieger, Linda Hamilton, ed. *Backlash Against the ADA: Reinterpreting Disability Rights*. Ann Arbor: University of Michigan Press, 2003.

McRuer, Robert. *Crip Times: Disability, Globalization, and Resistance*. New York: New York University Press, 2018.

Meekosha, Helen and Karen Soldatic. "Human Rights and the Global South: The Case of Disability." *Third World Quarterly* 32, no. 8 (2011): 1383-1397.

Miles, Angel L., Akemi Nishida, and Anjali J. Forber-Pratt. "An Open Letter to White Disability Studies and Ableist Institutions of Higher Education."

Disability Studies Quarterly 37, no. 3 (Summer 2017). https://doi.org/10.18061/dsq.v37i3.

Mitchell, David T. with Sharon L. Snyder. *The Biopolitics of Disability: Neoliberalism, Ablenationalism, and Peripheral Embodiment.* Ann Arbor: University of Michigan Press, 2015.

Mitchell, David T. and Sharon L. Snyder. "Is the Study of Debility Akin to Disability Studies without Disability?" *GLQ* 25, no. 4 (2019): 663-666.

Puar, Jasbir K. *The Right to Maim: Debility, Capacity, Disability.* Durham: Duke University Press, 2017.

Rabinow, Pual. *Essays on the Anthropology of Reason.* Princeton: Princeton University Press, 1996.

Rajan, Kaushik Sunder. *Biocapital: The Constitution of Postgenomic Life.* Durham: Duke University Press, 2006.

Rose, Nikolas. *The Politics of Life Itself: Biomedicine, Power, and Subjectivity in the Twenty-First Century.* Princeton: Princeton University Press, 2007.

Russell, Marta. *Capitalism and Disability: Selected Writings by Marta Russell.* Edited by Keith Rosenthal. Chicago: Haymarket Books, 2019.

Schalk, Sami. *Bodyminds Reimagined: (Dis)Ability, Race, and Gender in Black Women's Speculative Fiction.* Durham: Duke University Press, 2018.

Snyder, Sharon L. and David T. Mitchell. *Cultural Locations of Disability.* Chicago: The University of Chicago Press, 2006.

Titchkosky, Tanya. *Reading and Writing Disability Differently: The Textured Life of Embodiment.* Toronto: University of Toronto Press, 2007.

Yamashita, Karen Tei. *Through the Arc of the Rainforest.* Minneapolis: Coffee House Press, 1990. Reprint. Minneapolis: Coffee House Press, 2017. Citations refer to original edition.

Yavaş, Nesrin. "Ecocriticism and Magical Realism in Karen Tei Yamashita's *Through the Arc of the Rainforest.*" *Journal of Awareness* 3, no. 1 (2018): 1-12.

CHAPTER 9

STAR TREK, DISABILITY, AND LA FORGE: SEEING PAST THE VISOR

Craig A. Meyer

Jackson State University

Daniel Preston

Syracuse University

Abstract

Throughout its history, *Star Trek* has attempted to appropriately incorporate diverse characters, including those with disabilities. This chapter considers the *Star Trek: The Next Generation* character Geordi La Forge as a catalyst to discuss, educate, and further the understanding and positionality of people with disabilities. Focusing on specific episodes and scenes, we investigate how La Forge and his visual impairment are (re)presented. Our examination suggests that the medical model continues to inappropriately limit thinking about people with disabilities. We also recognize that representation matters, even though it is sometimes problematic. In addition, using the genre of science fiction and the character of La Forge, we illustrate the potential of technology to benefit society and how technology offers positive possibilities for our future. Our conclusion illustrates the importance of La Forge as a main character and how he positively represented those in disabled communities.

Keywords: Disability Studies, Star Trek, Visual Impairment, Popular Culture, Narrative Prosthesis

***

Science fiction has done much to eliminate the stigma of difference. As part of the genre, *Star Trek* made inroads to discussions about race and culture that remain notable and needed. For example, *Star Trek: The Original Series* (*TOS*) contained an interracial kiss between Communications Officer Nyota Uhura and Captain James T. Kirk, which helped open discussions about love and the concept of race. Another example from *TOS* was Spock, who was the first officer of Kirk's *Enterprise*. Being half human and half Vulcan, Spock was torn between two cultures, even two worlds, part of both and neither. Like the kiss, having a character of mixed heritage on screen allowed the show to offer commentary on difficult social questions in the imaginary world of science fiction. Despite these examples, *Star Trek* and many of its sequels still have trouble representing characters with disabilities in non-stereotypical ways, because they fall back on outdated disability tropes when telling stories involving characters with impairments. In this chapter, we investigate episodes within the *Star Trek* universe to demonstrate some ways that the franchise has negotiated this terrain.

As a focal point for our analyses, we consider *Star Trek: The Next Generation*'s (*TNG*) Geordi La Forge, a character with a visual impairment who uses a VISOR (Visual Instrument and Sensory Organ Replacement) to see. La Forge is part of storylines that use outdated tropes based on the medical model of disability or use disability as a major plot device (thereby reducing the on-screen character *to* their impairment). Both approaches to presenting disability on screen make use of what disability theorists David T. Mitchell and Sharon L. Snyder refer to as "narrative prosthesis,"[1] which draws attention to the impairment. What makes La Forge unique, however, is that he was also given stories that allowed him to advocate for people with disabilities.

Our goals in this chapter are threefold: primarily, we discuss specific episodes from *TOS* and *TNG* to demonstrate some of the ways that language, together with fictional technology, presented a character's visual impairment in negative and positive ways; second, we consider the potential of future technologies that may present themselves as benefiting specific groups and hopefully benefiting all. Moreover, as part of recognizing differing perspectives, we note the influence of *Star Trek* in popular culture and its utility in better understanding positionality. As we conclude, we explore the ways that La Forge and technology have created a more positive view of the future and shaped the lives of people in disability communities.

To See or Not to See: The Medicalizing of Visual Impairments in *Star Trek*

The medical approach to disability interprets *impairment* and *disability* as synonymous, and stigmatizes all impairment, erroneously, as negative. It also asserts what is deemed "proper" for a human body. As activist and poet Eli Clare writes, "The medical-industrial complex pushes normal weight, normal walking, normal ways of thinking, feeling, and communicating as if normal

---

[1] David T. Mitchell, and Sharon L. Snyder. *Narrative Prosthesis: Disability and the Dependencies of Discourse* (Ann Arbor: University of Michigan Press, 2000), 6.

were a goal to achieve and maintain,"[2] and we suggest that early episodes of *TOS* and *TNG* often relied on those ideas as well despite its overall claim of a completely inclusive and diverse future. After all, as *Star Trek* scholar and fan Lincoln Geraghty points out, "Roddenberry wanted to emphasize diversity within a community [. . . . Star Trek] was to be a series that promoted individual success and achievement through space travel as well as promoting diversity and equality within a utopian future."[3]

While investigating the ways people interact within groups, sociologist Erving Goffman uses the term "stigma" to refer to any characteristic that would mark an individual as different from the other members of a given group. According to Goffman, these stigmas can "spoil"[4] an identity and provide reasons for group members to deny membership.[5] The reality of Goffman's observation created the desire to hide visible impairments to be accepted. One of the most common ways for people to hide perceived physical stigmas is to use prosthetic devices to normalize themselves. As an example, consider an amputee who uses a prosthetic leg in public places. In Goffman's theory, the use of a prosthetic leg compensates for the missing limb by filling in the gap where the leg is expected thereby giving the appearance of social acceptance while the prosthetic is in place. Likewise, when Mitchell and Snyder explain their concept of narrative prosthesis, they write,

> In a literal sense a prosthesis seeks to accomplish an illusion. A body deemed lacking, unfunctional, or inappropriately functional needs compensation, and prosthesis helps to effect this end. Yet the prosthesizing of a body or a rhetorical figure carries with it ideological assumptions about what is aberrant. [. . . Similarly,] Narrative Prosthesis is first and foremost about the ways in which the ruse of prosthesis fails in its primary objective: to return the incomplete body to the invisible status of a normative essence.[6]

In other words, Mitchell and Snyder argue that narrative prosthesis fails to hide an impairment and instead calls more attention to it during the failed attempt. For La Forge, this means that each time the writers try to hide his visual

[2] Eli Clare, *Brilliant Imperfection: grappling with cure* (Durham: Duke University Press, 2017) Kindle, 173.

[3] Lincoln Geraghty, *Living with Star Trek: American Culture and the Star Trek Universe* (New York: I.B. Tauris, 2007), 2.

[4] Erving Goffman, *Stigma: Notes on the Management of Spoiled Identity.* 1986 Touchstone Reprint. New York: Simon & Schuster, 1963, 19.

[5] Goffman, *Stigma*, 2.

[6] Mitchell and Snyder. *Narrative Prosthesis*, 6-8.

impairment, it becomes more apparent. Here, our argument is that this visibility, while sometimes responding to outdated stereotypes of disability, also provides La Forge opportunities to educate others about his embodiment.

As a first step to demonstrate how narrative prosthesis operates alongside a stereotypical approach to disability, we offer one example from *TOS*, which is particularly relevant when discussing La Forge's character. In *TOS*'s third season episode, "Is There in Truth No Beauty?" audiences are introduced to Dr. Miranda Jones, who is a telepathic human and aide to a Medussan ambassador. Unknown to the audience at the beginning, Jones has a visual impairment. In the opening scenes, dialogue between various characters makes it clear that anyone who looks at a Medussan will be driven to madness. The one exception is if a Vulcan (like Spock) wears a special visor. In short, Spock can safely glimpse the ambassador without risk, if he wears the visor. However, in various scenes, Dr. Jones looks at the ambassador several times with and without a visor. As a human, this should not be possible, but she experiences no effects. To explain this, Jones points out that because of her telepathic abilities, she was raised on Vulcan and the mental discipline she learned there allows her to interact with the ambassador.

During the episode, the ship is trapped outside the known universe, and the Medussan is enlisted to help navigate the ship to safety. As Kirk, Spock, McCoy, and Jones discuss the possibilities for who should telepathically link with the ambassador and serve as pilot, McCoy reveals Miranda's impairment by saying "I realize you can do almost anything a sighted person can do, but you can't pilot a starship."[7] Until that moment, Miranda's impairment had not been named and was actively concealed by Jones. As a result, Spock logically concludes that her dress acts as a sensory net that allows her to maneuver around her surroundings and to conceal her impairment. Still, McCoy seems shocked by the suggestion that Jones could act as pilot. He confronts her and says, "I'm sorry, Miranda, but you must be realistic. You are blind, and there are some things you simply cannot do."[8] Jones is outed as impaired by McCoy, who assumes she is incapable of piloting the *Enterprise*. Once audiences discover the purpose of the dress (as a prosthesis to adjust for her impairment), the dress itself no longer serves as an effective narrative prosthesis because its presence reminds audiences of the impairment.

In addition to the dress, McCoy's assumption that she "cannot do" certain things because she has a visual impairment demonstrates the limited thinking

[7] "Is There in Truth No Beauty?" *Star Trek: The Original Series*, Season 3, episode 5. Directed by Ralph Senesky. Aired October 18, 1968: Paramount Pictures, 2004. DVD.
[8] "Is There in Truth No Beauty?"

of the era. McCoy's reaction is inappropriate, largely because it was based on the medical model. More problematic for us, though, is that McCoy reduces Miranda to her impairment. During that conversation, McCoy understands her *only* through her blindness. He ignores that she has adapted technology to suit her needs, which helps her navigate the world and might allow her to pilot a spacecraft. Instead, McCoy discounts her accomplishments and abilities, and he concludes that she *cannot* pilot a starship. Although we understand the reasoning behind the assumption for a world based in the 1960s, our concern here is *Star Trek's* failure to recognize the potential created within its own fictional and technological mythos.

Between the production of *TOS* and *TNG,* twenty years passed. In that time, disability activism and scholarship advanced so that (among other things) "disability" and "impairment" could be understood as separate ideas. Using these ideas, a person with a visual impairment *could* pilot a starship if the starship controls were modified sufficiently. Adding a character with a visual impairment to the main cast demonstrates how much the understanding of disability had changed. When viewers first meet Lt. Geordi La Forge in the pilot episode of *TNG,* "Encounter at Farpoint," he presents as an African American male with a dull golden, horizontal device covering his eyes and ending near, but not on, his ears, somewhat like sunglasses. It is this device that makes audiences curious about him. After his introduction, but before he goes to Farpoint Station, La Forge visits sickbay because of a headache, which is an effect of his using the VISOR. While there, he speaks with the Chief Medical Officer, Dr. Beverly Crusher:

> CRUSHER: Naturally I've heard of your case. The VISOR appliance you wear...
> LAFORGE: Is a remarkable piece of bio-electronic engineering by which I quote see much of the EM spectrum ranging from simple heat and infrared through radio waves et cetera, et cetera, and forgive me if I've said and listened to this a thousand times before.
> CRUSHER: You've been blind all your life?
> LAFORGE: I was born this way.[9]

Here, audiences get an explanation for La Forge's VISOR and learn that it replaces his biological vision. At this point, when La Forge makes it clear that he has adapted to it, and the prosthesis is identified. Likewise, the impairment draws more attention and is made more apparent to the audience. When the doctor offers him pain medication for the headache, La Forge explains that

---

[9] "Encounter at Farpoint." *Star Trek: The Next Generation.* Season 1, episode 1. Directed by Corey Allen. Aired September 28, 1987. CBS Studios, 2007. DVD.

using pain management medicine would affect the effectiveness of his VISOR and he refuses. As an alternative, she suggests exploratory surgery that would desensitize pain receptors in his brain. Unwilling to go through surgery, La Forge refuses again. To us, this indicates that La Forge recognizes the utility of his VISOR use and internalizes his disability. In other words, he accepts his impairment and using the VISOR as part of his life, only visits Dr. Crusher to minimize the pain rather than to erase his impairment. After speaking with her, he goes to Farpoint Station.

As part of the away team, the mission goals are to learn more about the station, and possibly provide a recommendation to Starfleet in order to make an agreement regarding the use of it. Beneath Farpoint Station are various tunnels that draw First Officer William Riker's interest, and he says to La Forge, "Geordi, I want your eyes down there."[10] After arriving in the darkened tunnels beneath the station, La Forge reports, "these tunnel walls are something I've never seen before."[11] Riker asks him, "How are you examining them?"[12] To which La Forge replies, "In every way: microscopically, thermally, electromagnetically. None of it is familiar."[13] For us, this represents the first noticeable moment of dichotomy regarding La Forge's visual impairment. On the one hand, characters do not outwardly mention La Forge's impairment; on the other, they acknowledge the impairment by utilizing the VISOR's technology. To demonstrate this point, we will focus on some of the earliest episodes that chose to utilize his advanced visual technology.

In another *TNG* episode, "Justice," Captain Jean Luc Picard asks La Forge to look at an unknown spacecraft near the ship that shows up on sensors but is not visible through the viewscreen. Picard directs La Forge to "Have a real look" and, after going to a window, La Forge says, "This is something I've never seen before, sir. After complete spectral analysis, well, it's as if it's not really there."[14] This dialogue calls attention to the narrative prosthesis with Picard's comment about having "a real look" and the technology of the VISOR rather than the person looking. Additionally, the reference to the analysis reminds audiences of La Forge's VISOR technology. Lastly, the exchange demonstrates that Picard and La Forge understand the VISOR's usefulness to a mission. Nevertheless, the VISOR is shown to be useful in other ways throughout the series.

---

[10] "Encounter at Farpoint."

[11] "Encounter at Farpoint."

[12] "Encounter at Farpoint."

[13] "Encounter at Farpoint."

[14] "Justice." *Star Trek: The Next Generation*. Season 1, episode 7. Directed by James L. Conway. Aired November 9, 1987: CBS Studios, 2007. DVD.

In the episode "Heart of Glory," Picard suggests using a device that will transmit what La Forge perceives back to the ship when he's on an away mission. When the away team arrives aboard a ship in distress, La Forge turns on the device, and Picard and the bridge crew receive the transmission of what La Forge "sees." When the transmission is projected on the bridge's viewscreen, several blurry shapes of various colors are displayed. As Picard takes in this visual, the following exchange occurs over the communication channel:

> PICARD: [whispers] Extraordinary. Now I'm beginning to understand him. [Then, to La Forge] Geordi, what was that? Over to the left.
> [. . .]
> LAFORGE: That's Commander Riker.
> PICARD: Ah, to me it's just an undefined form, standing in a visual frenzy. Can you filter out the extraneous information?
> LAFORGE: No, I get it all simultaneously.
> PICARD: But it's just a jumble. How can you make head or tail of it?
> LAFORGE: I select what I want and then disregard the rest.
> PICARD: But how is that possible?
> LAFORGE: Well, how, in a noisy room, can you select one specific voice or sound?
> PICARD: Of course, something you learn.
> LAFORGE: Exactly. It's something I have learned. Does that make it more clear?
> PICARD: Look over at Data. There's an aura around Data.
> LAFORGE: Well, of course. He's an android.
> PICARD: You say that as if you think that's what we all see.
> LAFORGE: Don't you?[15]

This scene is important for three reasons. First, when La Forge's visual input is received on the bridge, Picard says, "Now I'm beginning to understand him." This comment is troubling because although we appreciate Picard's acknowledgment that by understanding La Forge's vision, he can better understand La Forge; yet, Picard's comment once again reduces the character to his impairment, as if understanding his disability is the *only* way to understand him. What Picard learns from this experience is never fully described; however, it's clear in the rest of the exchange that La Forge sees differently. As they watch, audiences are expected to identify with Picard, and "work through" the difficult contrasts toward understanding La Forge given this added insight. As Picard struggles, so do viewers. Second, we argue that Picard's questions are designed to guide

---

[15] "Heart of Glory." *Star Trek: The Next Generation.* Season 1, episode 19. Directed by Rob Bowman. Aired March 21, 1988. CBS Studios, 2007. DVD.

viewers through the unique experience. To accomplish this, the writers relied on a trope that disability theorist Paul Longmore observes as common to this era of television. He writes that "[i]t becomes the responsibility of the disabled individual to 'educate' [nondisabled characters], to allay their fears and make them feel comfortable."[16] Throughout the scene in which La Forge uses the transmitter, he is educating the crew and the audience, which in turn helps them to understand him while showing the acceptance of his impairment. Third, the transmitter itself serves as a device that helps to maintain the prosthetic disruption of the story. Here is a second layer of technology (the transmitter) to explain the first (the VISOR), and it forces the audience to again recognize the ways that La Forge is unique. In this instance, the focus on his disability is used to educate Picard and the others, because although his VISOR can interpret more information than organic human eyes, the crew often normalizes La Forge's vision by thinking that he has the same vision experience that they do. La Forge's interpretation of the VISOR's signals and his ability to comprehend them during this scene highlight his difference yet again by providing the crew a visual display of the distressed ship while once more providing an opportunity for them to better understand him. This new experience for the crew (and audience) helps to maintain his difference, which helps to maintain the narrative prosthesis.

By the beginning of *TNG*'s second season, La Forge is promoted to Chief Engineer. La Forge's promotion signifies a level of trust from the captain and crew as well as an acknowledgment of an advanced understanding of engineering. In fact, according to popular culture writer Tamara Jude, La Forge was the character who was promoted fastest in *TNG*.[17] However, the promotion also challenges a metanarrative[18] association between blindness and knowledge. Disability scholar David Bolt, who himself has a visual impairment, notes various definitions of "blind," including "unable to see," "unable to recognize," "uncontrollable," "lacking awareness," "done unprepared,"[19] among others. In doing so, Bolt makes clear the perception of "blindness" is used in a disparaging

---

[16] Paul K. Longmore, "Screening Stereotypes: Images of Disabled People in Television and Motion Pictures." In *Images of the Disabled, Disabling Images*, edited by Alan Gartner and Tom Joe, 65-78 (New York: Praeger, 1987), 74.

[17] Tamara Jude, "Star Trek: 15 Things You Didn't Know about Geordi La Forge." ScreenRant, August 6, 2017. https://screenrant.com/geordi-la-forge-star-trek-next-generation-trivia-facts.

[18] Metanarratives, as we are using them here, refer to the stories created from prejudicial and stereotypical understandings of impairments.

[19] David Bolt, *The Metanarratives of Blindness* (Ann Arbor: University of Michigan Press, 2014), 18-19.

way. He also describes a time when a colleague thought he was a student and not a tutor, even though they were in a "staff"[20] only area. According to Bolt, his visual impairment made it difficult for his colleague to accept Bolt as a staff member. [21] Through the experience, he points out that some people still make assumptions based on preconceived notions; he explains, "Given the ubiquitous confusion between seeing and knowing, [. . .] it is more likely to be the case that for some people the idea of a tutor who has a visual impairment remains a contradiction in terms."[22] By positioning La Forge as Chief Engineer, *TNG* helps denaturalize the idea that impairment equates to inability.

Later in the second season, there are several episodes that show La Forge resisting the medical model and advocating for a more positive view of disability. For example, in season two's "Loud as a Whisper," the crew is working with a mediator named Riva, who has a hearing impairment and uses what he calls a "chorus" to communicate. The three-person chorus telepathically communicates with Riva, and they give voice to his thoughts. When Riva meets La Forge, they discuss the commonality of their impairments. When asked if he resents his VISOR or being visually impaired, La Forge says, "No, since they're both part of me, and I really like who I am, there's no reason for me to resent either one."[23] Riva expresses similar sentiments about his hearing impairment and his chorus.

Near the end of the episode, La Forge goes to sickbay to speak with Dr. Katherine Pulaski, the new Chief Medical Officer, about modifying his VISOR in an effort to once again ease the pain of using the VISOR. During the course of that discussion, Pulaski explains the possibility of a medical procedure that could regenerate his optic nerve. In addition, she would replicate "normal" eyes that would allow him to "see like everyone else." [24] Presented with this unexpected possibility, La Forge hesitates and says, "I don't know. I'd be giving up a lot."[25] Further, Pulaski notes that the procedure could fail and suggests he could lose all vision. In speaking with her, La Forge expresses his desire to keep his visual perception abilities, and when speaking with Riva, he recognizes the uniqueness of his impairment and how, at least in part, it makes him who he is.

---

[20] Bolt, *The Metanarratives of Blindness*, 3.

[21] Bolt, *The Metanarratives of Blindness*, 3.

[22] Bolt, *The Metanarratives of Blindness*, 3.

[23] "Loud as a Whisper." *Star Trek: The Next Generation.* Season 2, episode 5. Directed by Larry Shaw. Aired January 9, 1989. CBS Studios, 2007. DVD.

[24] "Loud as a Whisper."

[25] "Loud as a Whisper."

In La Forge's earlier discussion with Riva, he makes the point that "there's no reason to resent [the VISOR]." Since this is the final on-screen discussion regarding the modification of La Forge's vision, we argue that La Forge recognizes that his visual perception would, in his view, be limited with the procedure by Pulaski, if not lost altogether. For us, La Forge's choice demonstrates his rejection of "cure" that the medical model promises and requires. Within this exchange with Pulaski, La Forge acknowledges the potential loss to himself and perhaps the crew. Further, he recognizes that changing his VISOR (and his vision) might alter his social position within the crew because he (and the audience) knows that Picard and Riker have both utilized his unique vision to provide them with information that might not otherwise be available. More importantly, however, he establishes once again that he is comfortable with his identity and his abilities. La Forge's decision to keep his VISOR, despite any medical procedure that would make it unnecessary, remains unchanged throughout the series.

We recognize the conversations that La Forge has with Crusher, Pulaski, and Riva to effectively reject the "curing" of his vision as important moments for his character, and the audience's understanding of his character. Perhaps, too, La Forge channels what Clare means when he writes "cure doesn't only follow the lead of our body-mind yearnings; it also pushes us toward normality."[26] Clare suggests that cure inevitably leads to uniformity and implies dysfunction of existing bodies. Here, we note that La Forge resists the erasure of his disability since he has long accepted the reality of his embodiment. Even when presented with new medical procedures that would effectively erase this part of his current identity, his desire to maintain his embodiment overrides any desire for a cure, because as he noted, he would "be giving up a lot."

Despite La Forge's self-acceptance, in the episode "Measure of a Man," the technology of his VISOR and superior vision is used to demonstrate the power of normality. Although La Forge's VISOR enhances his vision, it also allows others to erroneously normalize it as well. This normalization allows, for the most part, the crew to think La Forge sees through biological eyes and therefore permits them to accept him. However, the following discussion demonstrates that acceptance is determined on a case-by-case basis. While fighting an order to be dismantled and cataloged for scientific experimentation and possible replication, the android Data discusses his rights as a Starfleet officer and a sentient being with Captain Picard. Data says, "Sir, Lieutenant La Forge's eyes

---

[26] Clare, *Brilliant Imperfection*, 180.

are far superior to human biological eyes. True?" [27] Here, Captain Picard appears to nod and to acknowledge Data's point. In effect, as Picard realizes that La Forge's vision is superior, so does the audience. The scene continues:

> DATA: Then why are not all human officers required to have their eyes replaced with cybernetic implants? [Picard looks away] I see. It is precisely because I am not human.
> PICARD: That will be all, Mister Data.[28]

Data's insight is undeniable regarding disability studies and normality. In his article titled "Bodies of Difference," disability scholar Lennard Davis argues that the concepts of "normal" and "disability" developed linguistically alongside the creation of the bell curve and its determination of "average" so that "normal"[29] was at the height of the curve and any deviation from average was undesirable. Clare supports this as he writes:

> The standards called normal [. . .] are promoted as averages. They are posed as the most common and best states of being for body-minds. They are advertised as descriptions of who "we" collectively are—a we who predictably is white, male, middle- and upper-class, nondisabled, Christian, heterosexual, gender-conforming, slender, [and] cisgender.[30]

Both Davis and Clare reason that most people understand the world through binaries—that people are natural *or* unnatural, normal *or* abnormal—rather than acknowledging the existence of a more complex spectrum.

In the scene above, Picard and Data acknowledge the superiority of La Forge's VISOR and vision. In so doing, Picard and the audience are forced to recognize that the replacement of an officer's biological eyes with cybernetic implants would be outside the understanding of normality, *even if* the replacements are superior. Thus, suggesting that anything outside *normal* is undesirable. Moreover, Picard and Data seem to realize the myriad of ethical and invasive concerns involving human bodies and that other humans would never be forced to give up their existing eyes for implants. However, as the rest of the episode shows audiences, those same concerns were negotiable for androids or other artificial lifeforms, because they are *not* human. This scene demonstrates

---

[27] "Measure of a Man." *Star Trek: The Next Generation.* Season 2, episode 9. Directed by Robert Scheerer. Aired February 13, 1989. CBS Studios, 2007. DVD.

[28] "Measure of a Man."

[29] Lennard J. Davis, "Bodies of Difference: Politics, Disability, and Representation." In *Disability Studies: Enabling the Humanities,* edited by Brenda Jo Brueggemann, Rosemarie Garland-Thomson, and Sharon Snyder, 100-108 (New York: MLA, 2002), 103-104.

[30] Clare, *Brilliant Imperfection,* 173.

that there is an unspoken standard of normal and acceptable. While La Forge's VISOR is acceptable, the scene demonstrates he is unique and even his superiority will not cause others to modify or enhance their natural vision. Through this discussion, we recognize that the future will remain challenged by technological advances, and they will complicate disability rights and justice as society moves into the future.

Their Eyes Uncovered: La Forge Teaching Others about Difference

Mitchell and Snyder argue that a narrative prosthesis ultimately fails because it draws more attention to the impairment that traditional prosthetic devices attempt to hide.[31] Another way that a prosthetic narrative operates is to make use of disability as a major plot device in a story. There are several episodes of *TNG* where the technology the VISOR uses becomes crucial to the plot, and the story revolves around La Forge's visual impairment. In what follows, we focus on two that highlight the VISOR's use as a plot device. Not only do these episodes center on technology solving problems, but they allow La Forge to inform others about disability in a positive way, which improves the representation of people with disabilities on television. Up to this point, we have demonstrated how narrative prosthesis presents the disability as a "crutch on which literary narratives lean for the representational power,"[32] but it ultimately fails as a prosthetic because it forces audiences to notice how crew members make use of his VISOR to reduce his usefulness to one of analysis. In these next examples, the technology surrounding his VISOR still highlights La Forge's impairment and still fall back on a trope of disability television but allow him to advocate for a more positive outlook regarding disability.

The season three episode, "The Enemy," rejects normalizing La Forge's impairment and characterizes him as innovative and powerful. He contributes *because* of his impairment. To help illustrate, Mitchell and Snyder, analyze the use of disability in *Oedipus the King,* they point out that Oedipus solves the Riddle of the Sphinx based on his own knowledge and experience using a cane (due to the binding of his feet as a child).[33] In other words, impairment informed his solution to the riddle. Likewise, La Forge applies knowledge from his own bodily experience to solve a problem. In this episode, La Forge is left behind on a planet that is experiencing several electrical storms that wreak havoc on humanoid nervous systems and have prevented the crew from

---

[31] Mitchell and Snyder, *Narrative Prosthesis*, 8.

[32] Mitchell and Snyder, *Narrative Prosthesis*, 49.

[33] Mitchell and Snyder, *Narrative Prosthesis*, 61.

locating him. In an attempt to coordinate with La Forge, the crew launch a probe at the surface that emits a special beam that La Forge can notice with his VISOR, even with the interference. Recognizing the beam, La Forge realizes he has to adjust the beam to show where he is, so the crew can teleport him up. As he's working his way to the probe, Bochra, an enemy Romulan officer, attacks him. Since he's been on the planet longer than La Forge, Bochra is in poor condition, because the planet's electrical storms are affecting his nervous system too. As Bochra appears to have difficulty, La Forge notices this change, and as Bochra denies having any distress, the following exchange occurs:

> LAFORGE: Wrong. Your heart rate just shot way up. [taps the VISOR] It translates a wide range of radiation into neural impulses. Allows me to see.
> BOCHRA: Without it, you're blind?
> LAFORGE: Yes.
> BOCHRA: How did this happen?
> LAFORGE: I was born that way.
> BOCHRA: And your parents let you live?
> LAFORGE: What kind of question is that? Of course they let me live.
> BOCHRA: No wonder your race is weak. You waste time and resources on defective children.[34]

Bochra sees La Forge as weak and as taking up resources that would be better used on non- "defective" children. Bochra and his fellow Romulans seem to understand the elimination of all children with impairments as absolute and necessary, which is a sub theme in another episode we will return to shortly.

As the episode progresses, atmospheric conditions on the planet soon make the connection between La Forge and his VISOR impossible. Because he is now unable to perceive his surroundings, he and Bochra must work together to rig the VISOR so it can work as a directional beacon to the probe and then help each other to it. In effect, for both characters to survive, they need to trust an enemy, and Bochra needs to overcome his understanding of disability and recognize La Forge's capabilities. By using his VISOR to resolve the situation, the focus becomes its technology. At the same time, these scenes call attention to La Forge's disability, as both characters realize that without his VISOR technology, they will likely not survive.

Technology helps us create, adapt, and meet the challenges of our future. By extension, we hope humanity continues to embrace and accept differences and diverging perspectives. One episode points explicitly to the power of additional

[34] "The Enemy." *Star Trek: The Next Generation.* Season 3, episode 7. Directed by David Carson. Aired November 6, 1989: CBS Studios, 2007. DVD.

perspectives and to the advantages of future technologies. In the episode "The Masterpiece Society," La Forge attempts to find a solution to the threat of a stellar core fragment for an inhabited planet, which will destroy all structures on the planet and poses considerable risk to the inhabitants. After working a number of hours with Hannah, the planet's lead scientist, and not finding a working solution, La Forge takes off his VISOR. Then, Hannah asks about his visual impairment. She realizes that in asking, she may have embarrassed him. La Forge responds that he is not embarrassed by his blindness and that he's always been blind. He speaks openly about it and points out that it is simply a difference between him and others. Unfamiliar with his VISOR and its technology, Hannah asks to see it, and La Forge holds it up to her. He then asks her if he were conceived in her world if he would have been allowed to be born. She responds in the negative and says,

> HANNAH: It was the wish of our founders that no one had to suffer a life with disabilities.
> LAFORGE: Who gave them the right to decide whether or not I should be here? Whether or not I might have something to contribute.[35]

Again, like the scene with Bochra, La Forge is visibly upset by the idea that someone with a disability would not be given a chance to live. Nevertheless, La Forge's comment about contributing to society sets up the coming solution, which he develops as he describes how the VISOR works.

> LAFORGE: Well, the VISOR scans the electromagnetic spectrum between one hertz and one hundred thousand terahertz, converts it all to usable frequencies and then transmits that information directly to my brain.
> HANNAH: What about the data conversion rates? How do you avoid a sensory overload?
> LAFORGE: A bank of pre-processors compresses the data stream into pulses, you see. That way, my visual cortex never. [he pauses] Wait a minute. Wait just a minute. We should be able to send a high-energy pulse through the tractor system. If it's short enough, it shouldn't overload the emitters. The technology is right here [La Forge touches his VISOR].[36]

After some brief discussion of making the idea work, La Forge soon realizes that his VISOR's technology will be the thing that saves Hannah's planet. With a

---

[35] "The Masterpiece Society." *Star Trek: The Next Generation.* Season 5, episode 13. Directed by Winrich Kolbe. Aired February 10, 1992. CBS Studios, 2007. DVD.
[36] "The Masterpiece Society."

slight tone of contempt, he says, "[T]he answer to all of this is in a VISOR created for a blind man who never would have existed in your society."[37] This scene reinforces the idea that those with disabilities can and do contribute to society in ways others may not recognize, and more importantly, their contributions can have a powerful impact.

While speaking with La Forge and collectively solving the issue, Hannah realizes the missed opportunities of her world and secretly devises a plan to correct what she believes is a failure in her planet's dominant thinking—that those with disabilities are not worthy of life. Later, an alarm sounds on the planet and Hannah is called to find the cause. Having found the problem, an apparent breach of the protective shield, Hannah is alone with La Forge. She scans the shield and points out the breach, but La Forge, with the help of his VISOR, knows the shield has no breaches, and he says: "Hannah, my VISOR's positronic scan would have detected the leak. Its molecular pattern enhancer would have picked up even the smallest crack."[38]

By revealing there is no breach, La Forge exposes Hannah's lie about the failing shield. After being caught in her deception, Hannah admits her plan to dismantle the shield and change the dominant thinking of the planet. She laments the idea that she, one of the best scientific minds on her planet, could not have even conceived of technology like La Forge's VISOR. She continues,

> HANNAH: And I've got to ask myself, if we're so brilliant how come we didn't invent any of these things?
> LAFORGE: Well, maybe necessity really is the mother of invention. You never really look for something until you need it.
> HANNAH: But all my needs have been anticipated and planned for before I was even born. All of us in this colony have been living in the dark ages. It's like we're victims of a two hundred year old joke. Until you came, all we could see was to the wall of our biosphere. Suddenly our eyes have been opened to the infinite possibilities.[39]

By this point, he's at peace with his earlier flash of contempt and switches to a perspective that allows Hannah to recognize that her pre-planned and engineered life is not as perfect as it seems. Hannah's hubris crashes down as she recognizes the value of La Forge's experience, which is partly derived from his unique vision. She begins to accept the idea that different embodiments

---

[37] "The Masterpiece Society."

[38] "The Masterpiece Society."

[39] "The Masterpiece Society."

lead to unique perspectives and innovations. This realization, that differences generate more complete understanding of people, is a foundational concept for disability studies.

La Forge's disability would not have given him the opportunity to live on Hannah's planet, "[b]ecause," as Rosemarie Garland-Thomson writes, "disability is understood to disqualify us from access to the benefits and status of the properly human."[40] Since science fiction is not bound by (dis)ability or reality, it allows for discussions to develop like this and the earlier ones noted. Additionally, science fiction provides an opportunity for disabilities to be reimagined as non-stigmatized differences. In both "Masterpiece Society" and "The Enemy," La Forge's visual impairment and his VISOR serve as the element that saves a society and an adversary. Through these episodes, and due in large part to La Forge's efforts to teach other characters about himself, the audience is shown that having an impairment does not equate to helplessness. Additionally, La Forge demonstrates that different embodiments can lead to new ideas and innovations

The previous examples demonstrate some of the ways in which La Forge's VISOR acts as a narrative prosthesis that propels a plot to a conclusion. Although it is occasionally problematic, it becomes a meaningful focal point regarding the utility of disability and differences in science fiction. The presence of the VISOR suggests a future where innovations based on disability continue to enhance humanity, because it offers its users a unique perspective. As we've noted, La Forge's VISOR is often seen as an asset. In her work on *Star Trek* and disability, Llana Lehmann suggests that such adaptive technology "allows people with disabilities to perform 'as if' they were not otherwise impaired."[41] Given the rate of innovation, humanity will continue to confront questions about disability, technology, and what it means to be human. Over the years, several innovations have been made based on *Star Trek*'s fictional technology. The cellular phone, co-developed by Martin Cooper, was partly based on the communicator from *TOS*. Other innovations like the iPad, Google Glass, and voice interactions with computers were also partly based on *Star Trek* tech. As such, the franchise will likely continue to offer possibilities for future technologies.

---

[40] Rosemarie Garland-Thomson, "The Case for Conserving Disability." *Bioethical Inquiry* 9, no. 3 (September 2012): 339-55, 340.

[41] Llana Lehmann, *All You Need to Know about Disability Is on Star Trek* (Vancouver: Mind Meld Media, 2014), 222.

Looking Ahead: La Forge and Our Future

The technology of La Forge's VISOR provides insight into our future and the potential of technology to mitigate stigma. Present technologies like Google Glass and Argus II suggest scientists are not far away from developing VISOR-like visual assistance devices. While these are forthcoming, we also note other technologies *Star Trek* provided as possible future technologies. For example, throughout *TNG*, audiences see La Forge have complete access to the ship controls without difficulty, and there was no mention of assistance, or accommodation because of his visual impairment. There are no curb cuts or canes, no specialized computers, or visual enhancements on instruments, just an occasional painkiller for a headache is all he seems to need. In fact, through most of the series, La Forge's sight is not discussed or referred to at all, and he functions as the main officer at the conn and later as the chief engineer of the most prestigious ship in Starfleet, and very little attention is given to his eyesight. In other words, this *lack* of special attention demonstrates that the crew has largely accepted La Forge's vision and VISOR use, and part of the reason for this omission could be the ubiquity of adaptive technology, which helps La Forge to accomplish his tasks.

Although adaptive technology was not specifically mentioned during *TOS or TNG*, the shift in awareness and the environment around later shows made mentioning ideas of universal design and accessibility easier. During one episode of *Star Trek: Voyager*, Tuvok, Voyager's Security Chief, was temporarily visually impaired. Despite the impairment, he continued to serve as Security Chief. In one scene, he arrives on the bridge and calls to his workstation, "Computer, activate tactile interface."[42] The importance of those latter three words provides an opportunity for some discussion. Notably, he was still able to function in his role as chief of security. More notable, the computer console had a *built-in* tactile interface that he understood and was able to use *as part of the design*. How this interface operated was never explained, but it is one of those aspects of *Star Trek* that suggest a future with more tactile interfaces and inclusive capabilities for differences (i.e., universal design). Even now with cell phones, many have pressure sensors that can determine how hard one is pushing on the screen and various kinds of vibration to signify different actions. In other words, tactile-type interfaces are being developed for various reasons, including gradations of visual acuity.

This awareness brings us to one of our final points. *Star Trek* is a part of popular culture. The various television series and movies have become a part

---

[42] "Year of Hell, Part I." *Star Trek: Voyager.* Season 4, episode 8. Directed by Allan Kroeker. Aired November 5, 1997. Paramount Pictures, 2004. DVD.

of how society understands itself and what we might hope to become. However, there are two understandings of *Star Trek*: on the one hand, are the actual TV shows and movies—presented and perceived as entertainment—and on the other hand are the ways popular culture appropriates the entire franchise, and sometimes the entire genre of science fiction under the broad category of "Star Trek." While here, we have discussed only the former. We recognize the latter as an important element to mention, because it has also influenced our society. This popular culture understanding of Star Trek, includes the various technologies that are currently not possible and well-known sayings, such as "Beam me up, Scotty." Most people understand what the phrase means and even where it comes from, but interestingly, it was never said on any *Star Trek*. In addition, this phrase has taken on its own meaning beyond the franchise (for example, "get me out of here") and, as such, become part of the mythos or lore that is Star Trek.

By extension, this lore demonstrates how La Forge and his futuristic VISOR have impacted society. In an interview with *Rolling Stone*, LeVar Burton, the actor who played La Forge, says, "Geordi's visor is iconic. You know exactly what you're looking at when you see it. The idea that young people, male and female, put headbands over their eyes and play Geordi La Forge, is proof positive that it is an iconic image."[43] Thus, not only has *Star Trek* driven innovation, but the *idea* of Star Trek coupled with the positive image that La Forge presented, drives cultural change and understanding as well. As we close this chapter, however, we recognize the ongoing problem that representation presents. As Mitchell and Snyder remind us:

> Representation inevitably spawns discontent. All portrayal (artistic or documentary) proves potentially allegorical in the sense that the act of characterization encourages readers or viewers to search for a larger concept, experience, or population. Thus, the effort to represent is inevitably fraught with politics. The question of disability's service to "negative" portrayals is profoundly complex and central to our thinking about narrative prosthesis. Any response is riddled with difficulty because the question is, first and foremost, social in its making. What one generation of interpreters views as "humane" can be challenged by the next, and so on and so forth. This is particularly true of the representation of disability.[44]

---

[43] Angie Martoccio, "The Last Word: LeVar Burton on the Upside of Losing the 'Jeopardy!' Gig and What 'Star Trek' Gave Him." November 26, 2021. https://www.rollingstone.com/tv/tv-features/levar-burton-last-word-interview-jeopardy-star-trek-1245262/.

[44] Mitchell and Snyder, *Narrative Prosthesis*, 40-41.

Like science fiction and technology, different embodiments have the potential to offer new perspectives, which, in turn, provide for new discoveries and new ideas. Because science fiction constantly challenges what we know about the universe, abilities are redefined. Audiences can, then, reconsider the potentials and perspectives of people with disabilities, even when disability is not a main focus, as was often the case with La Forge. Further, his VISOR was the prosthesis that motivated many plot lines and forced others to recognize his skills despite a visual impairment.

After studying the history of La Forge, we believe that his (dis)ability ultimately transcended stereotypes to create a definitive character who helped shape disability portrayals on television and in society. Through *TNG*, La Forge also started conversations among audience members about disabilities. According to Jude, "The cultural significance of Geordi La Forge is a legacy that remains to this day. Not only was he one of the few African American characters on science fiction TV, but he was also one of the few engineers. However, his largest impact has been in the portrayal of a sci-fi character with a disability."[45] Through the example of La Forge and the *Enterprise* crew, we recognize *Star Trek*'s potential to mitigate disability, to create acceptance, and to foster understanding between people with disabilities and people currently without them. Further, science fiction provides an ideal medium for understanding and reconceptualizing identity, embodiment, and what it means to be human. In the future, we foresee humanity looking beyond the concept of "disability" and accommodating differences by, for example, including people of all embodiments into the design and testing phases of new innovations. Throughout much of his work with disability studies, Davis has made a similar argument and has theorized that "diversity"[46] should replace normalcy. In other words, identity markers have become so fluid and embodiment so diverse that "normalcy" is an outdated concept. We hope society will recognize diversity as a center point for unique perspectives and skills, while following the example presented by La Forge.

Bibliography

Bolt, David. *The Metanarratives of Blindness*. Ann Arbor: University of Michigan Press, 2014.

Clare, Eli. *Brilliant Imperfection: grappling with cure*. Durham: Duke University Press, 2017. Kindle.

---

[45] Jude, "Star Trek."

[46] Lennard J. Davis, *The End of Normal: Identity in a Biocultural Era*. (Ann Arbor: University of Michigan Press, 2013), 3.

Davis, Lennard J. "Bodies of Difference: Politics, Disability, and Representation." In *Disability Studies: Enabling the Humanities*, edited by Brenda Jo Brueggemann, Rosemarie Garland-Thomson, and Sharon Snyder, 100-108. New York: MLA, 2002.

Davis, Lennard J. *The End of Normal: Identity in a Biocultural Era*. Ann Arbor: University of Michigan Press, 2013.

"Encounter at Farpoint." *Star Trek: The Next Generation*. Season 1, episode 1. Directed by Corey Allen. Aired September 28, 1987. CBS Studios, 2007. DVD.

Garland-Thomson, Rosemarie. "The Case for Conserving Disability." *Bioethical Inquiry* 9, no. 3 (September 2012): 339-55.

Geraghty, Lincoln. *Living with Star Trek: American Culture and the Star Trek Universe*. New York: I.B. Tauris, 2007.

Goffman, Erving. *Stigma: Notes on the Management of Spoiled Identity*. 1986 Touchstone Reprint. New York: Simon & Schuster, 1963.

"Heart of Glory." *Star Trek: The Next Generation*. Season 1, episode 19. Directed by Rob Bowman. Aired March 21, 1988. CBS Studios, 2007. DVD.

"Is There in Truth No Beauty?" *Star Trek: The Original Series*, Season 3, episode 5. Directed by Ralph Senesky. Aired October 18, 1968: Paramount Pictures, 2004. DVD.

Jude, Tamara. "Star Trek: 15 Things You Didn't Know about Geordi La Forge." ScreenRant, August 6, 2017. https://screenrant.com/geordi-la-forge-star-trek-next-generation-trivia-facts.

"Justice." *Star Trek: The Next Generation*. Season 1, episode 7. Directed by James L. Conway. Aired November 9, 1987: CBS Studios, 2007. DVD.

Lehmann, Llana. *All You Need to Know about Disability Is on Star Trek*. Vancouver: Mind Meld Media, 2014.

Longmore, Paul K. "Screening Stereotypes: Images of Disabled People in Television and Motion Pictures." In *Images of the Disabled, Disabling Images*, edited by Alan Gartner and Tom Joe, 65-78. New York: Praeger, 1987.

"Loud as a Whisper." *Star Trek: The Next Generation*. Season 2, episode 5. Directed by Larry Shaw. Aired January 9, 1989. CBS Studios, 2007. DVD.

Martoccio, Angie. "The Last Word: LeVar Burton on the Upside of Losing the 'Jeopardy!' Gig and What 'Star Trek' Gave Him." November 26, 2021. https://www.rollingstone.com/tv/tv-features/levar-burton-last-word-interview-jeopardy-star-trek-1245262/

"Measure of a Man." *Star Trek: The Next Generation*. Season 2, episode 9. Directed by Robert Scheerer. Aired February 13, 1989. CBS Studios, 2007. DVD.

Mitchell, David T. and Sharon L. Snyder. *Narrative Prosthesis: Disability and the Dependencies of Discourse*. Ann Arbor: University of Michigan Press, 2000.

"The Enemy." *Star Trek: The Next Generation*. Season 3, episode 7. Directed by David Carson. Aired November 6, 1989: CBS Studios, 2007. DVD.

"The Masterpiece Society." *Star Trek: The Next Generation*. Season 5, episode 13. Directed by Winrich Kolbe. Aired February 10, 1992. CBS Studios, 2007. DVD.

"Year of Hell, Part I." *Star Trek: Voyager*. Season 4, episode 8. Directed by Allan Kroeker. Aired November 5, 1997. Paramount Pictures, 2004. DVD.

ABOUT THE CONTRIBUTORS

Agnibha Banerjee is a PhD Fellow in the Department of English at Rice University. Before moving to the US, he worked as Assistant Professor in the Department of English at Adamas University, India. His research and teaching interests include posthumanism, speculative fiction, critical race theory, postcolonialism, ecocriticism, and Marxism. In the summer of 2022, he won a fellowship to participate in the Bucknell Summer Institute's two-week workshop on Non/Humanity: Revisioning the Centrality of the Human in the Humanities at Bucknell University, Pennsylvania. His recent work has been published in *Derrida Today*, the *South Central Review*, and the *SFRA Review*.

Edmond Y. Chang is an Assistant Professor of English at Ohio University. His areas of research include technoculture, race/gender/sexuality, video games, RPGs, and LARP, feminist media studies, cultural studies, popular culture, and 20/21C American literature. Recent publications include "Imagining Asian American (Environmental) Games" in *AMSJ*, "Why are the Digital Humanities So Straight?" in *Alternative Historiographies of the Digital Humanities*, and "Queergaming" in *Queer Game Studies*. He is an editor for *Analog Game Studies* as well as the website *Gamers with Glasses*.

Lucas Cober is a doctoral candidate at Quebec's Concordia University. He studies health and disability in both the Bible and in modern religious institutions, and is interested in the ways that health, disability, religion and popular culture intersect and how historical and fictional narratives can and do affect real people.

Stevi Costa earned her PhD in English from the University of Washington, specializing in nineteenth and twentieth-century American literature through the lenses of feminism, queer theory, and disability studies. Her work articulates theories embodied across narratives of bodily difference, and combines approaches from literary theory, cultural studies, and performance studies. She has been published in *The Journal of Multimodal Rhetorics*, the *European Journal of American Cultural Studies*, and *In Media Res*. She teaches at Cornish College of the Arts and writes theatre criticism for *Deconstruct*.

Elliot Mason is a PhD candidate in the department of Religions and Cultures at Concordia University in Montréal. There, he teaches the classes Religion and its Monsters; Magic, Witchcraft, and Religion; and The History of Satan. His research focuses on the articulation of marginalized identity through the figure of the monster, particularly in science-fiction, fantasy, and horror. He holds advanced degrees in Medieval Studies, Russian Literature, and Religious Studies, and is currently authoring a chapter on monstrosity and nature in the twenty-first century for Bloomsbury's Cultural History of Monsters series.

Craig A. Meyer, PhD, is an Associate Professor of English and Director of the Writing Program at Jackson State University. His research areas include histories of rhetoric, academic writing, writing pedagogy, creative writing, disability studies, popular culture, and practical rhetoric.

Sean Mock is an assistant professor of adult basic education at Umpqua Community College, primarily focusing on advocacy and academic preparation for students with disabilities. His research investigates the intersection of disability and popular culture, with particular reference to fantasy/magical tropes and disability identity. Engaging with diverse topics—from dwarfism in the Middle Ages to neurodivergence and chronic illness in contemporary science fiction—Sean's work seeks to destabilize the normative ableism so casually perpetuated in modern and contemporary popular culture.

Jeana Moody is a scholar, workshop facilitator and writer. They hold a Master's degree in Women, Gender and Sexuality Studies from Oregon State University, where they studied exclusionary language and its affective consequences for trans, queer, and other minoritized populations. Their research interests include sociolinguistics, feminist speculative fiction, disability and queer studies, and critical race theory. They have held positions such as Program Coordinator for the University of Idaho Women's Center and Associate Lecturer at Prague City University.

Daniel Preston is ABD at Syracuse University and has taught English courses at SUNY Oswego and SUNY Albany. He specializes in the intersections between disability studies, popular culture, and education. He has published work on *Batman, Star Trek, Finding Nemo*, and *The Breakfast Club*, as well as the intersections of parenting and disability.

Samuel Z. Shelton, MA (they/them/theirs) is an accessibility coordinator at Iowa State University. Sam received their MA degree in Women, Gender, and Sexuality Studies from Oregon State University, and they earned three bachelor's degrees from Iowa State University in English, Sociology, and Women's Studies. Sam's research focuses on the complex intersections of social justice, critical trauma studies, and transformative, anti-oppressive education.

T. Wesley is a PhD candidate in the Department of English & Literary Arts at the University of Denver.

INDEX

www.ingramcontent.com/pod-product-compliance
Lightning Source LLC
Chambersburg PA
CBHW072128020426
42334CB00018B/1713